Adda

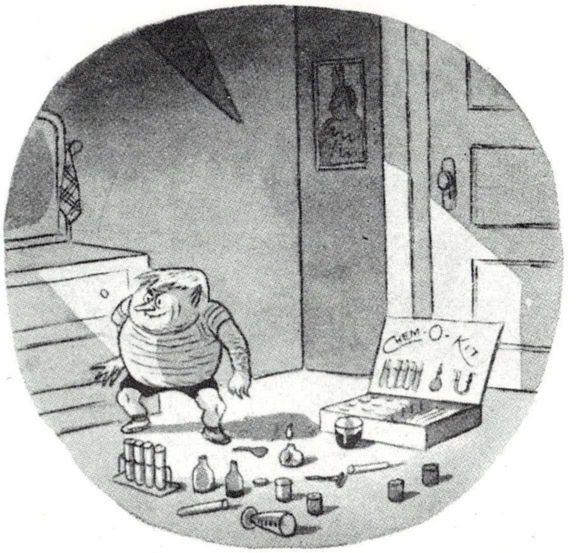

METHUEN HUMOUR CLASSICS

Alphonse Allais
A WOLF IN FROG'S CLOTHING
Selected, translated and introduced by Miles Kington

H. M. Bateman
THE MAN WHO . . . AND OTHER DRAWINGS

Noël Coward
THE LYRICS OF NOËL COWARD
A WITHERED NOSEGAY

A. P. Herbert
UNCOMMON LAW
MORE UNCOMMON LAW

Paul Jennings
GOLDEN ODDLIES

Jerome K. Jerome
THREE MEN IN AN OMNIBUS

Osbert Lancaster
THE LITTLEHAMPTON SAGA

Tom Lehrer
TOO MANY SONGS BY TOM LEHRER

Frank Muir and Denis Norden
THE COMPLETE AND UTTER 'MY WORD!' COLLECTION

S. J. Perelman
THE LAST LAUGH
THE MOST OF S. J. PERELMAN

W. C. Sellar and R. J. Yeatman
1066 AND ALL THAT
AND NOW ALL THIS

James Thurber
LET YOUR MIND ALONE!
THE MIDDLE-AGED MAN ON THE FLYING TRAPEZE

In preparation
Ogden Nash
CANDY IS DANDY: THE BEST OF OGDEN NASH

X-mas 87

ADDAMS AND EVIL

Dear M & P -

Happy bed-time reading! Love Suz

An Album of Cartoons

Charles Addams

A Methuen Humour Classic

First published in the United States of America in 1947
First published in Great Britain in 1985
by Methuen London Ltd
11 New Fetter Lane, London EC4P 4EE

Originated and printed in Great Britain
by BAS Printers Ltd, Over Wallop, Hampshire

ISBN 0 413 57190 4 (hardback)
0 413 55370 1 (paperback)

For Barbara

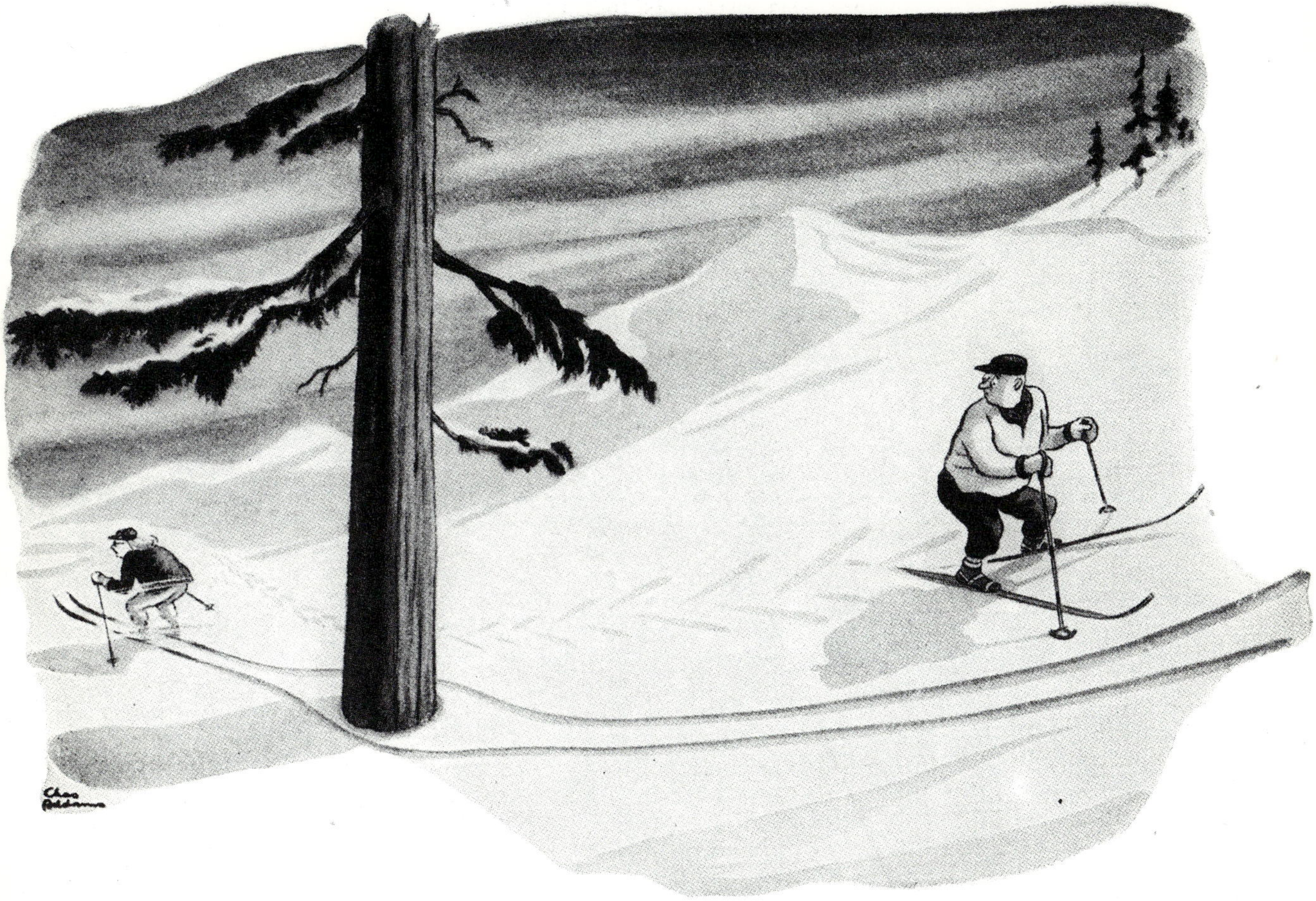

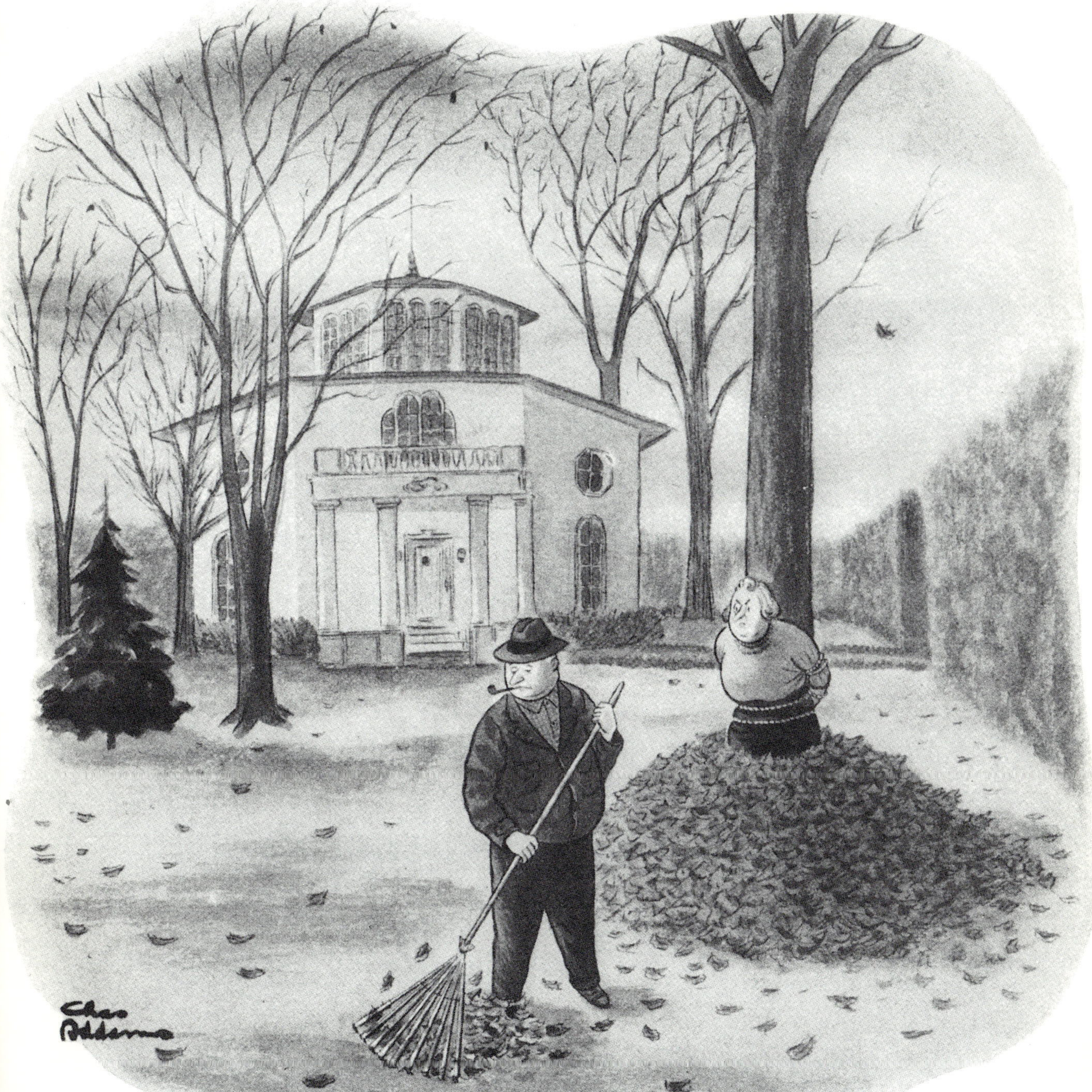
Chas
Addams

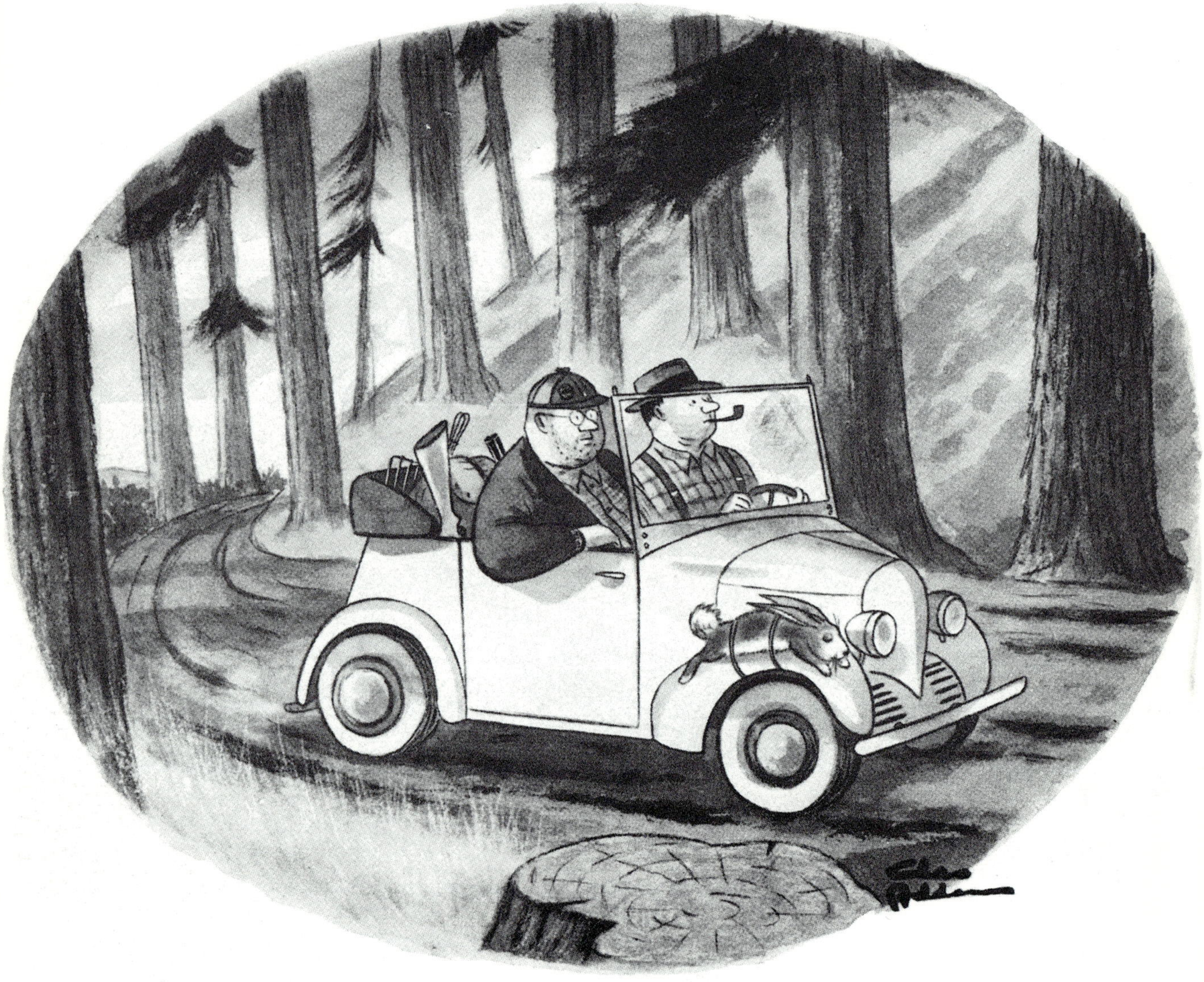

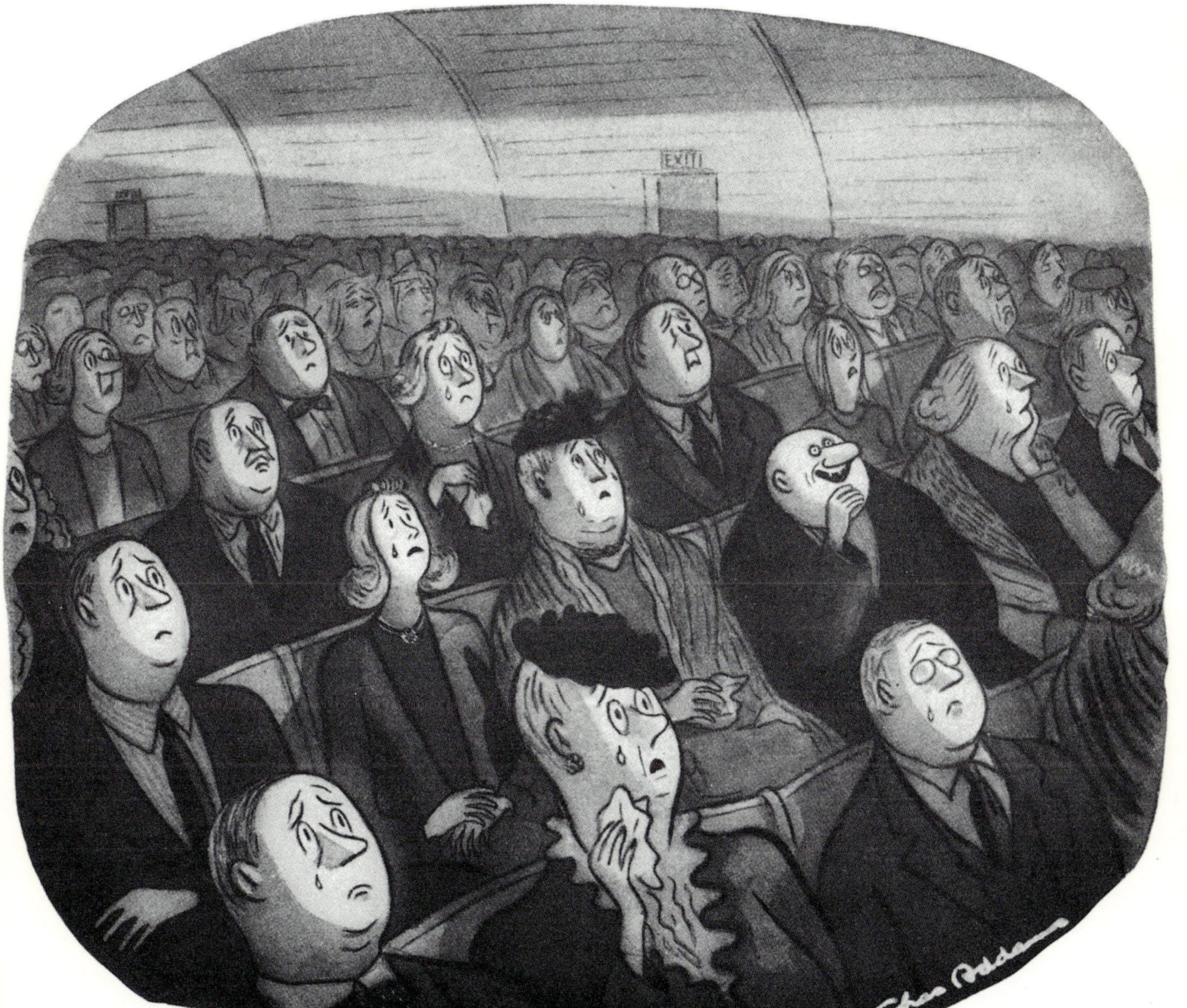
EXIT
Chas Addams

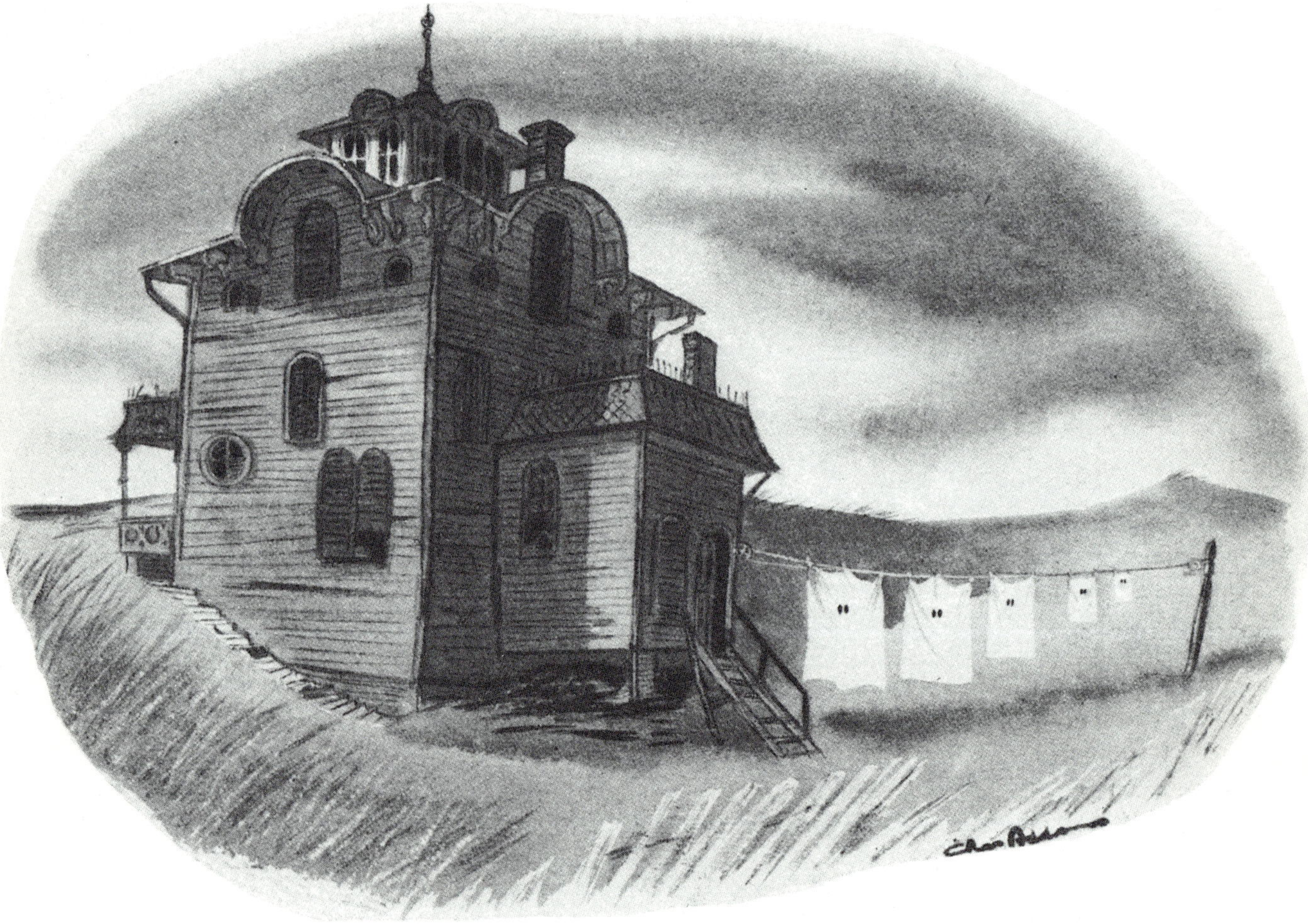

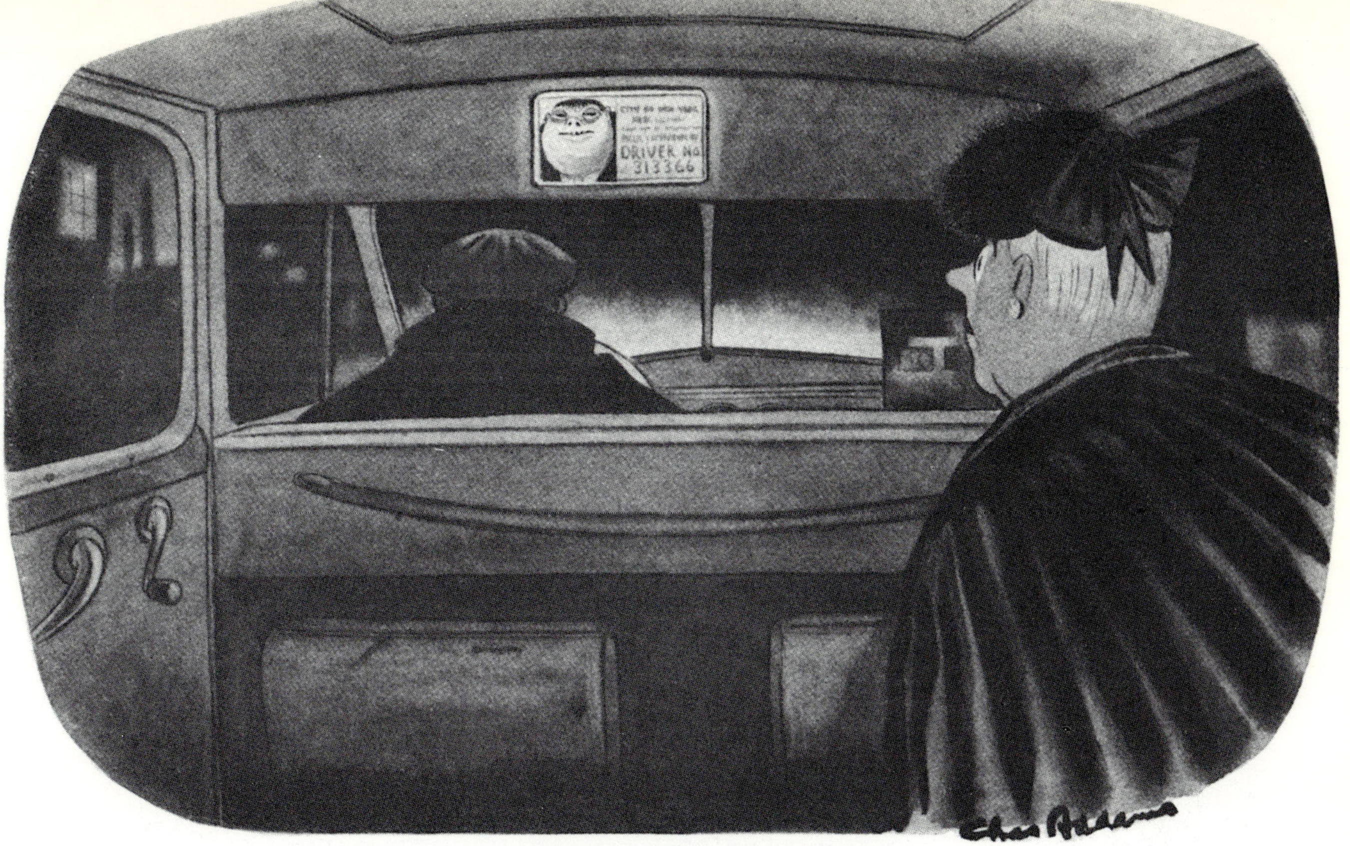
DRIVER No
313366
Chas Addams

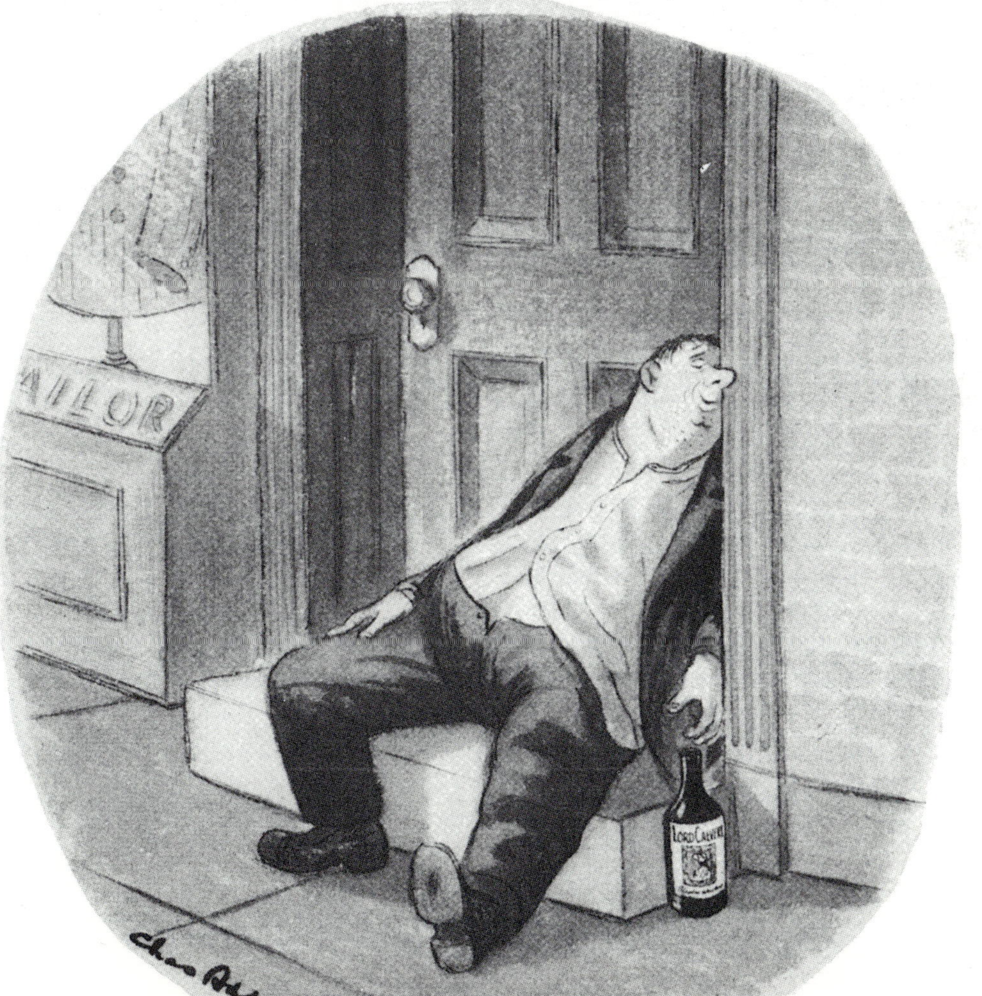
AILOR
Chas Addams

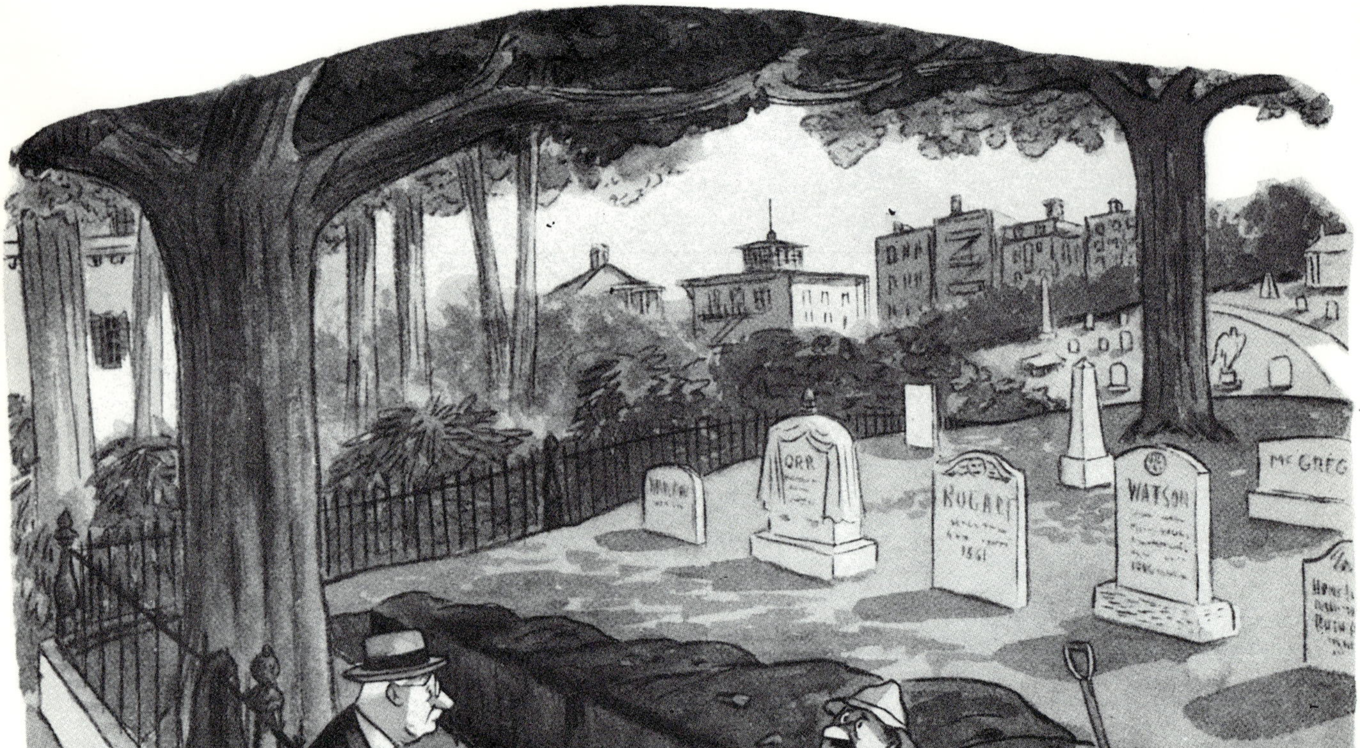

'Oh, my goodness, no! Just a water main.'

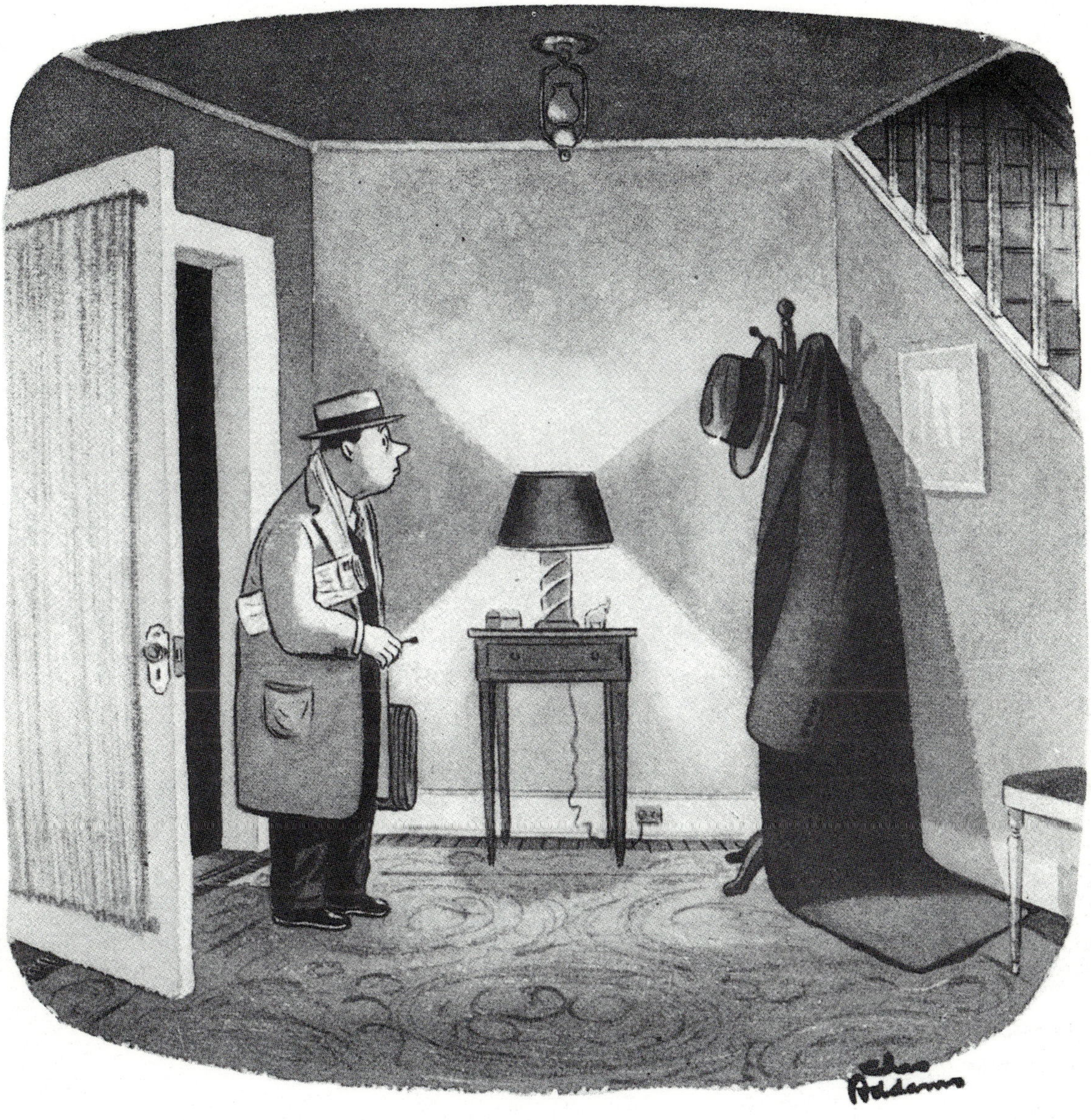
Chas Addams

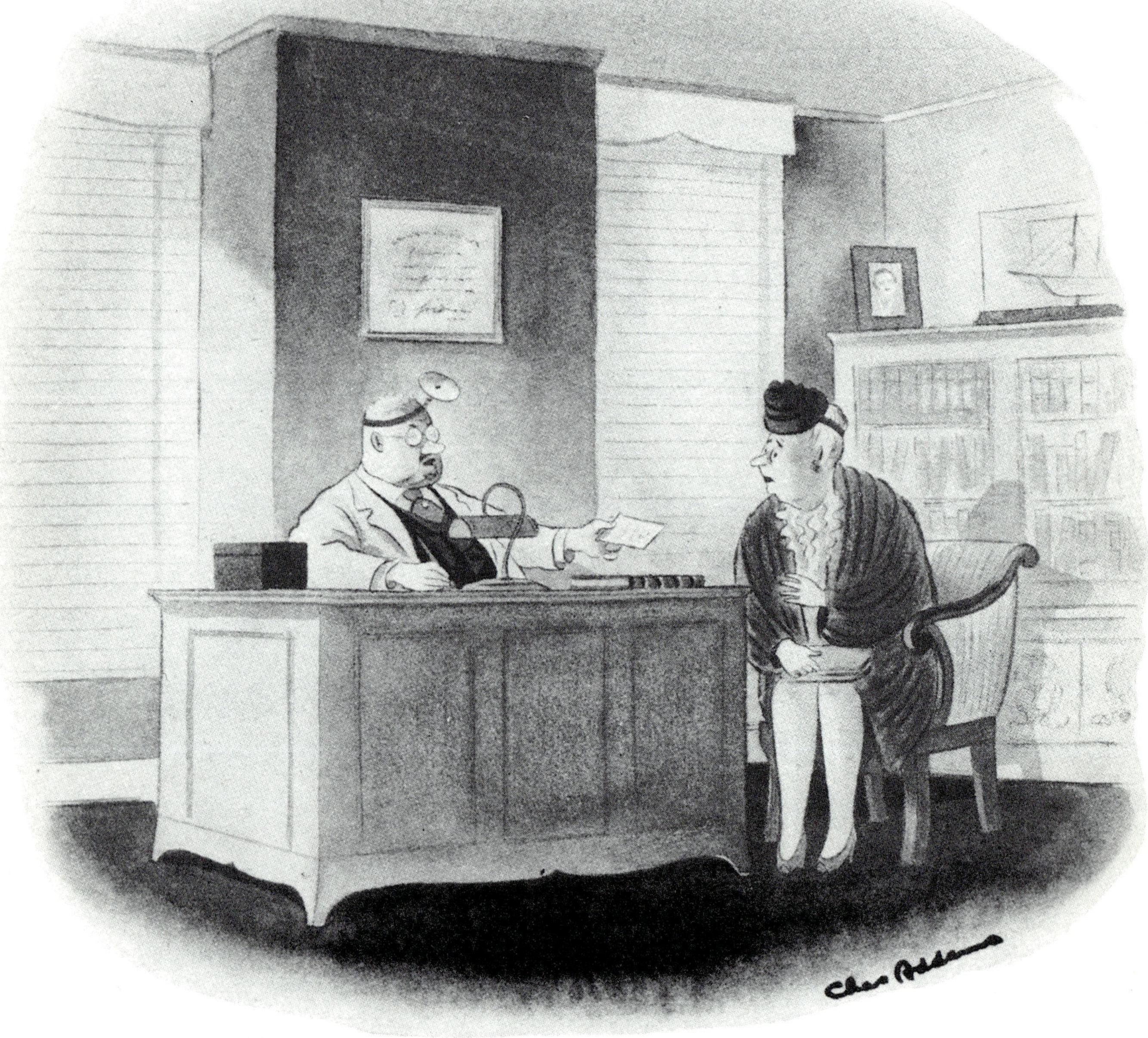

'Now have this prescription filled and take as directed.
Then, two nights after the first full moon, procure the left hind leg
of a he-frog and a root of St John's-wort . . . .'

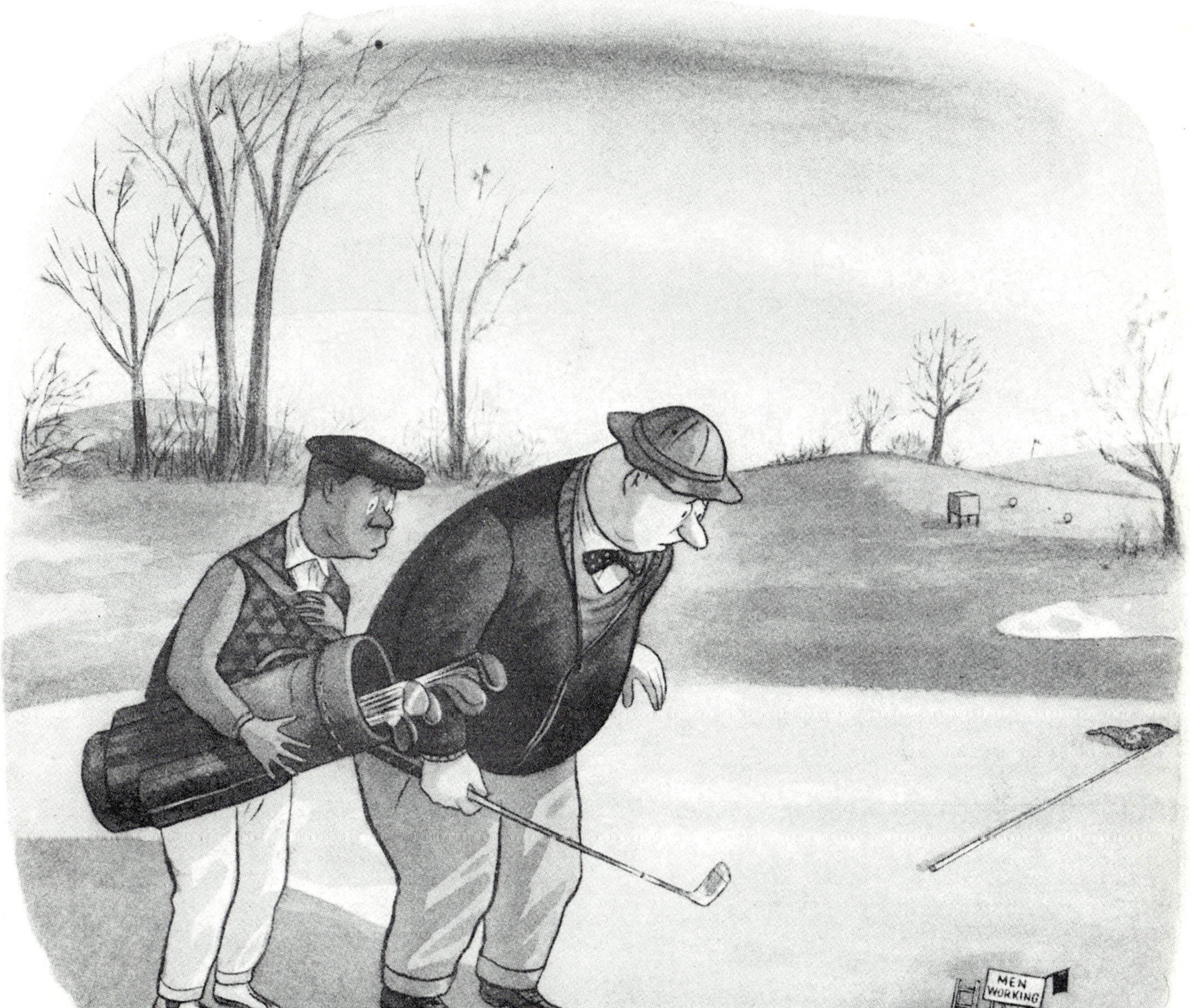
MEN WORKING
Chas Addams

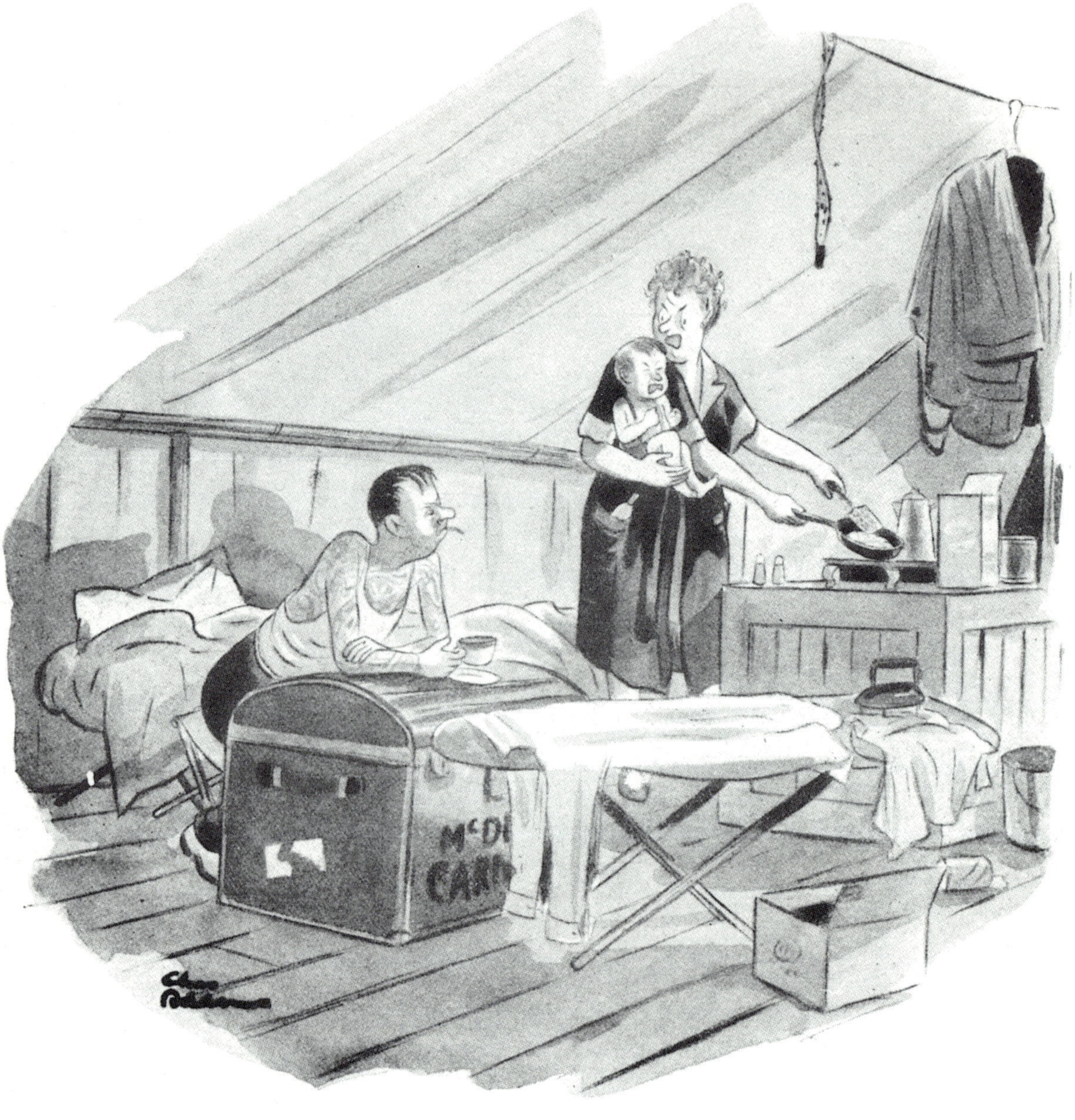

'Wait a minute, can't you? I've only got three hands.'

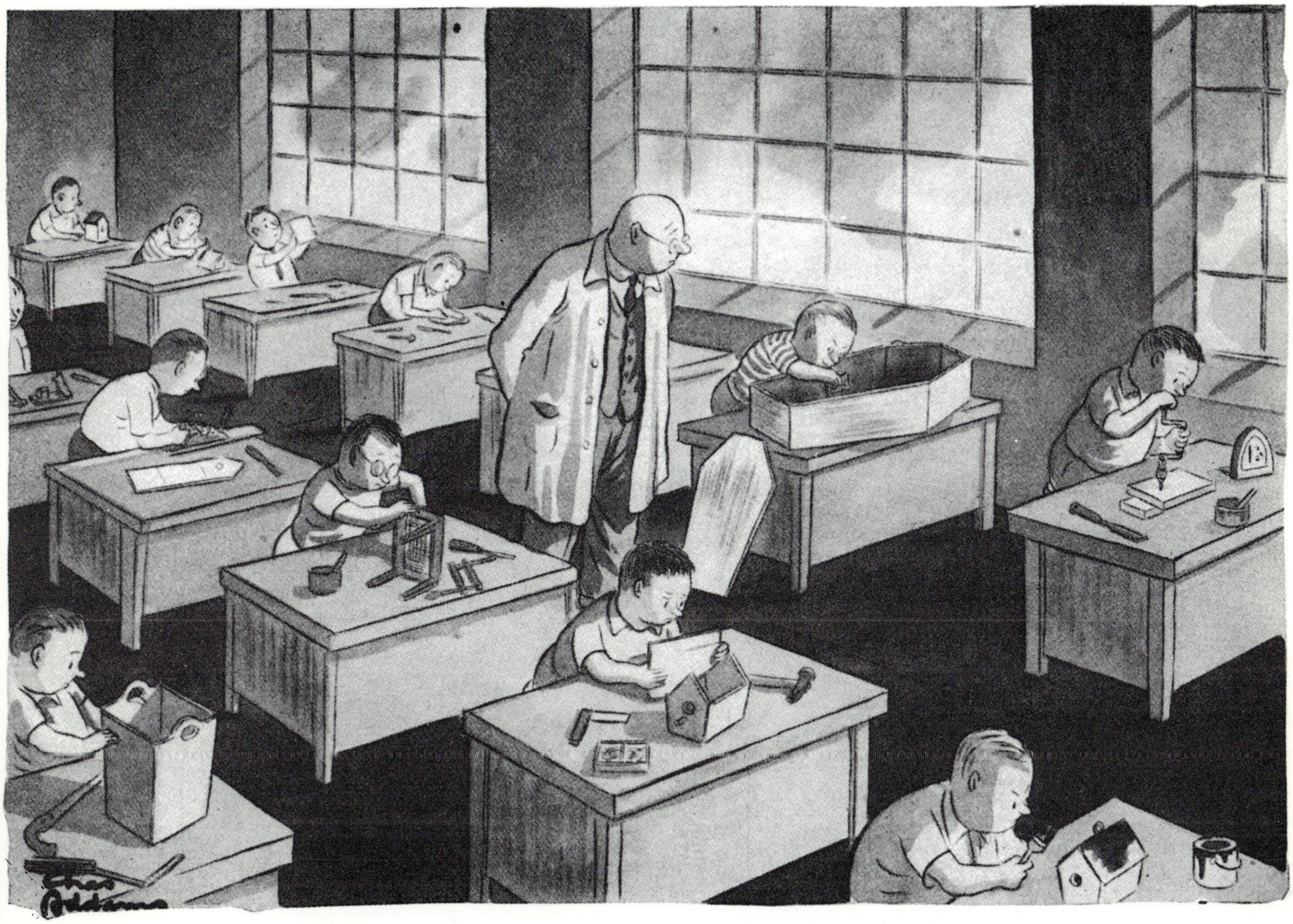
Chas Addams

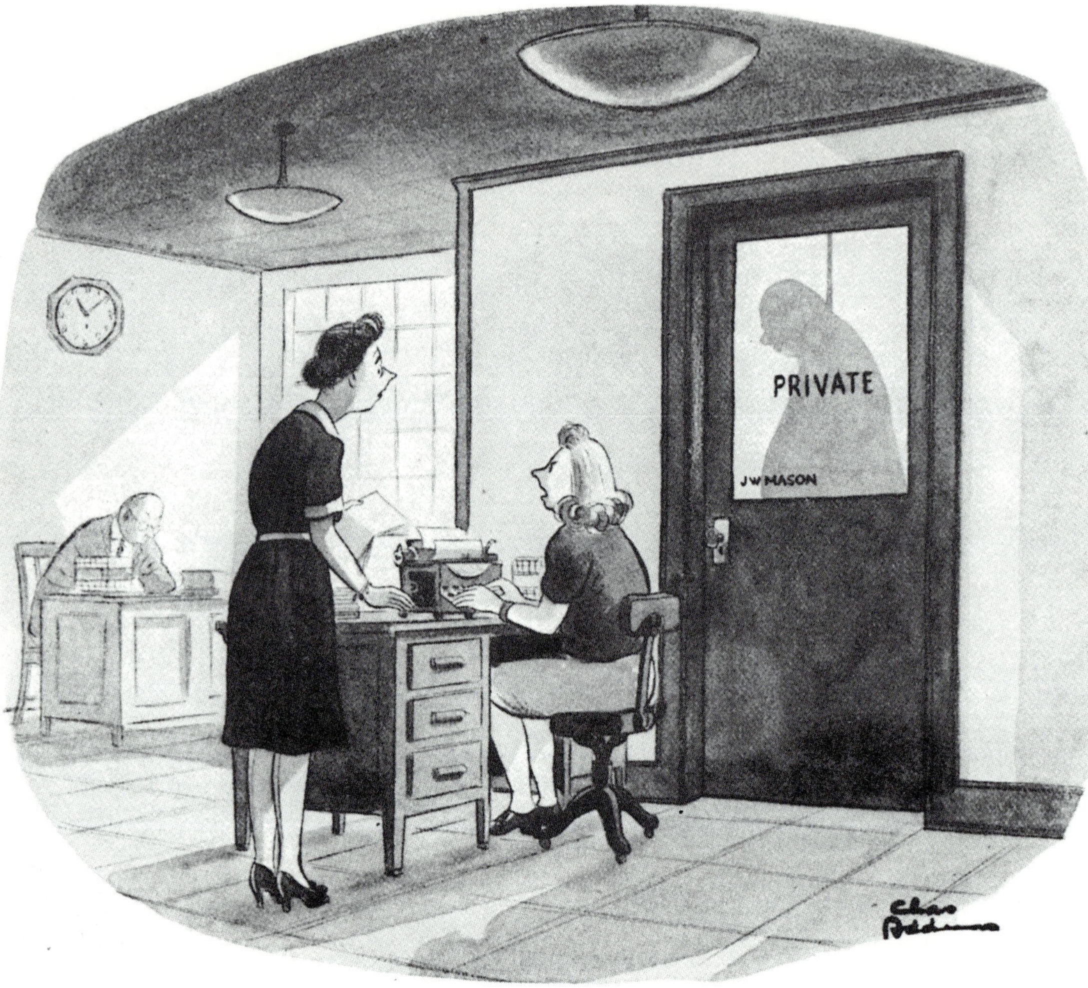

‘I know, but I don’t go in unless he buzzes.’

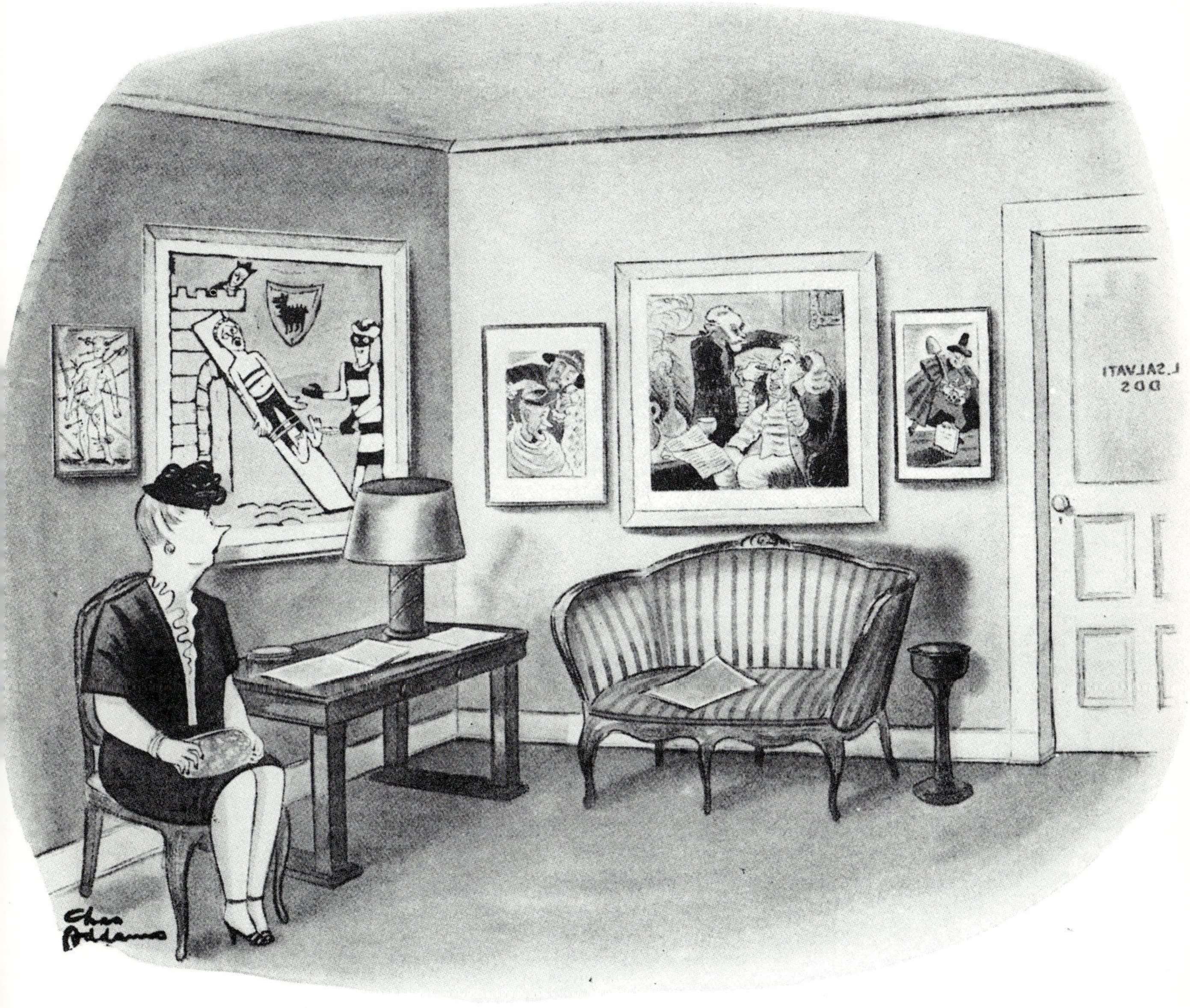
L. SALVATI
DDS
Chas Addams

1

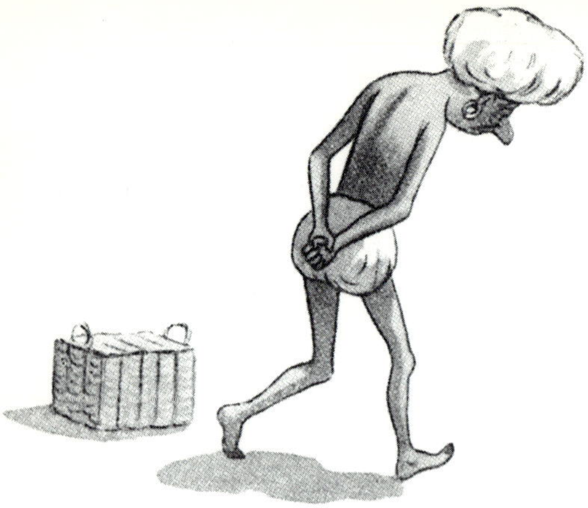

2

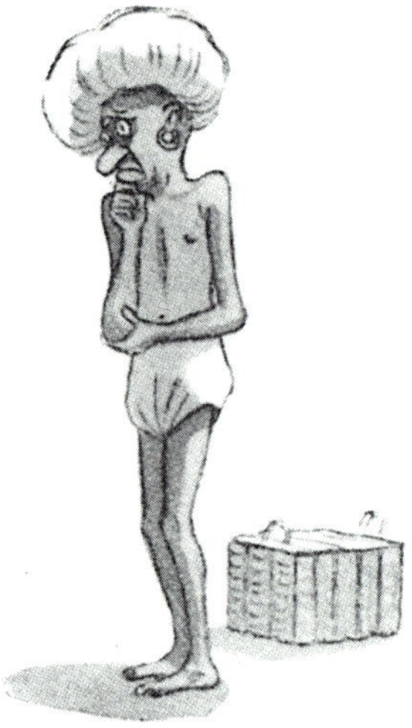

3

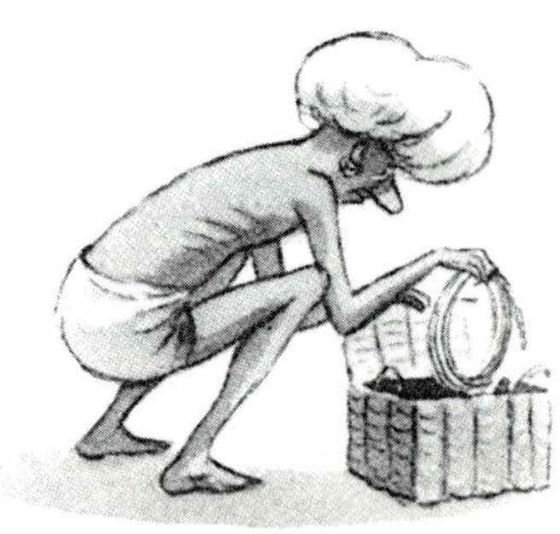

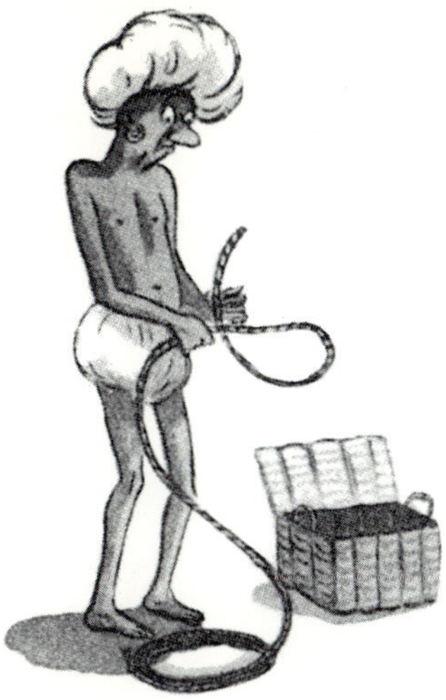

5

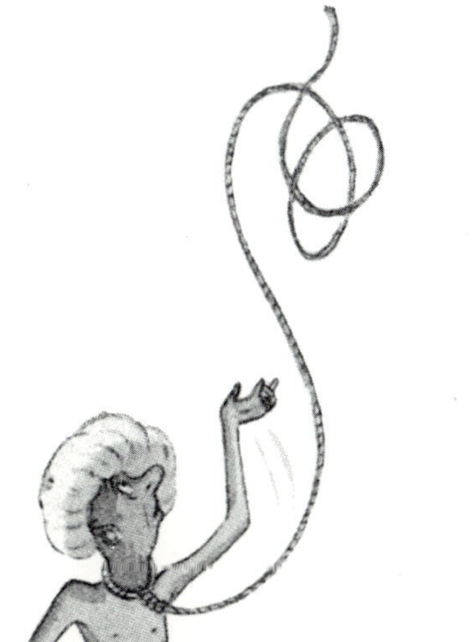

6

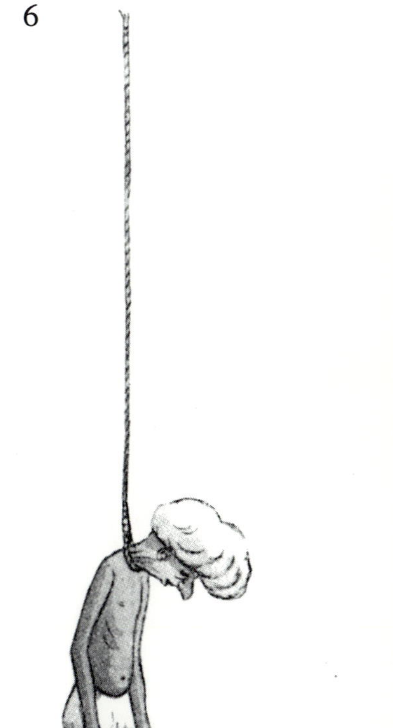

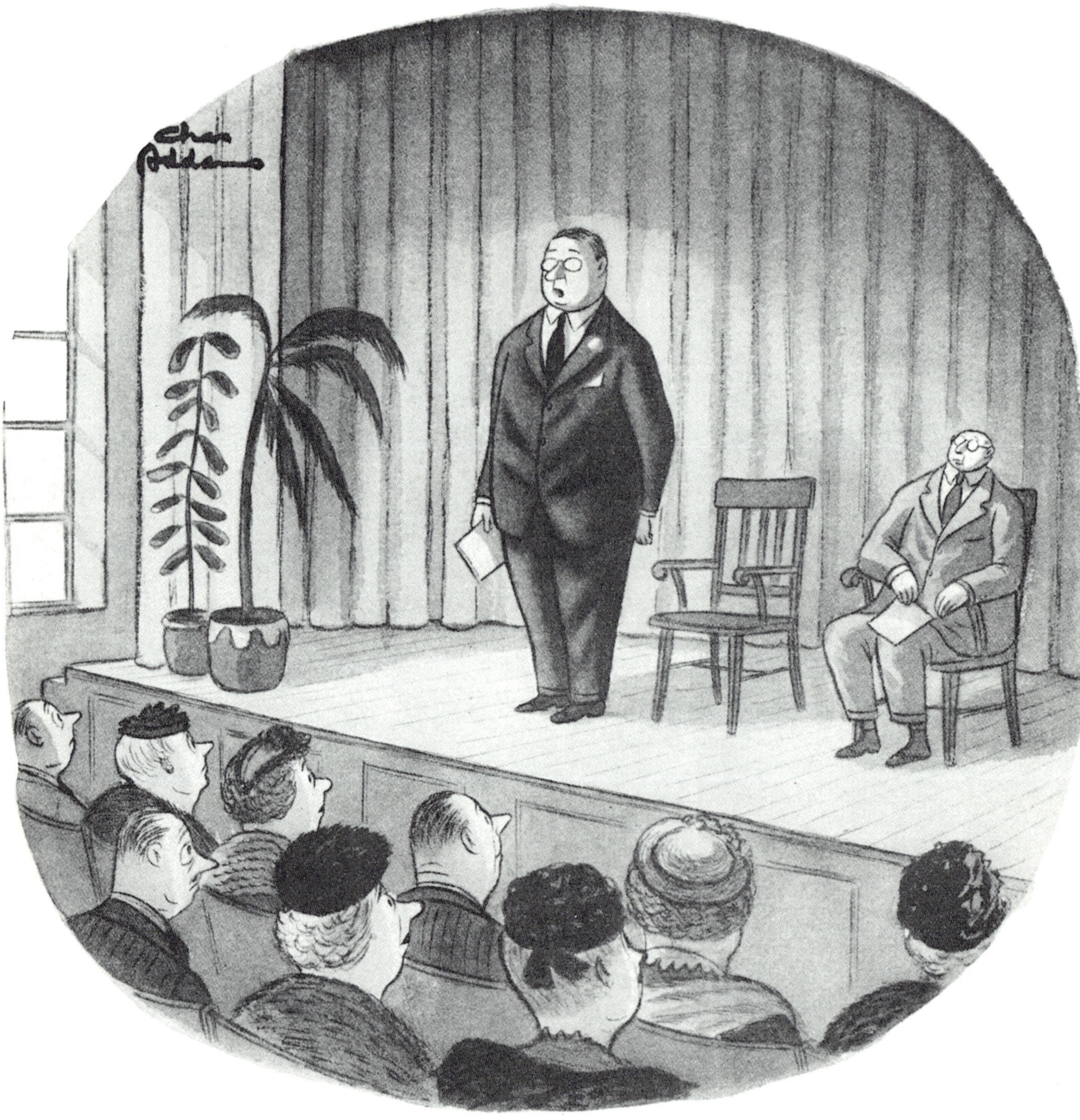

'Dr Fairburn is going to tell us about some of his interesting experiences among the head-shrinking tribes of Ecuador.'

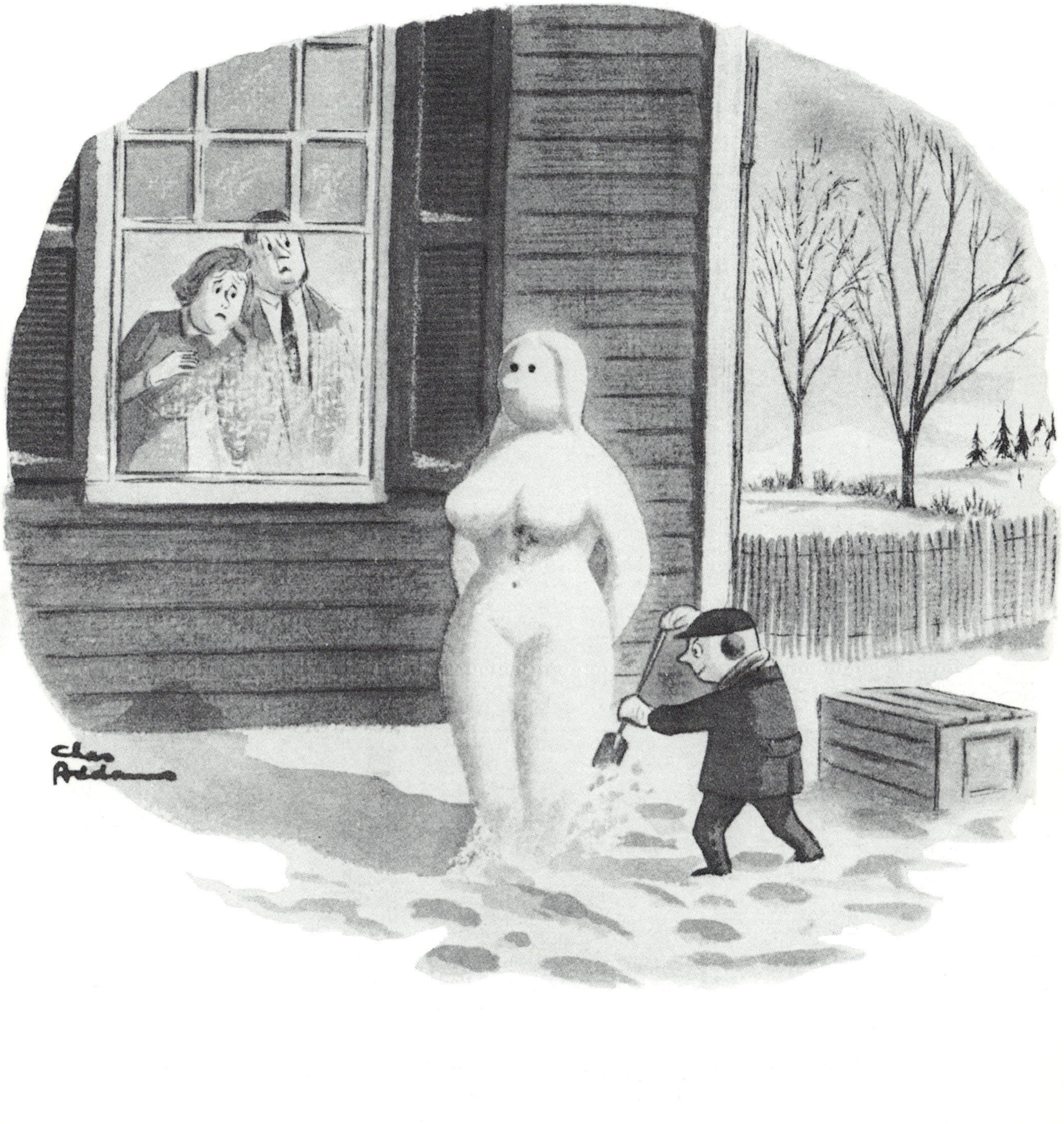
Chas Addams

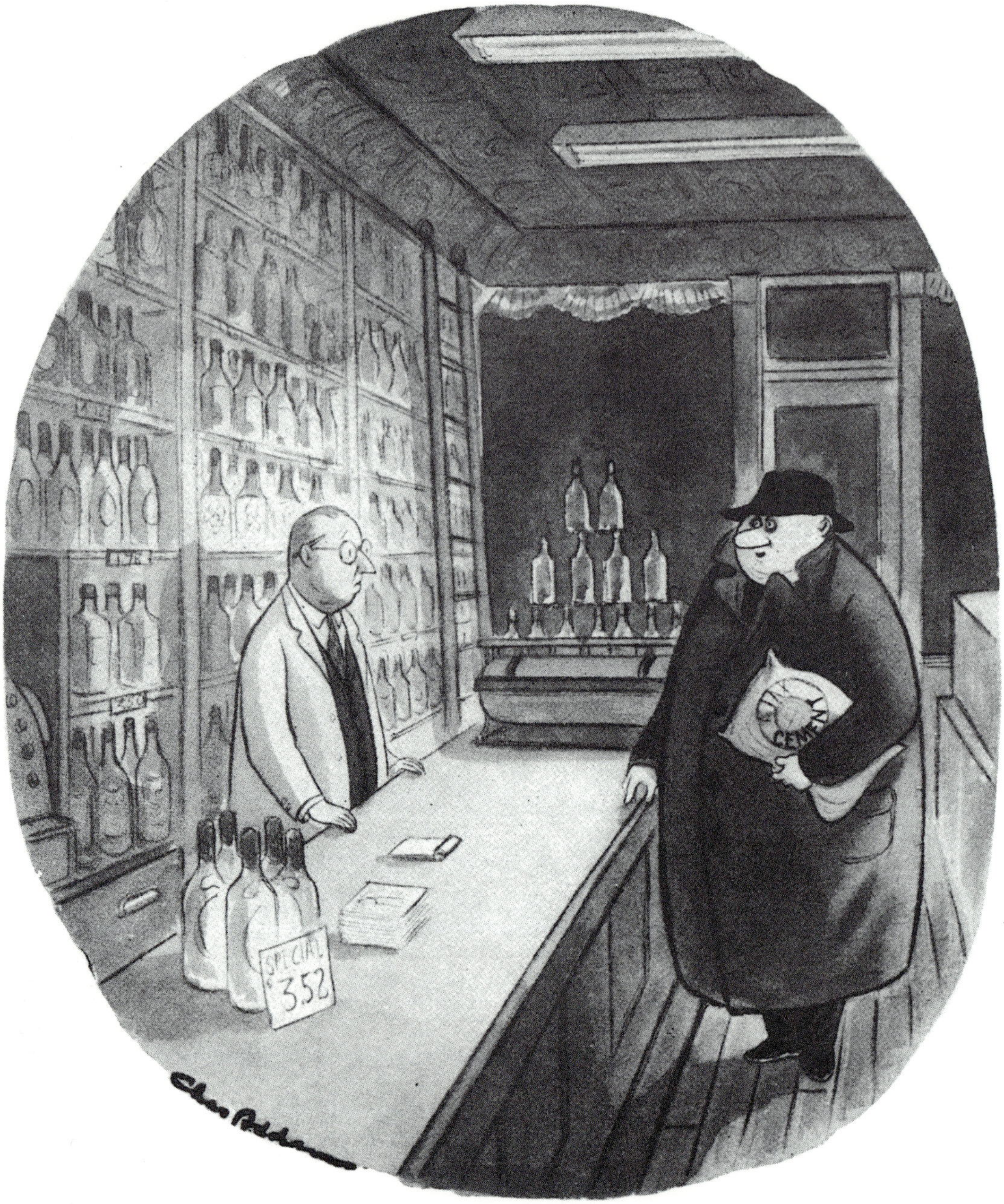

'A cask of Amontillado, please.'

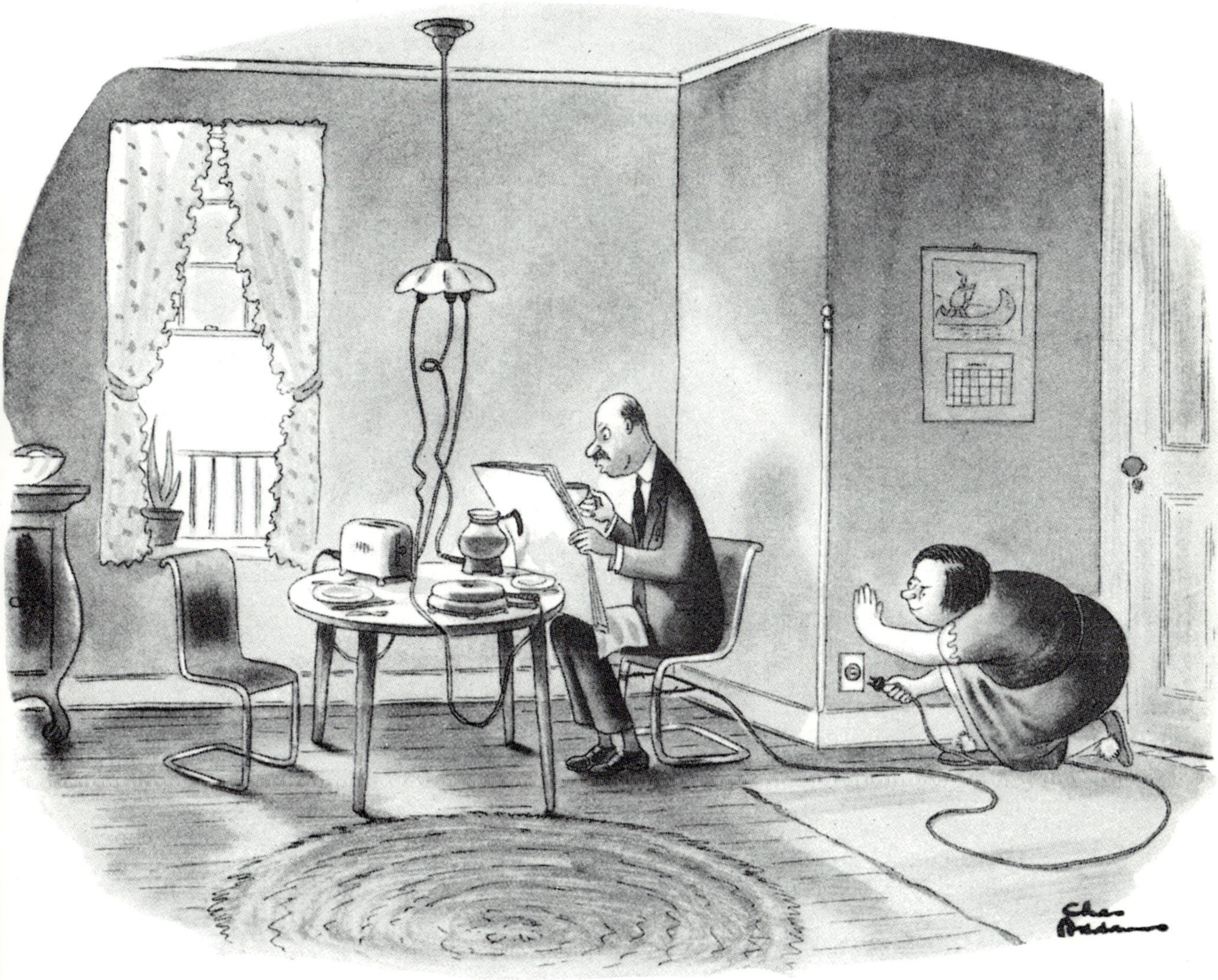

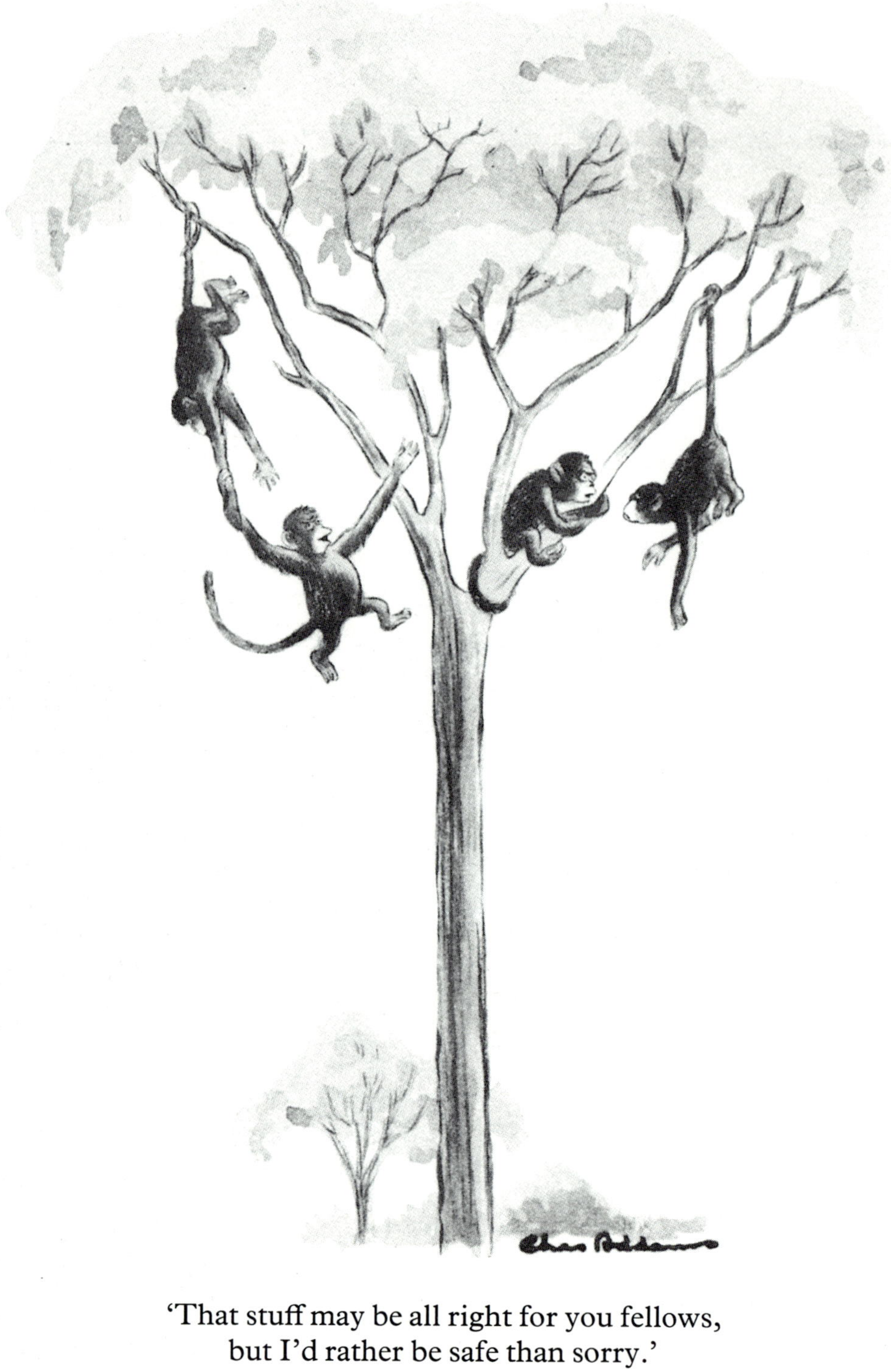

'That stuff may be all right for you fellows,
but I'd rather be safe than sorry.'

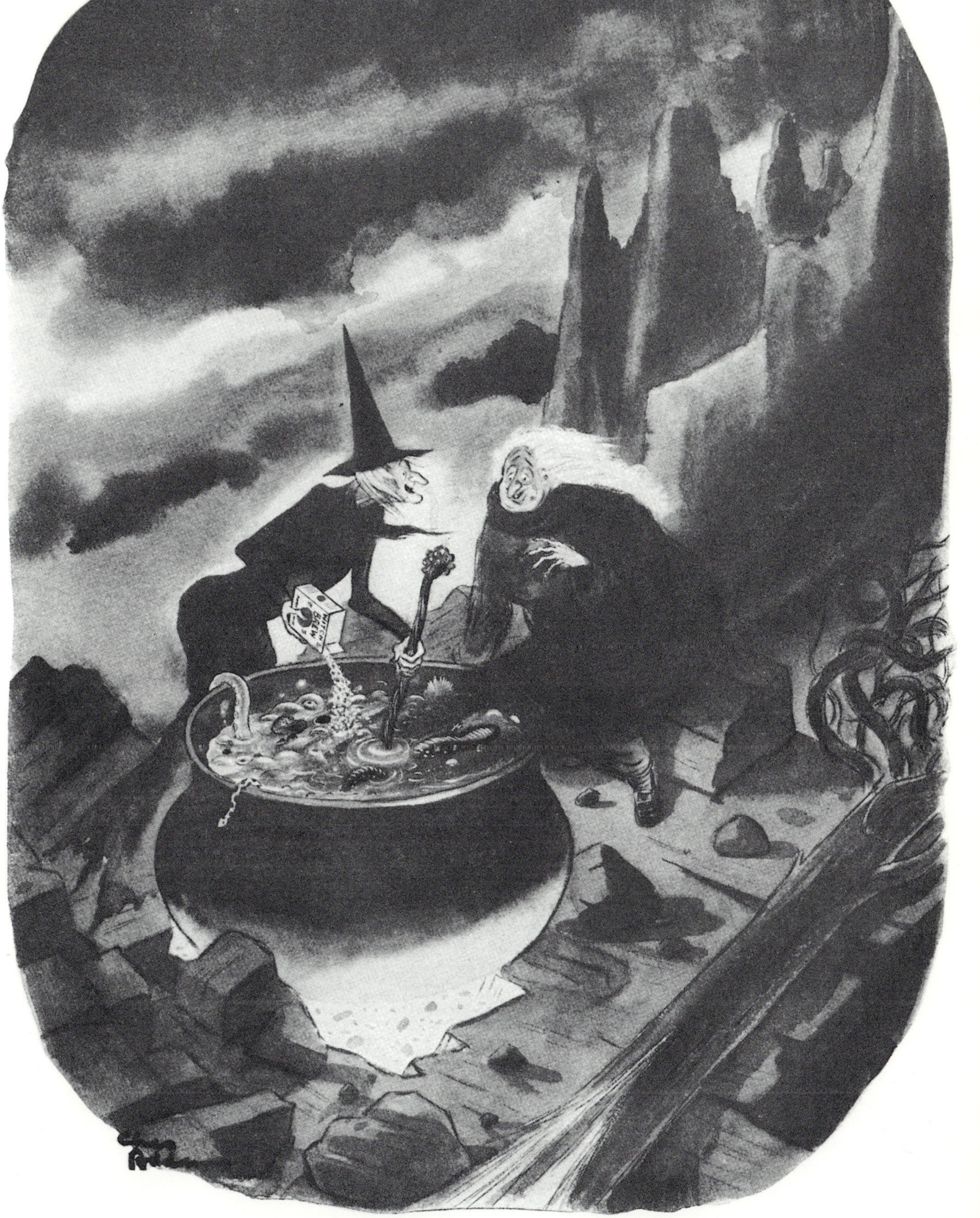

'It's marvellous! All you do is add water.'

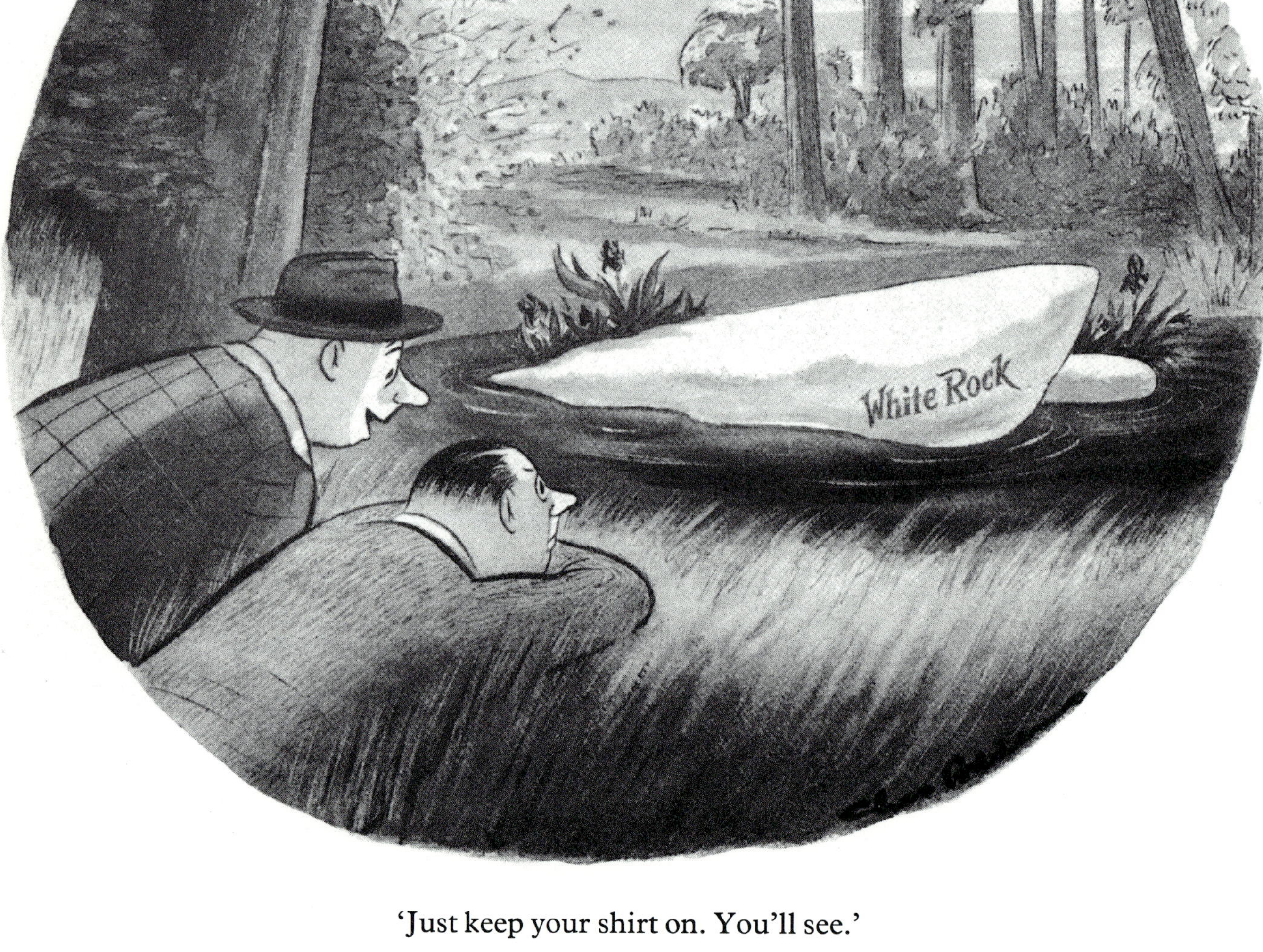

'Just keep your shirt on. You'll see.'

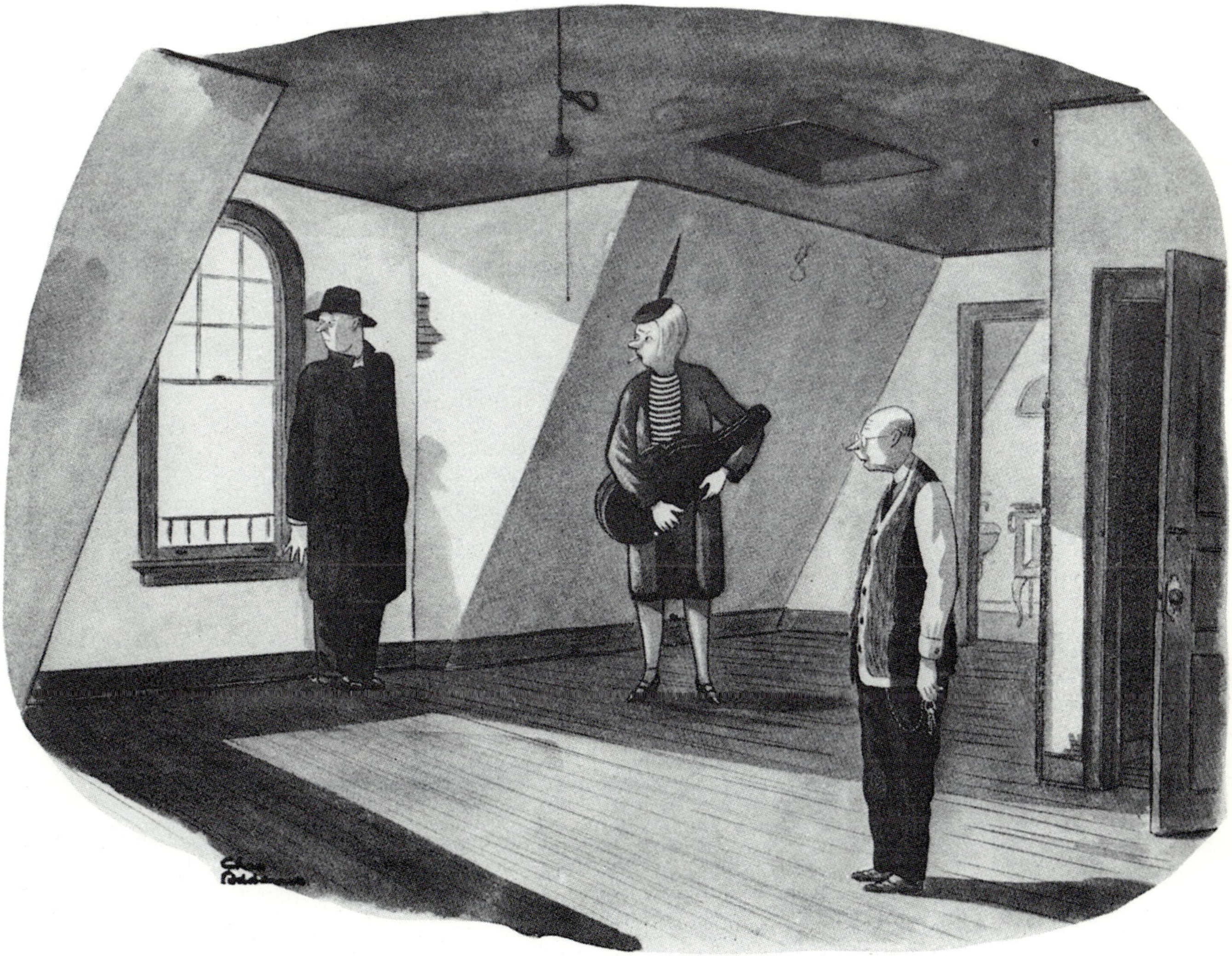

‘Any children?’

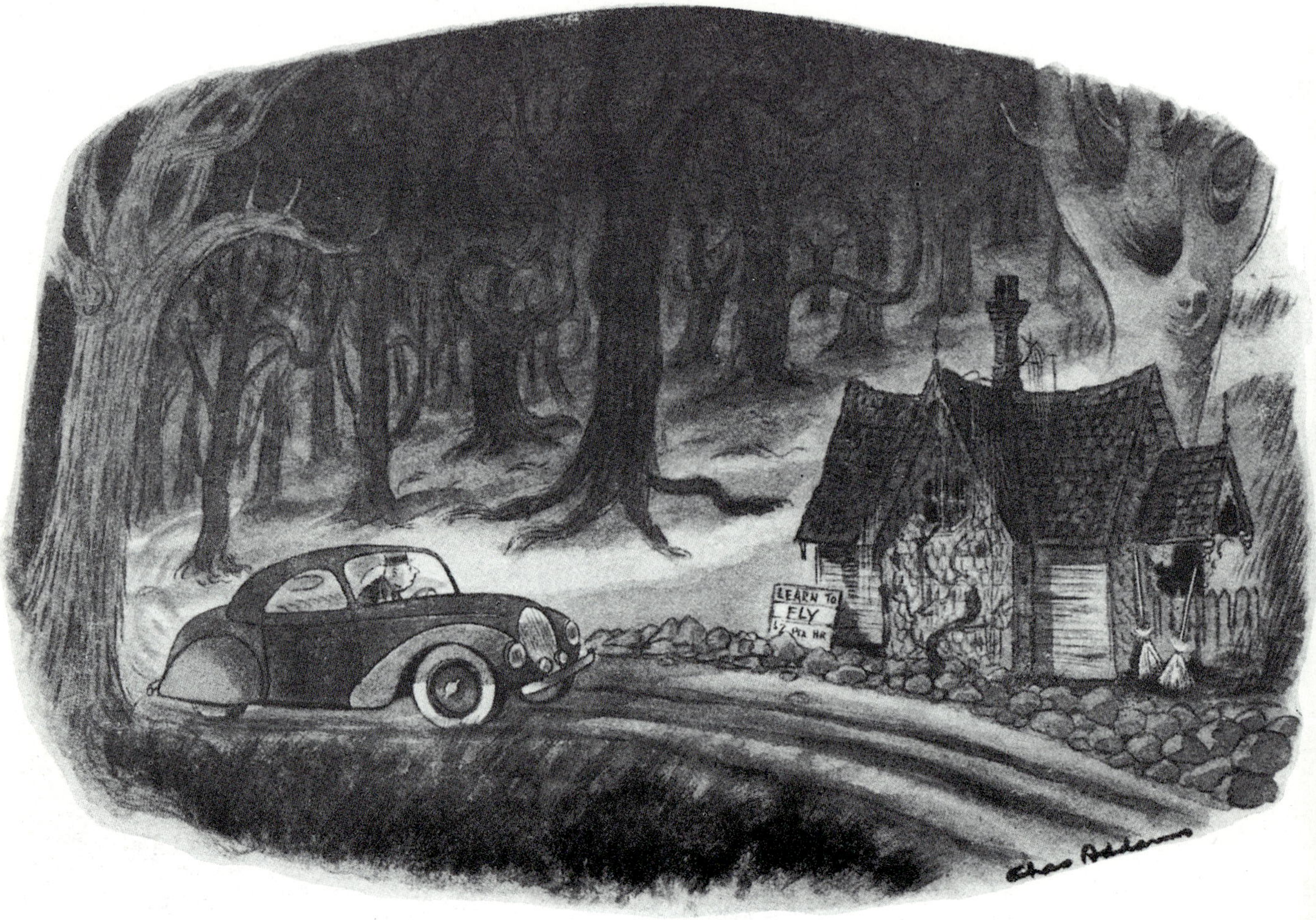
LEARN TO
FLY
Chas Addams

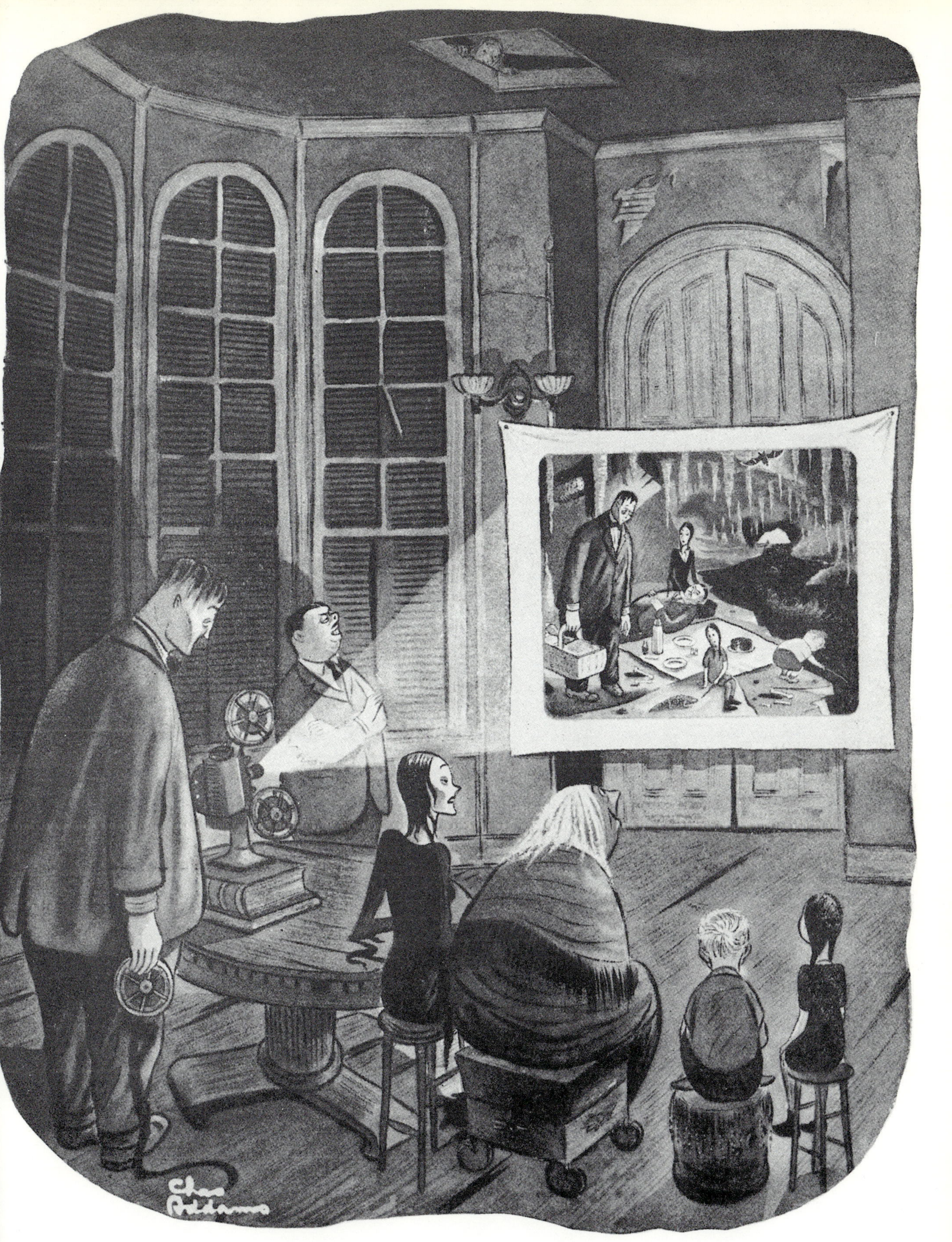

'It's a lovely spot – so unspoiled.'

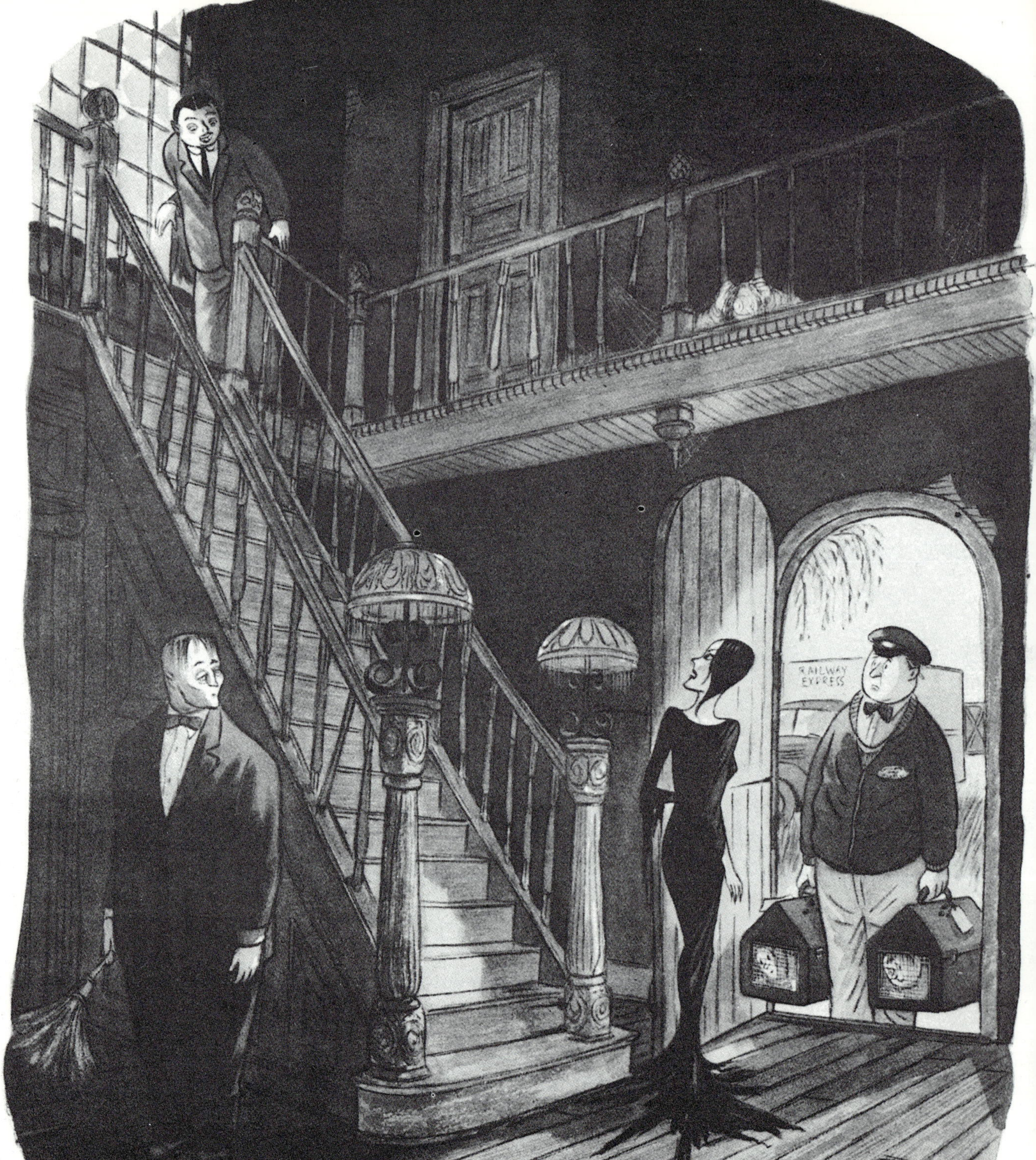

'It's the children, darling, back from camp.'

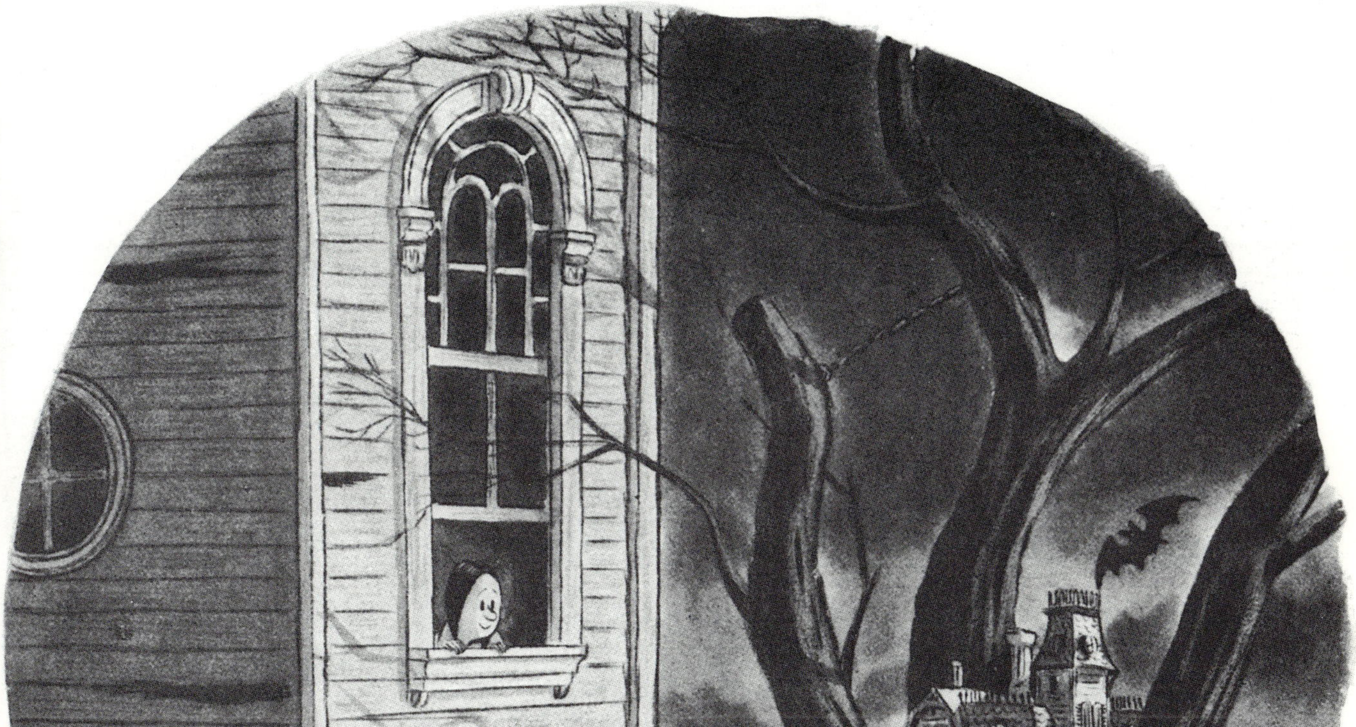

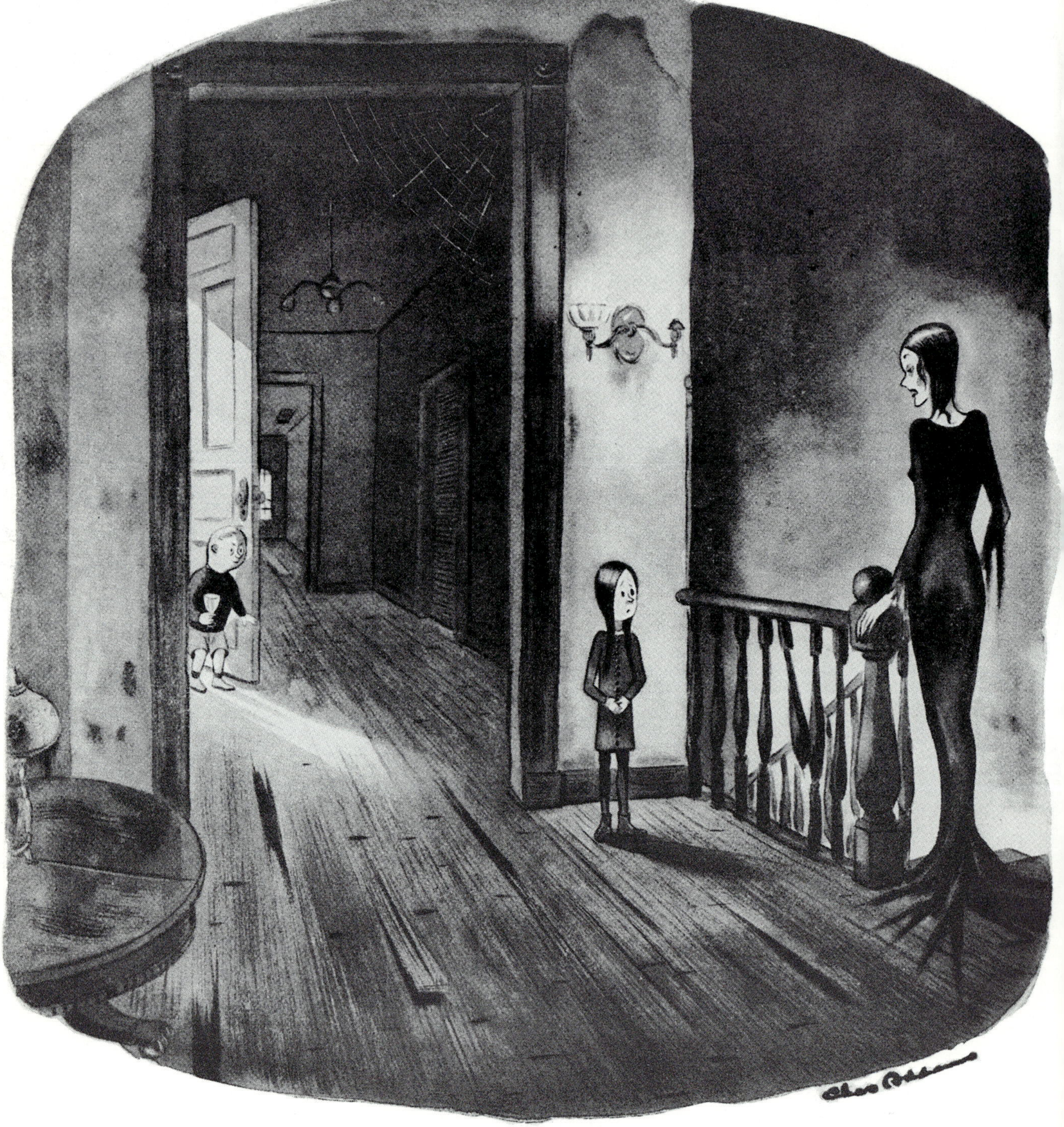

'Well, don't come whining to me.
Go tell him you'll poison him right back.'

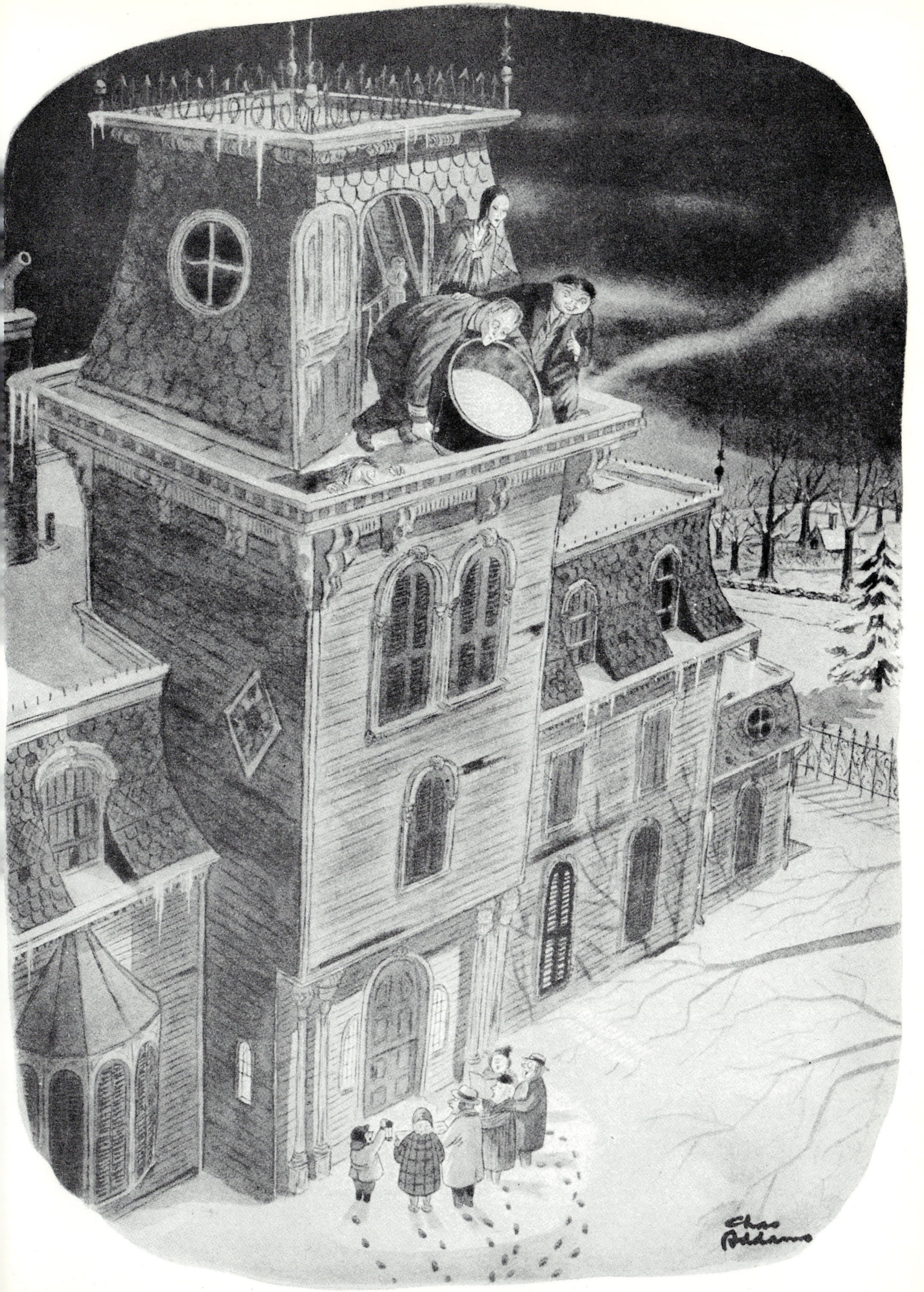
Chas Addams

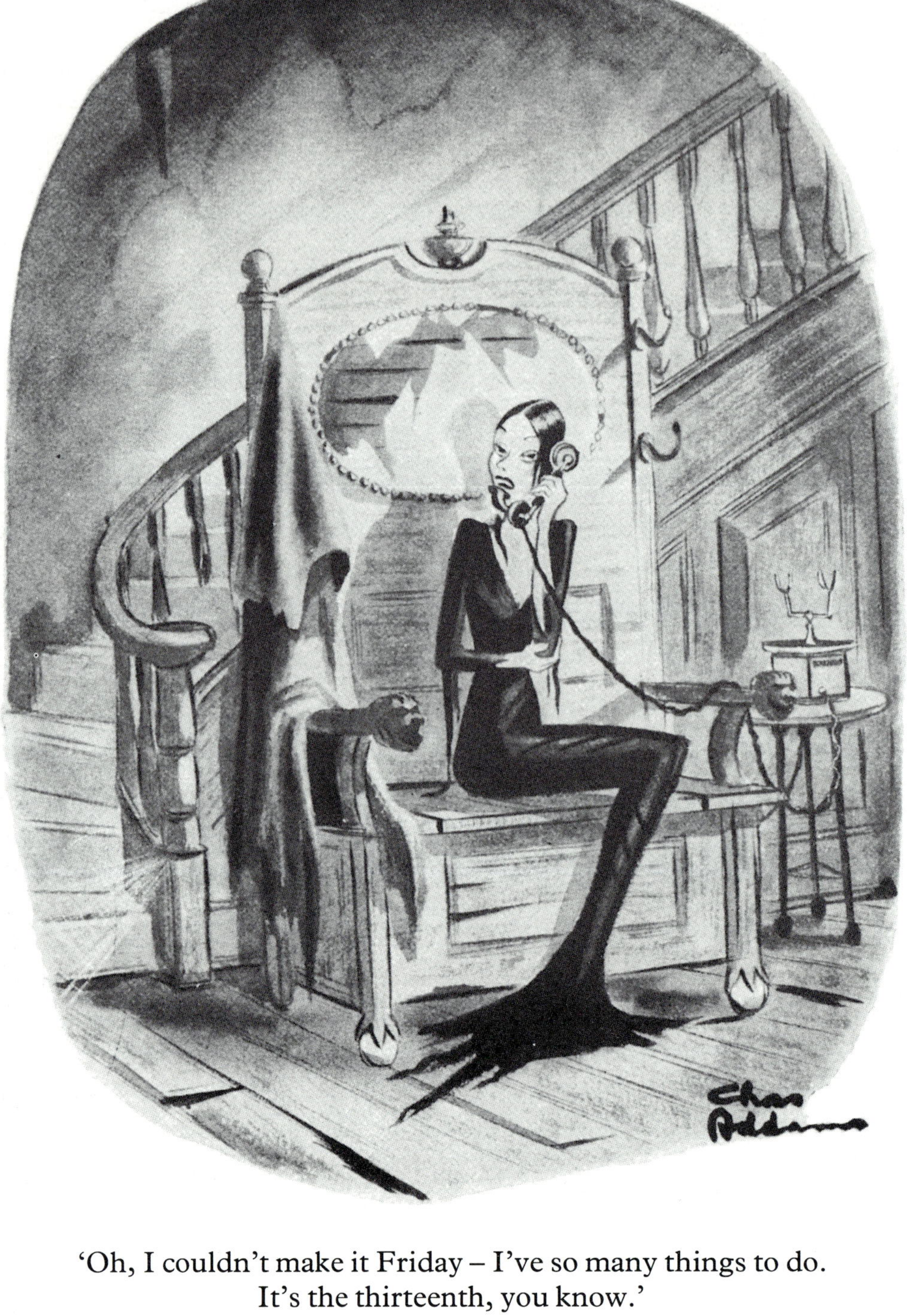

'Oh, I couldn't make it Friday – I've so many things to do.
It's the thirteenth, you know.'

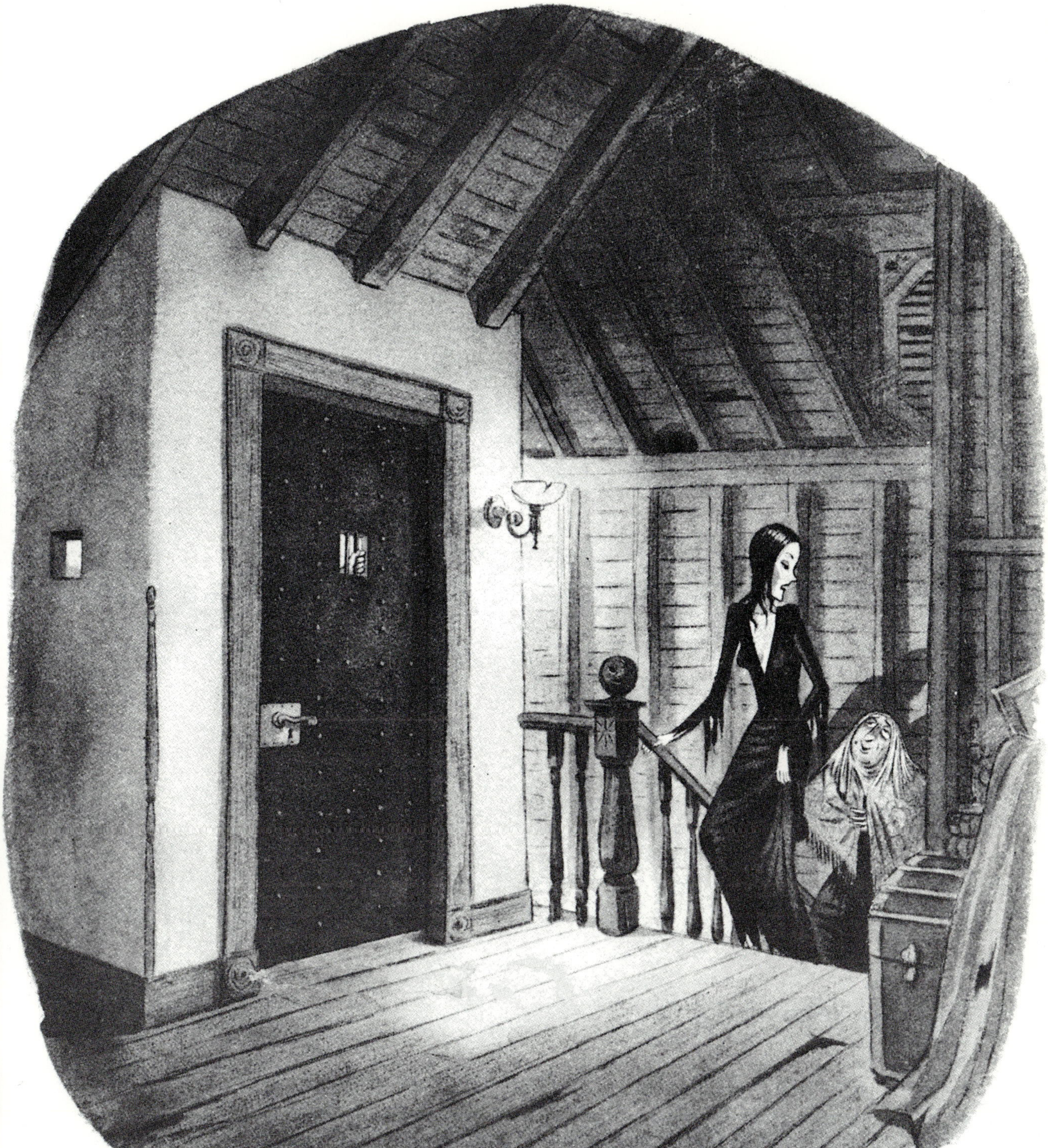

'We've had part of this floor finished off for Uncle Eimar.'

1

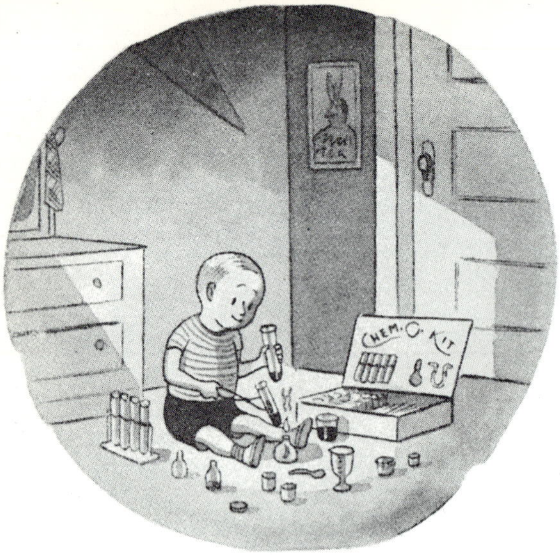

2

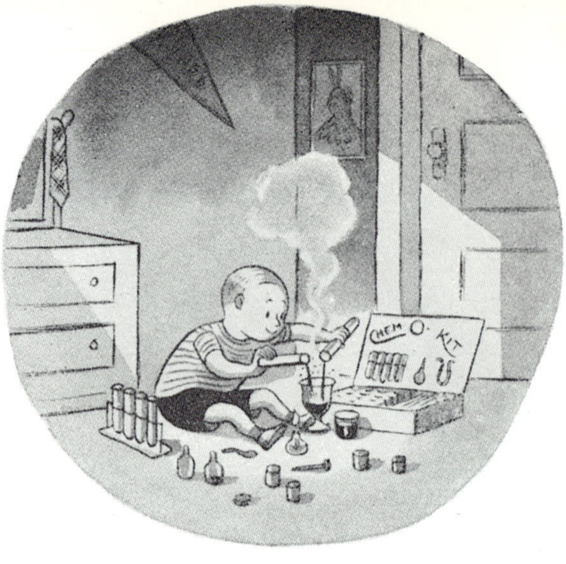

3

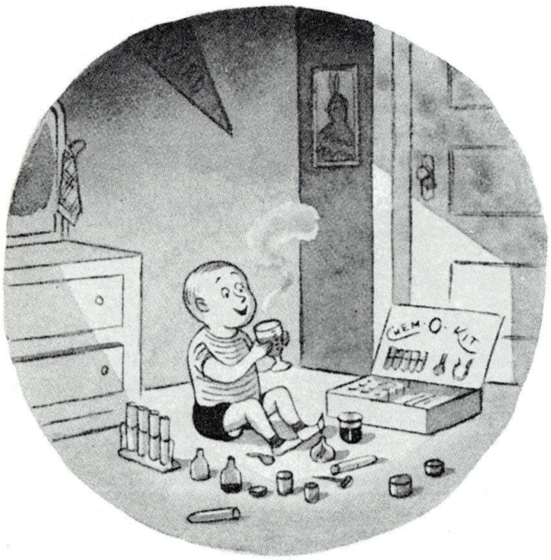

4

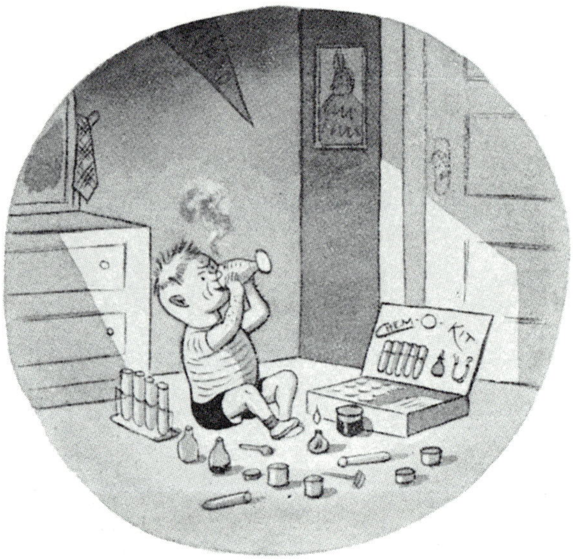

5

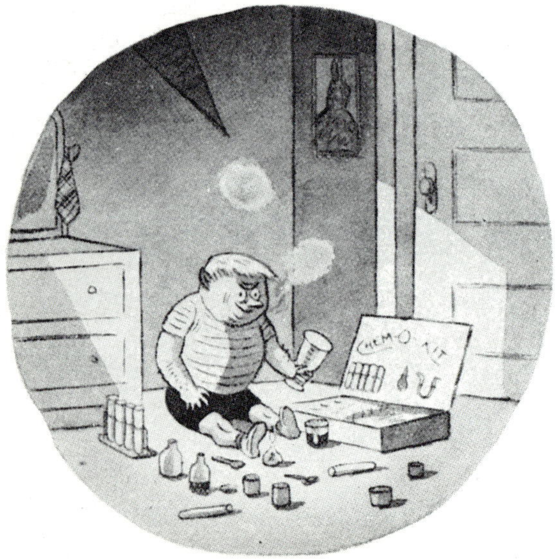

6

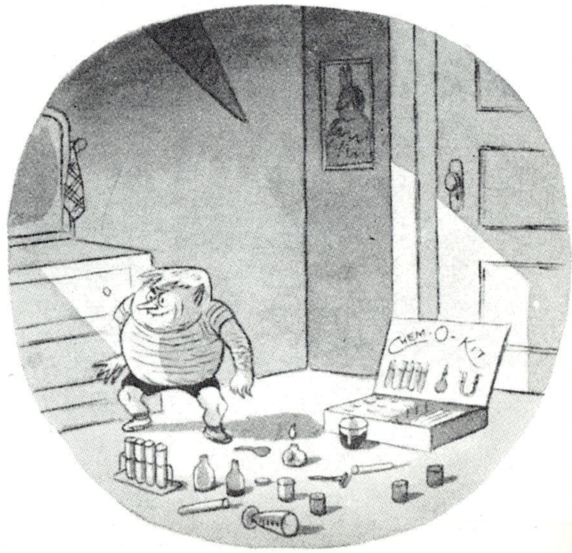

7

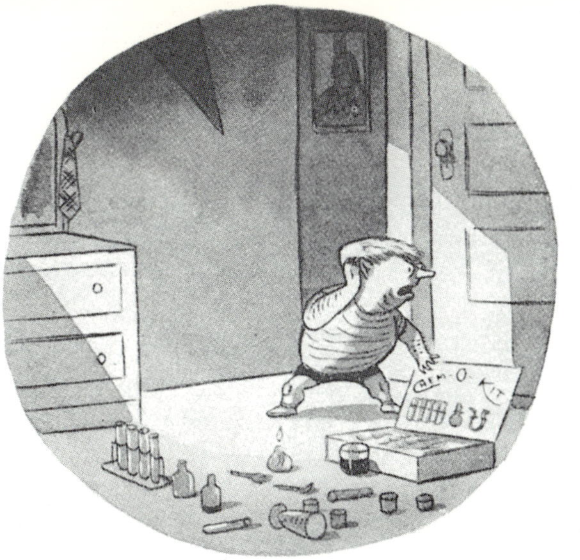
CHEM-O-KIT

8

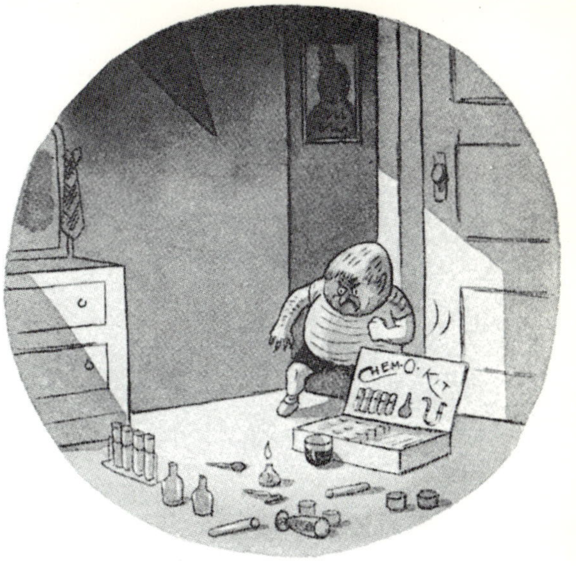
CHEM-O-KIT

9

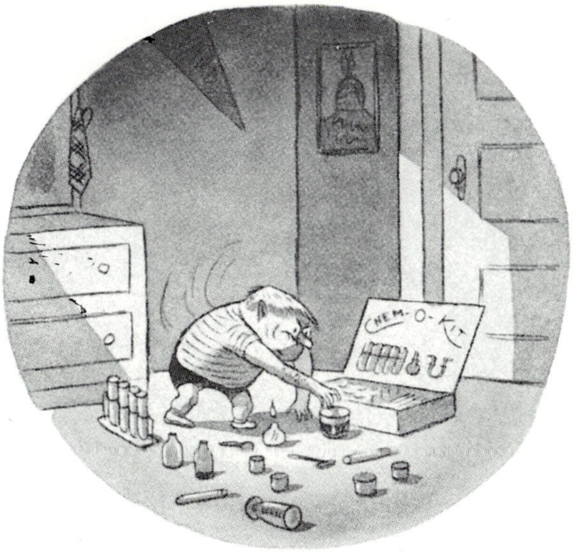
CHEM-O-KIT

10

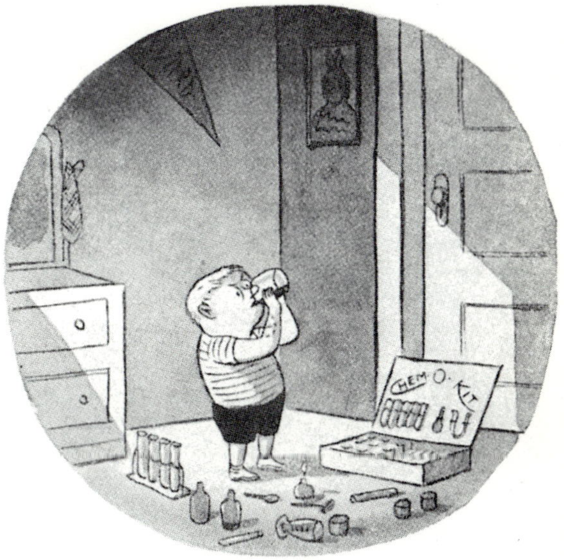
CHEM-O-KIT

11

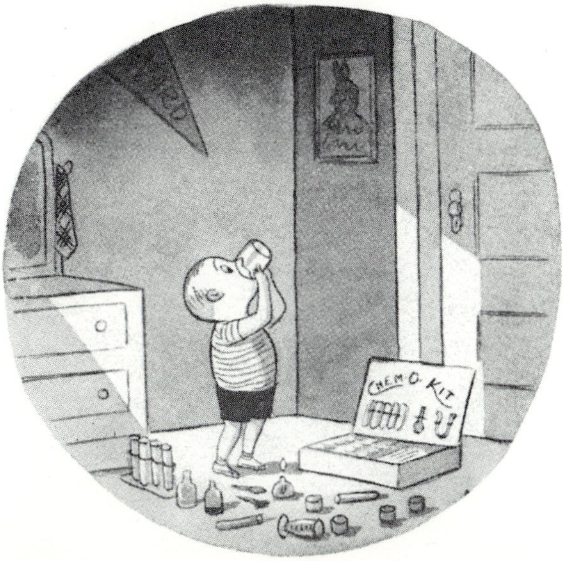
CHEM-O-KIT

12

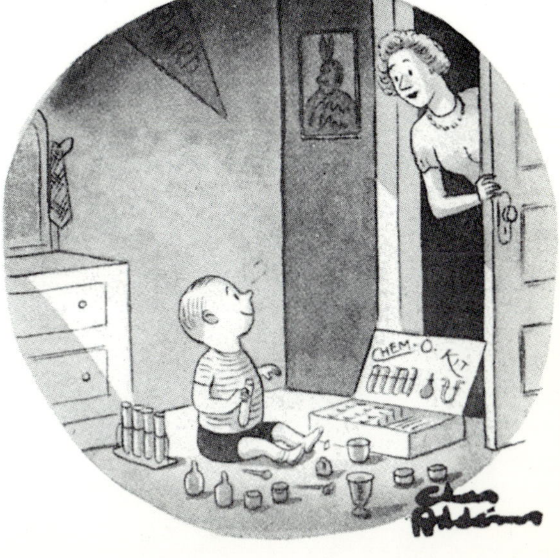
CHEM-O-KIT
Chas Addams

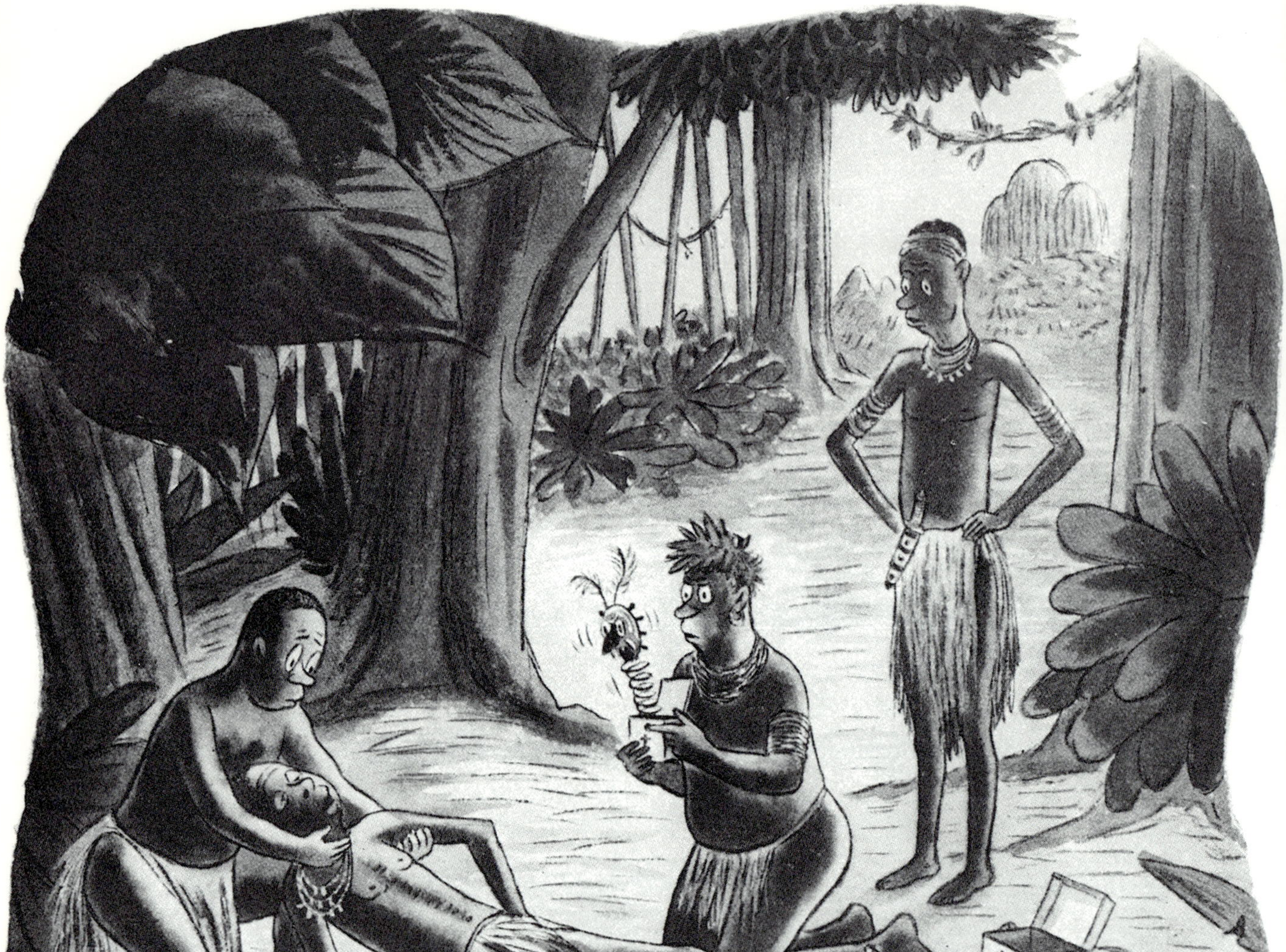
FIRST AID
Chas Addams

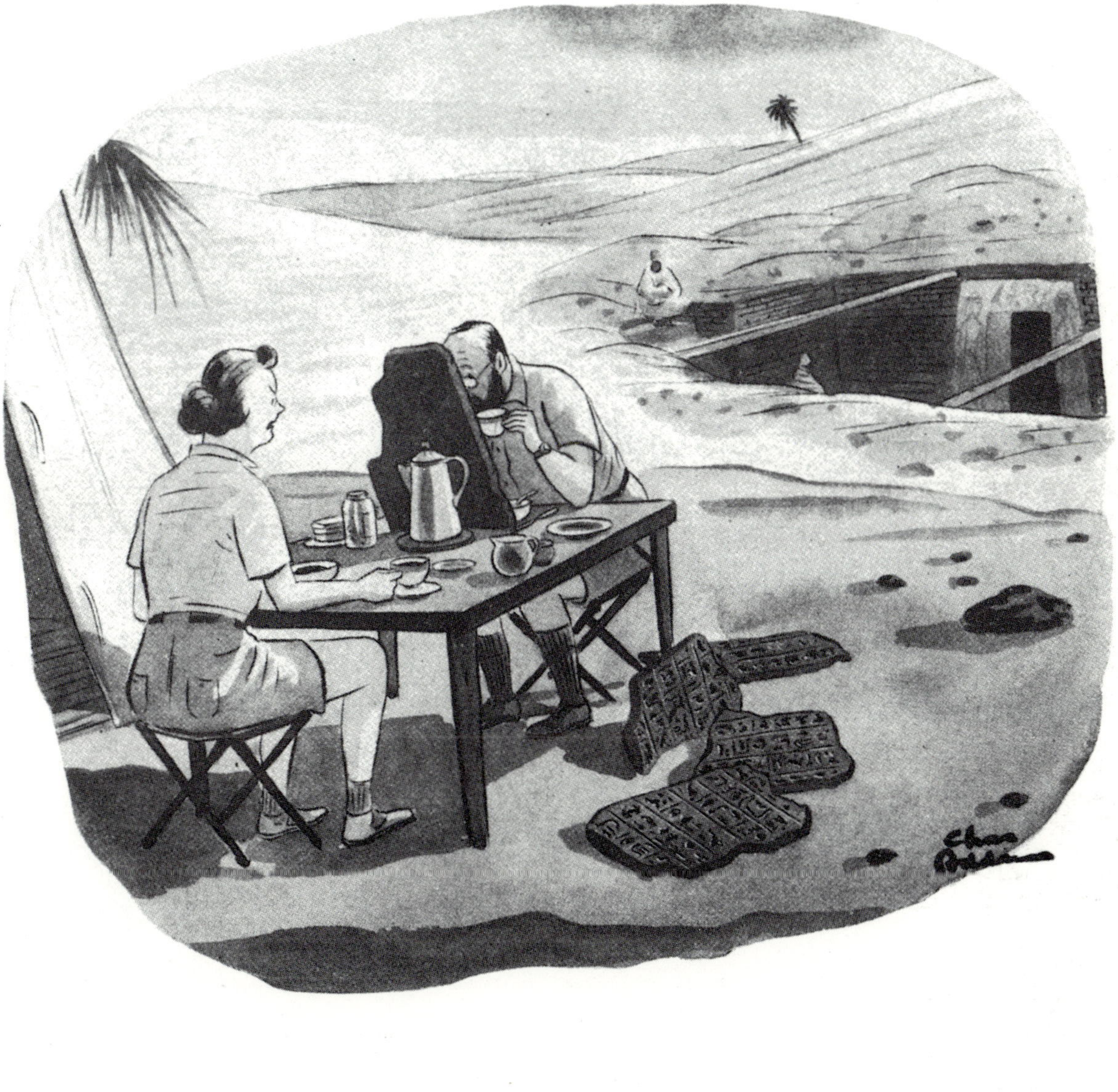

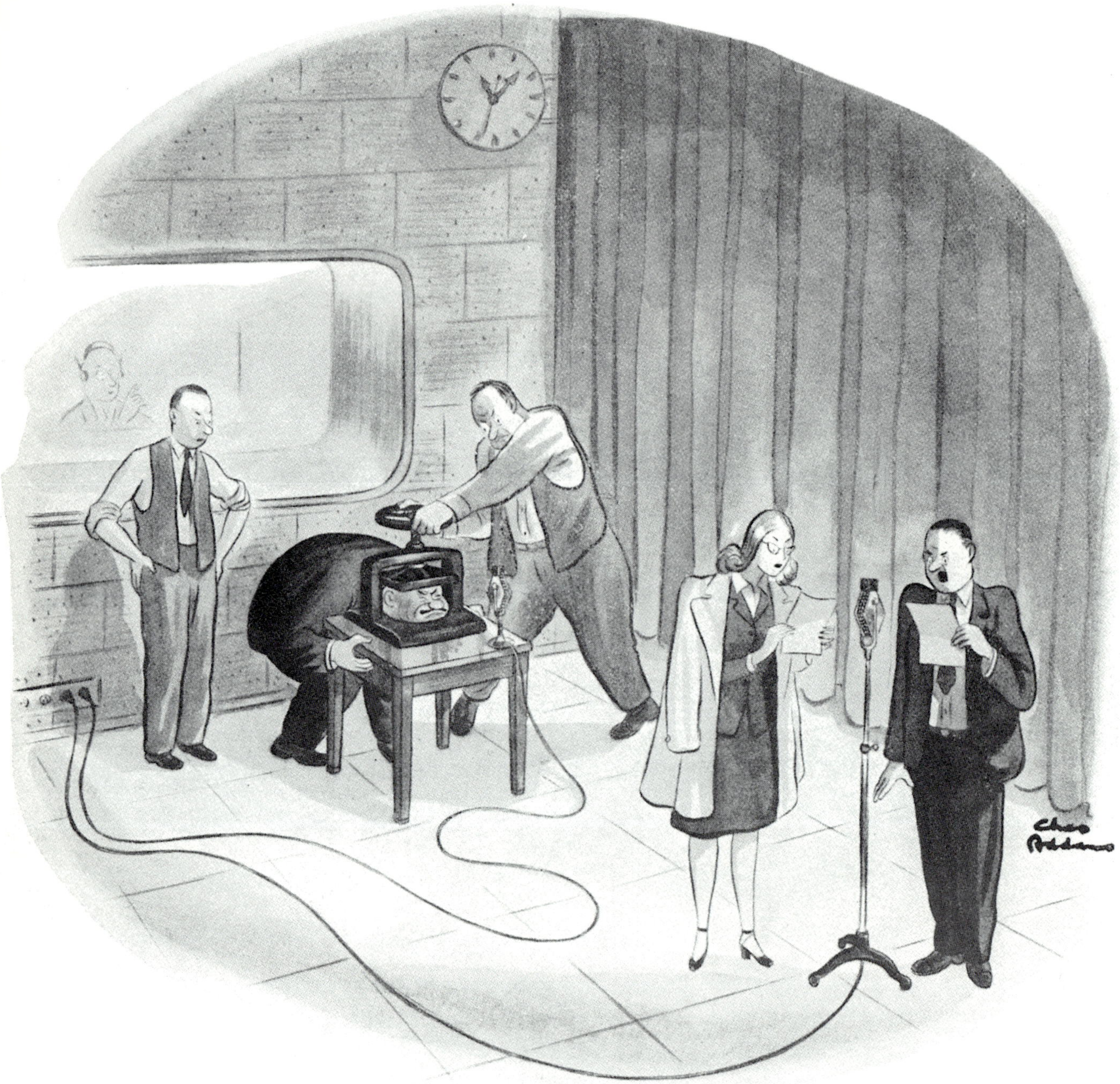

'Listen! Was that a moan I heard?'

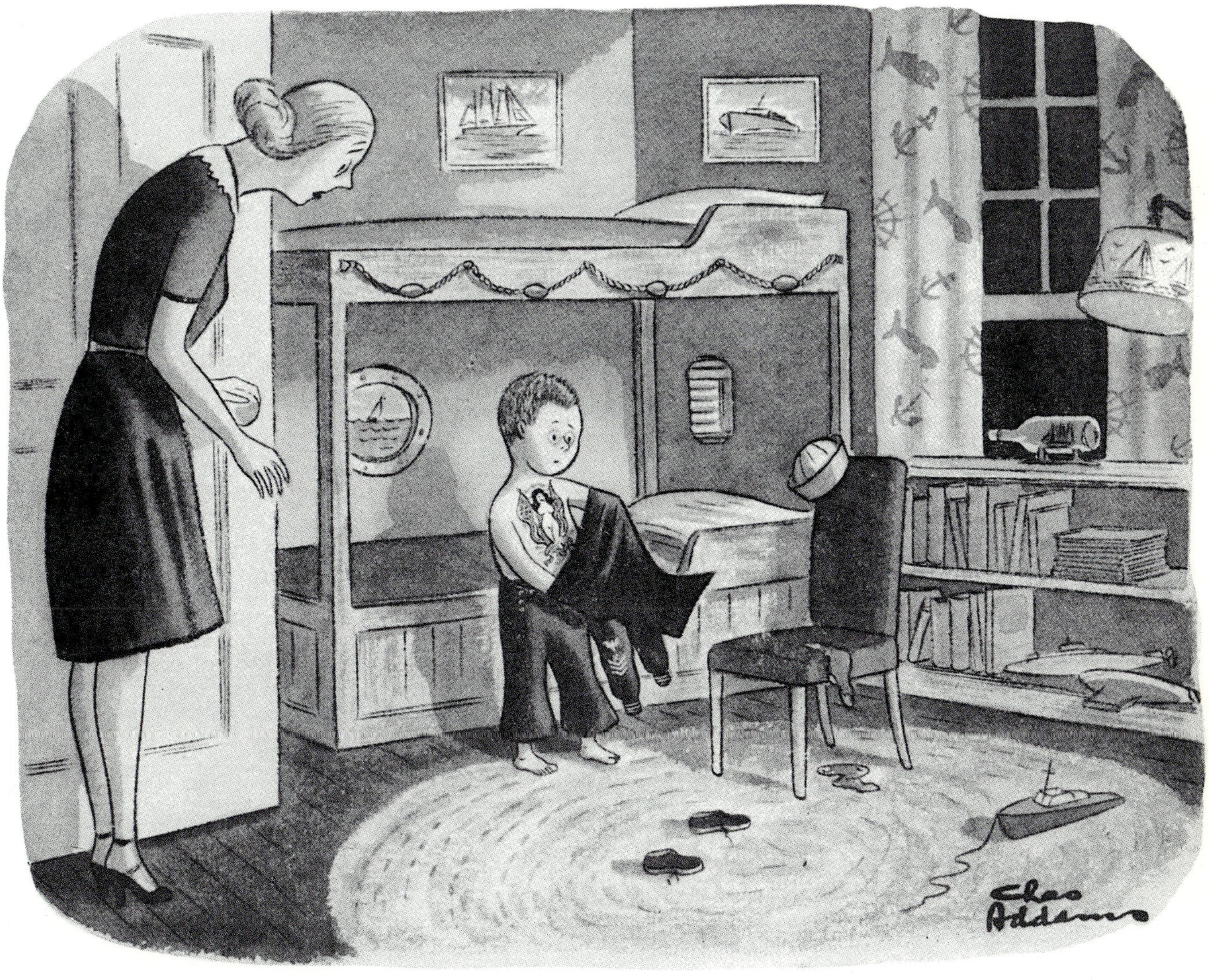
Chas Addams

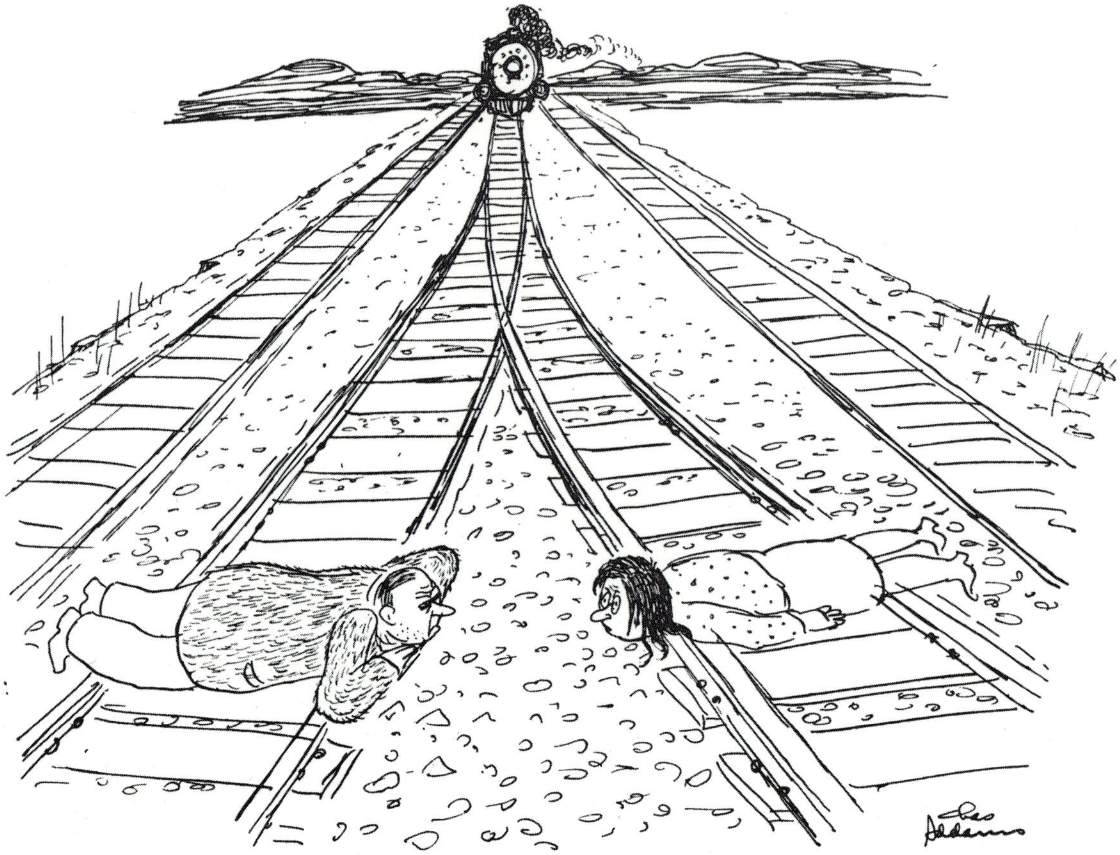

Suicide Pact

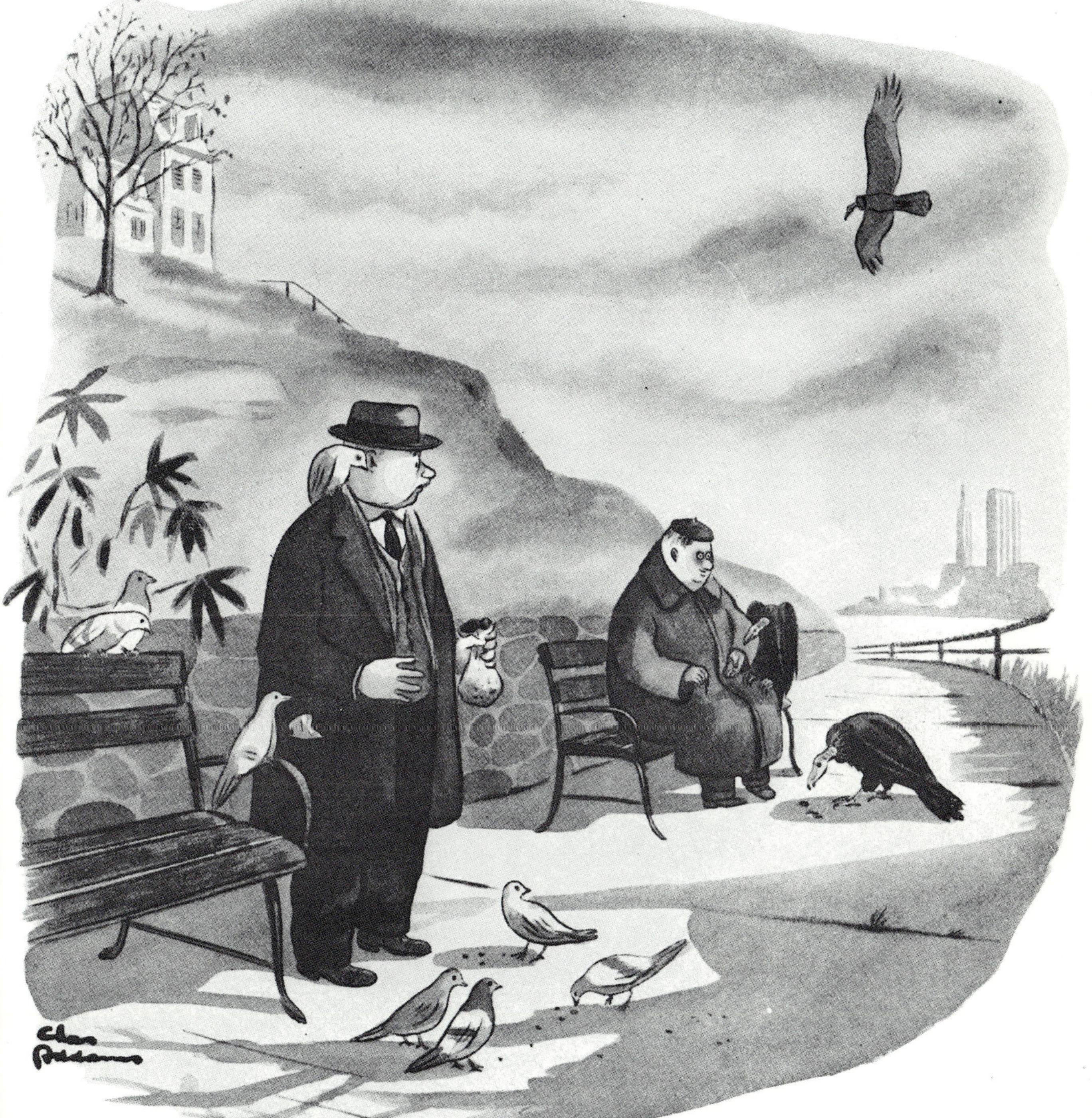
Chas Addams

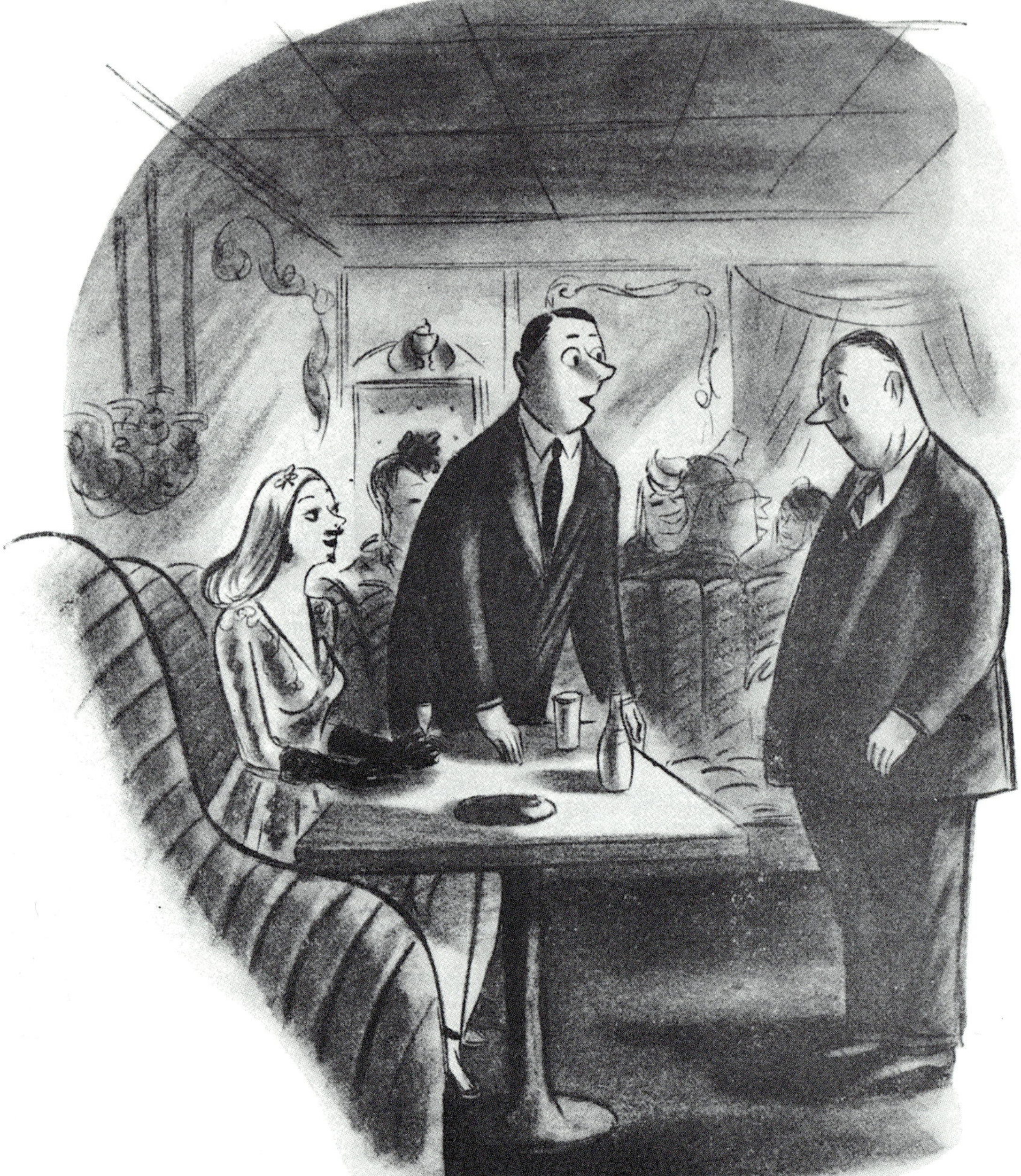

'Miss Osborne poses for subway posters.'

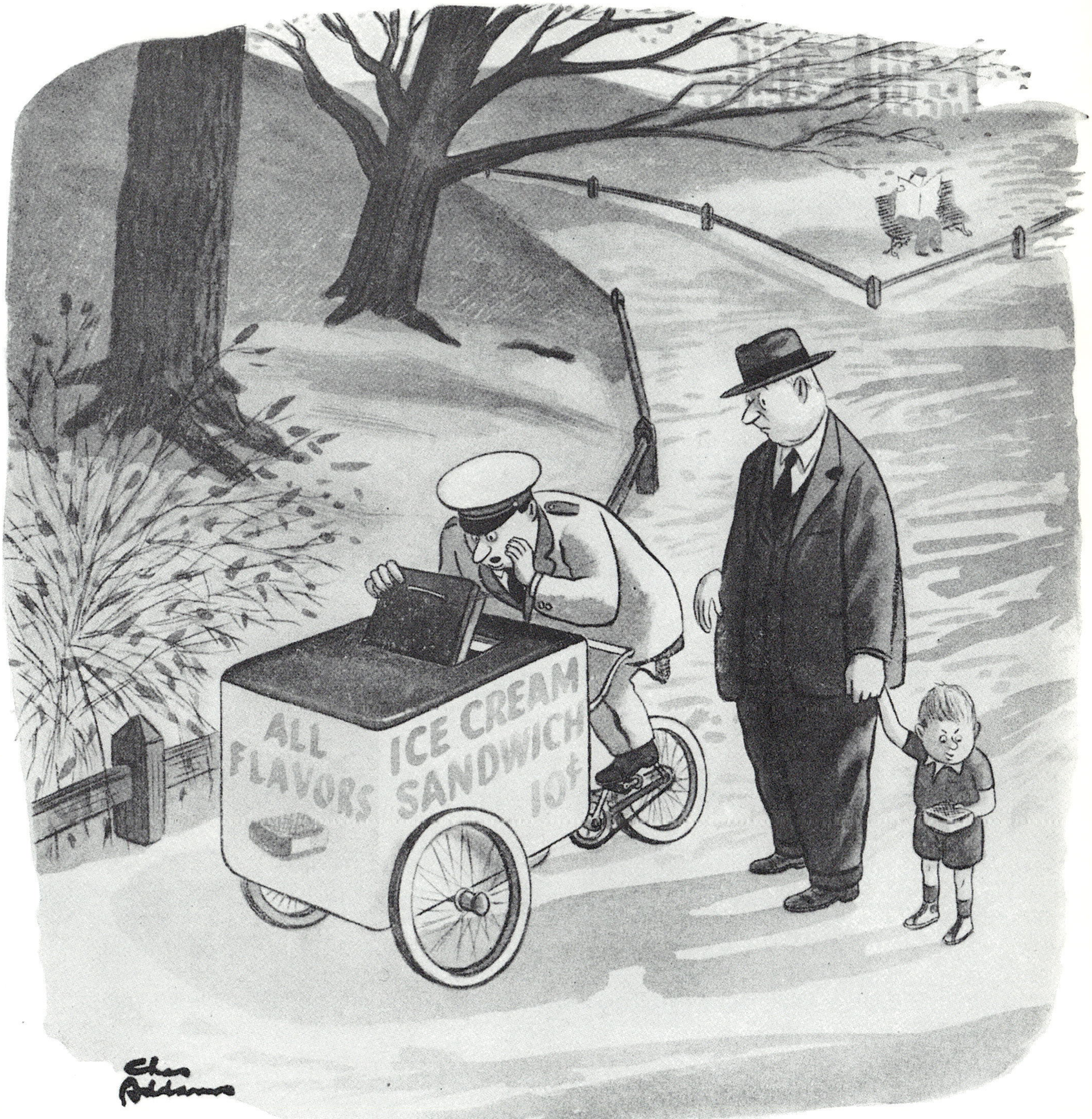

'Another vanilla, Benny.'

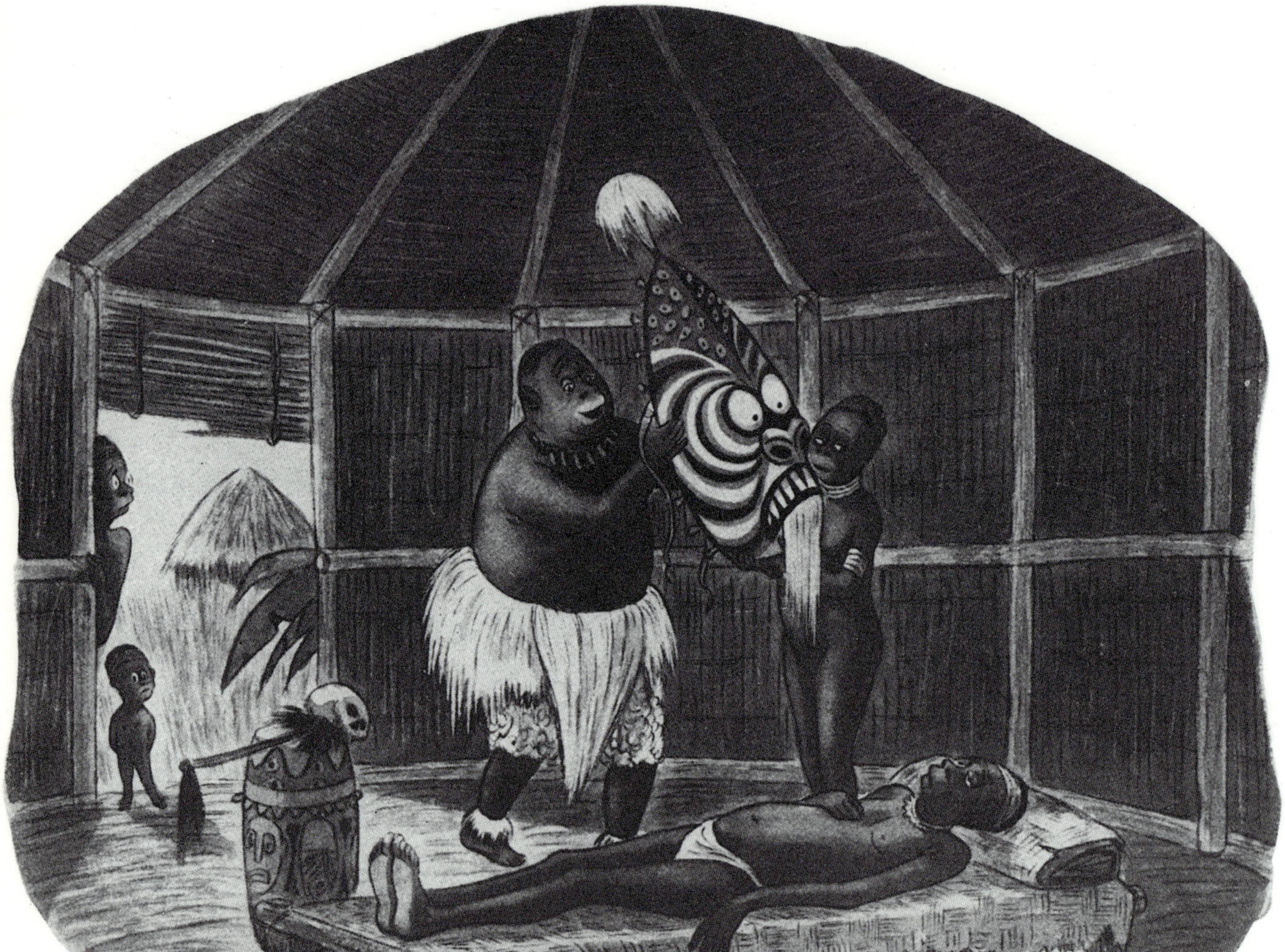

'Now, this may frighten you just a little bit.'

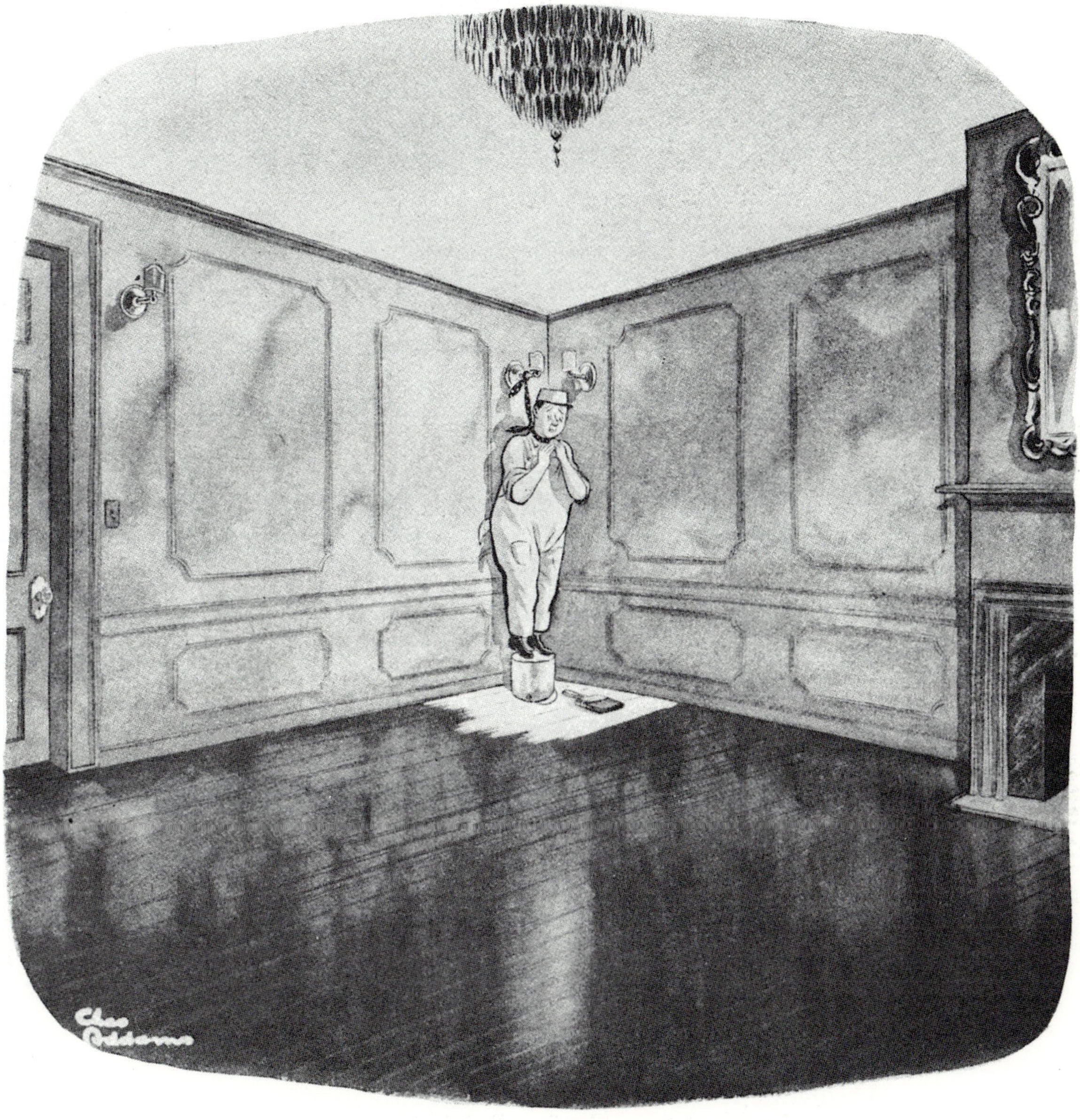
Chas Addams

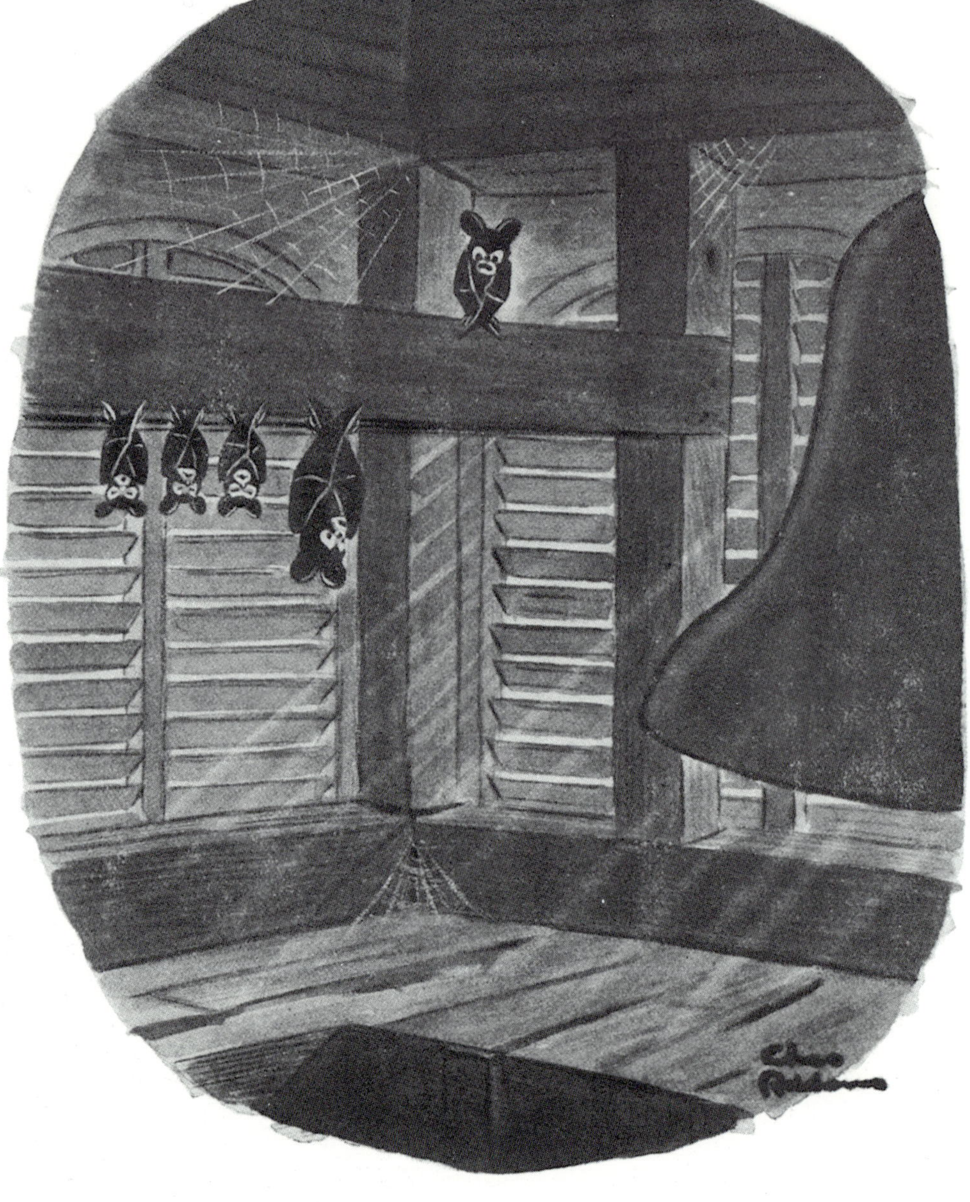

'I tell you, Mama, the blood keeps going to my head.'

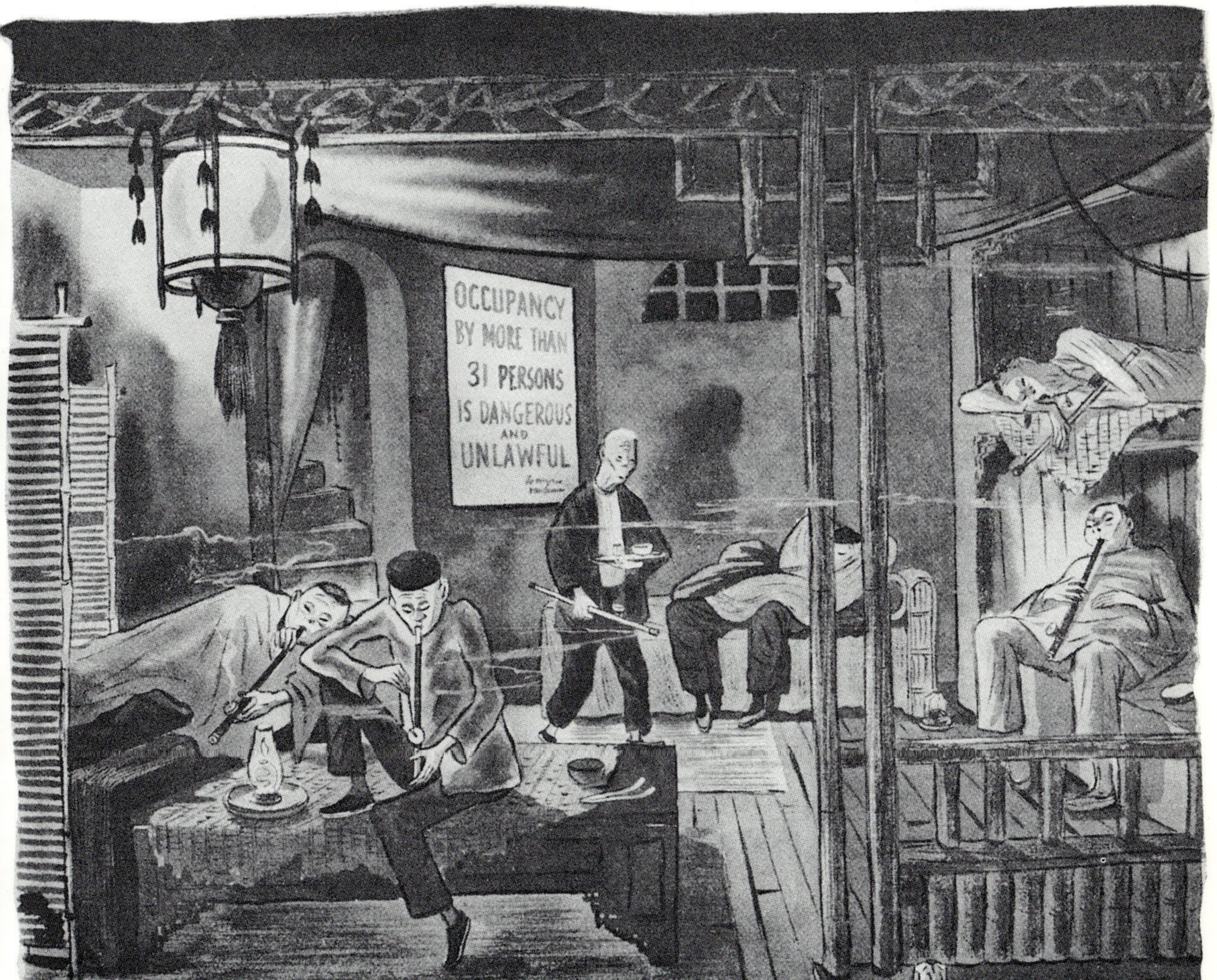
OCCUPANCY
BY MORE THAN
31 PERSONS
IS DANGEROUS
AND
UNLAWFUL
Chas Addams

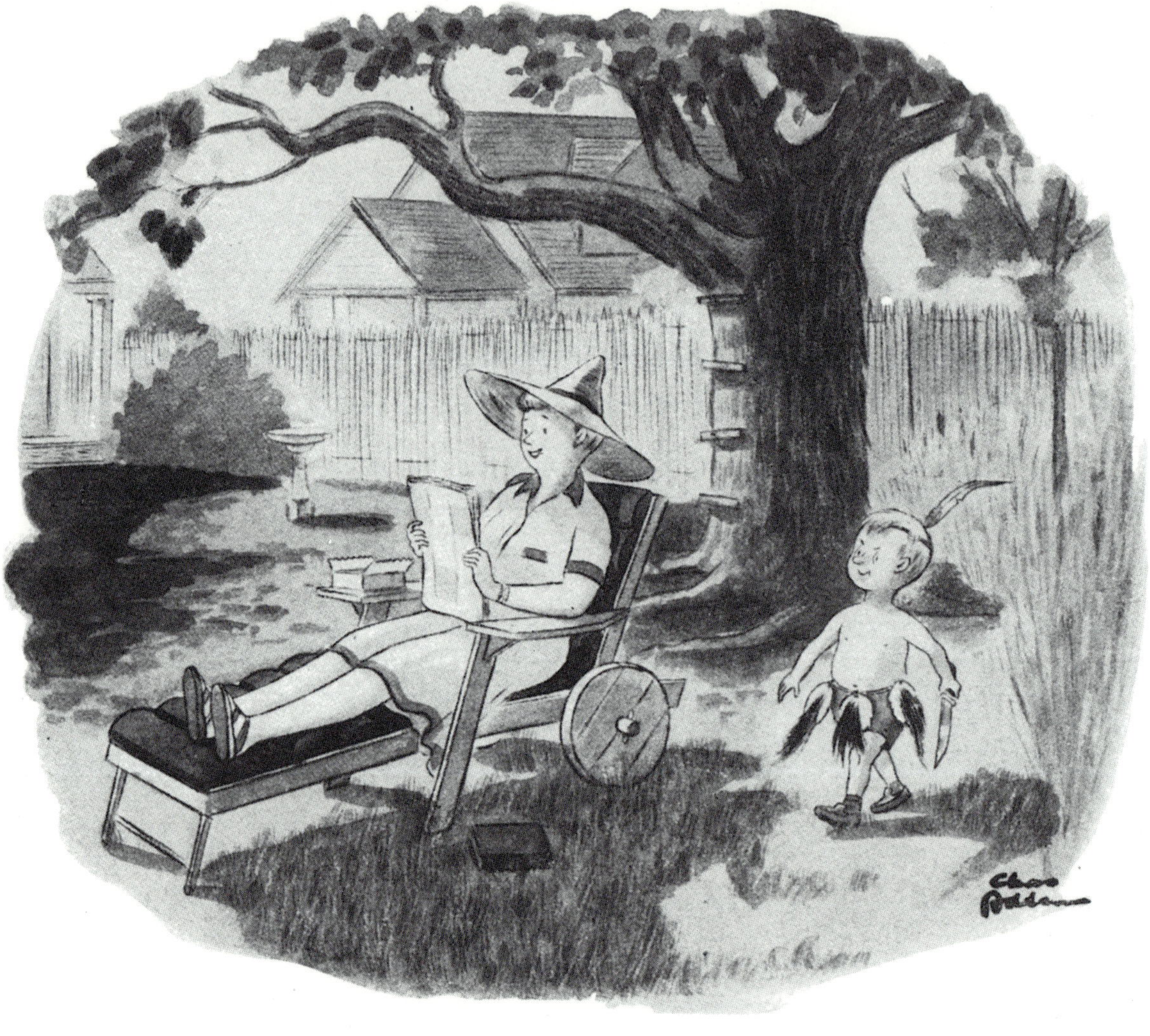

'Well, dear, was it fun playing Indian?'

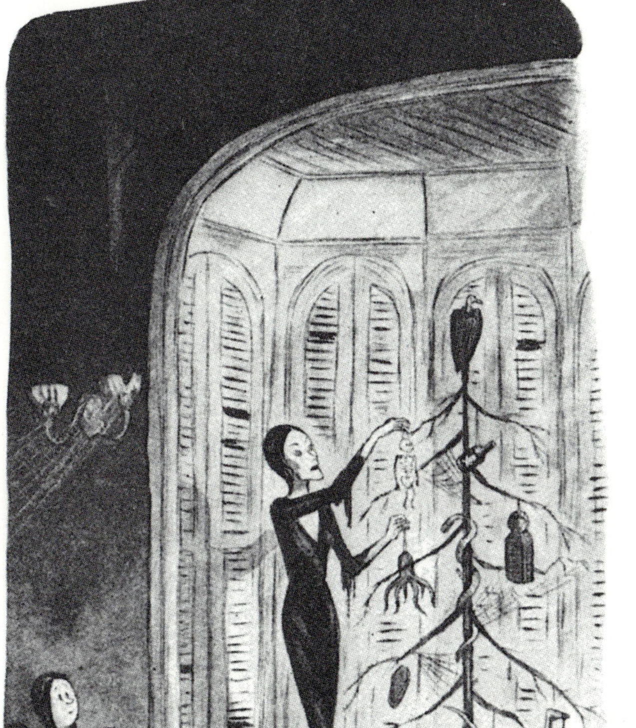

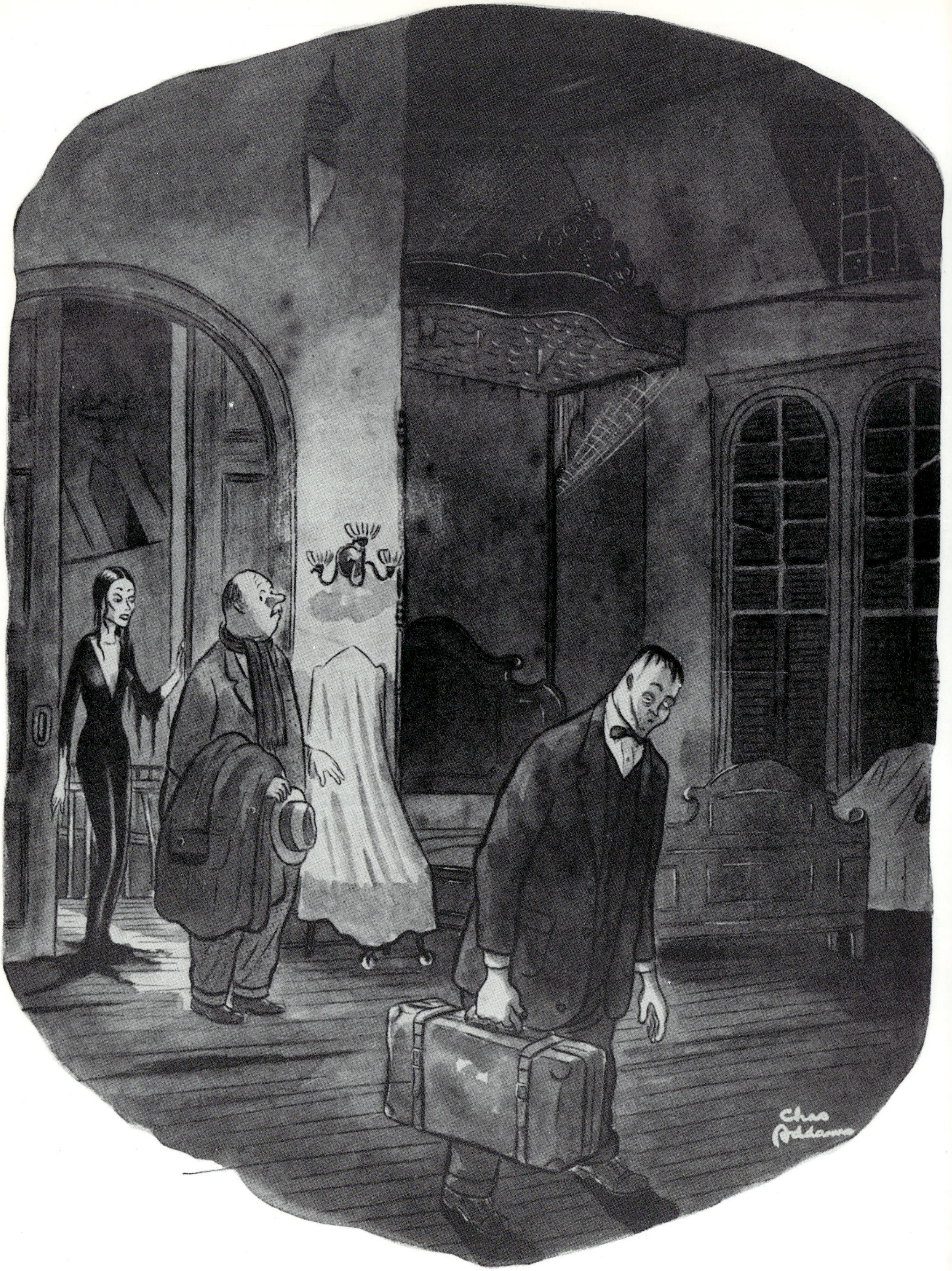

'This is your room. If you should need anything, just scream.'

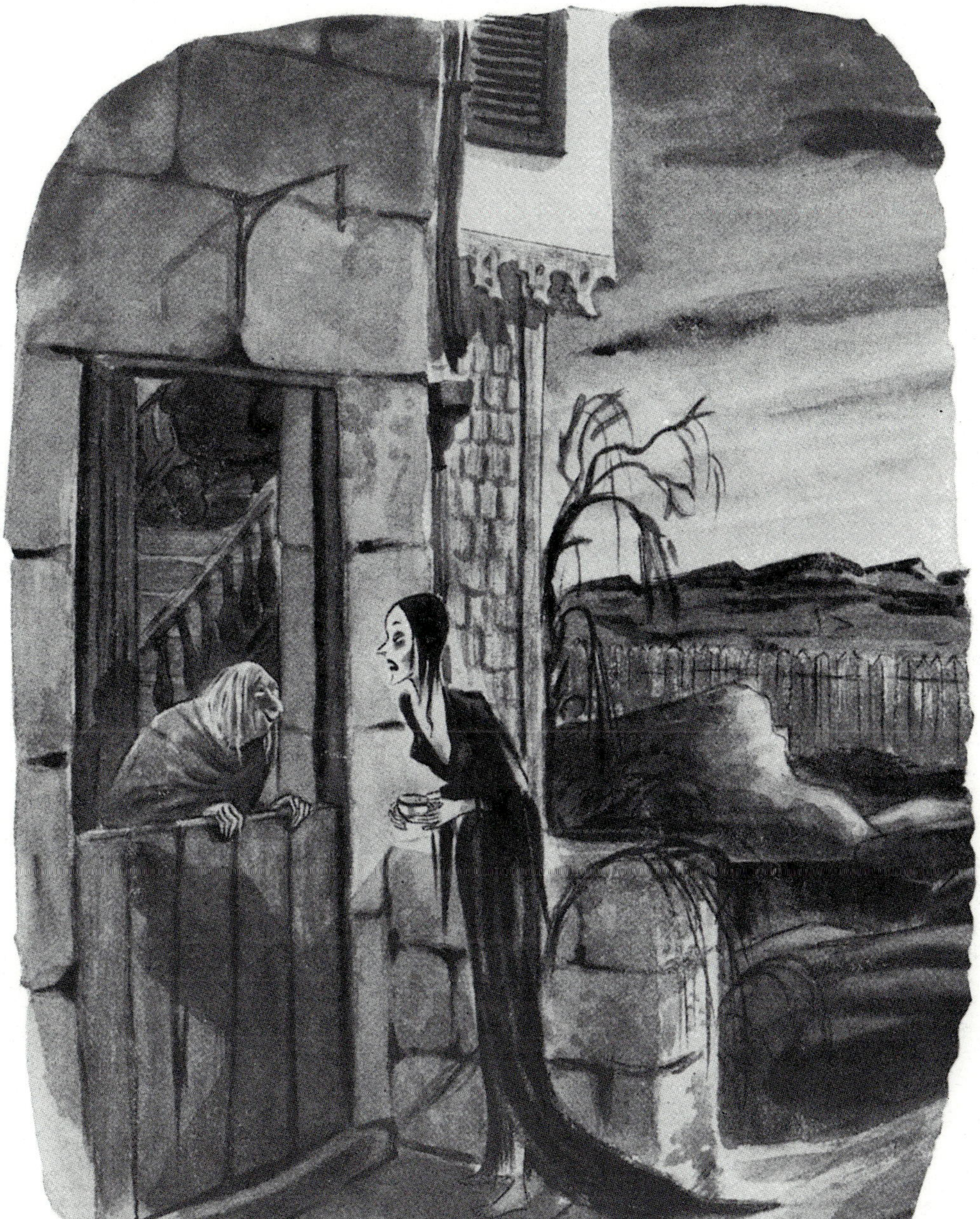

'May I borrow a cup of cyanide?'

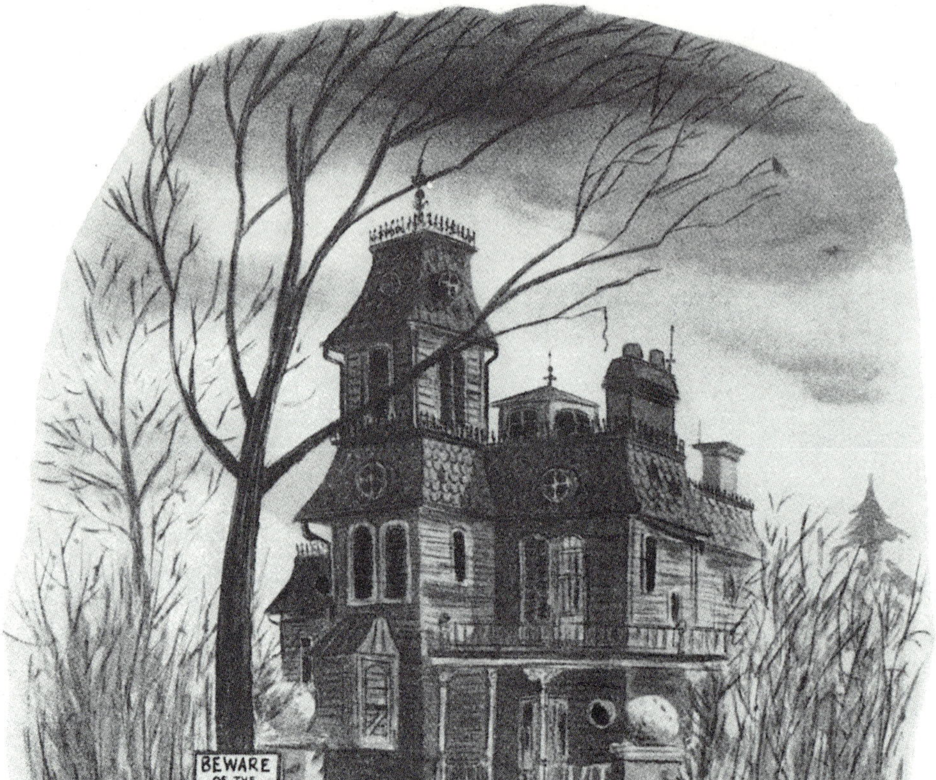
BEWARE
OF THE
THING

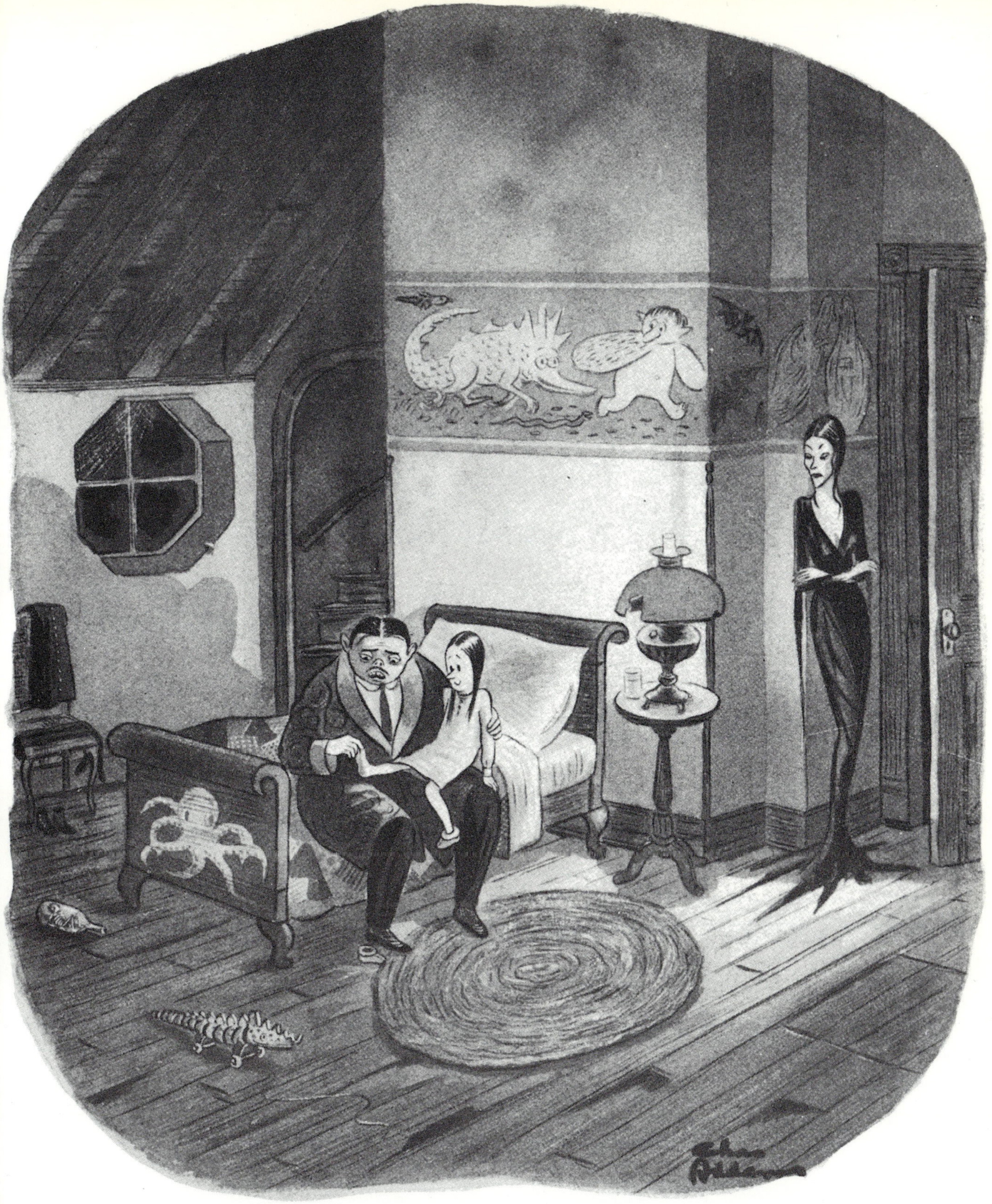

'This little piggy went to market,
This little piggy stayed at home,
This little piggy had roast beef,
This little piggy had none,
This little piggy went wee wee wee all the way home,
And this little piggy . . .'

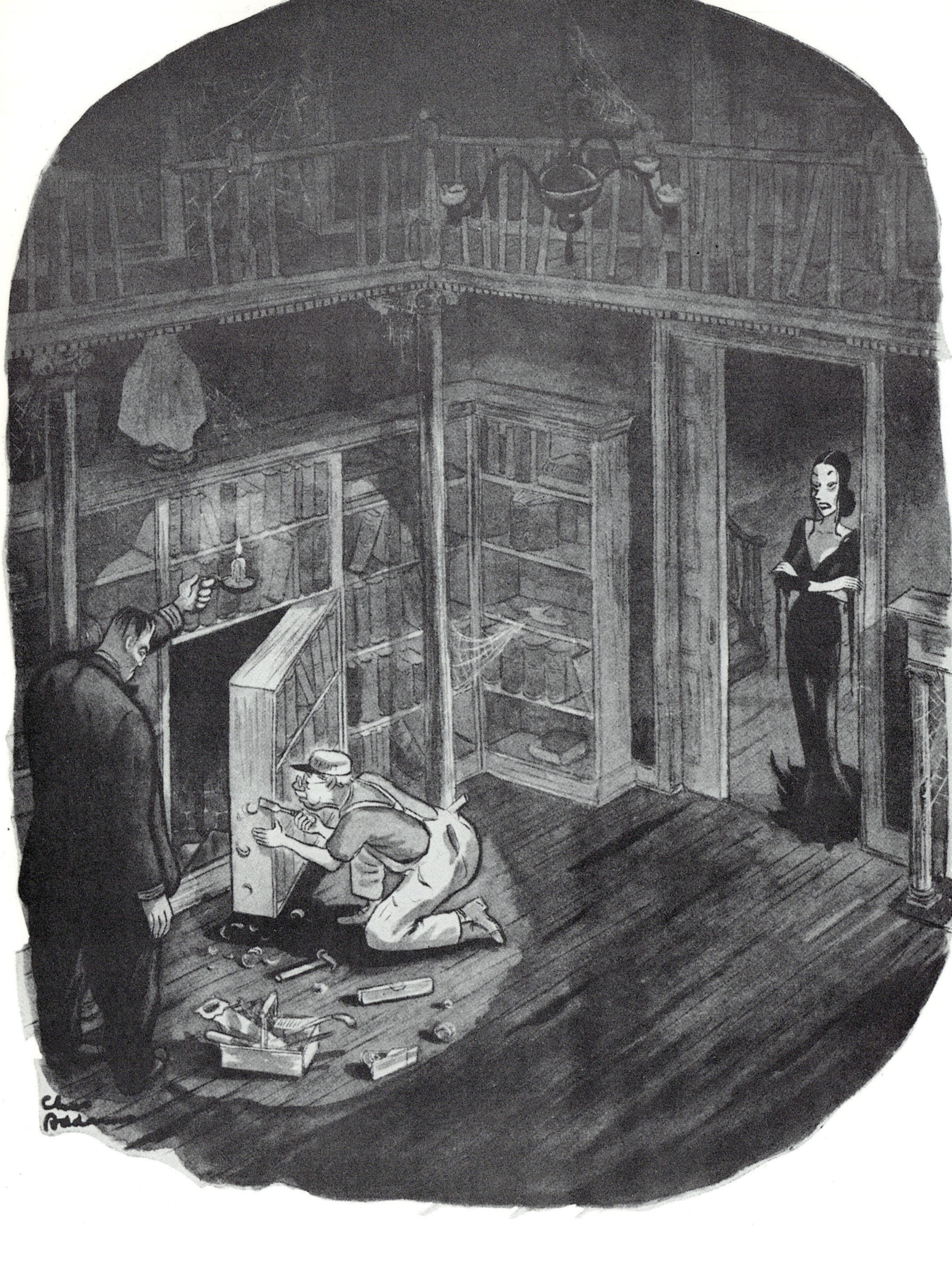

‘While you’re here,
there’s a squeaky trap door I’d like you to look at.’

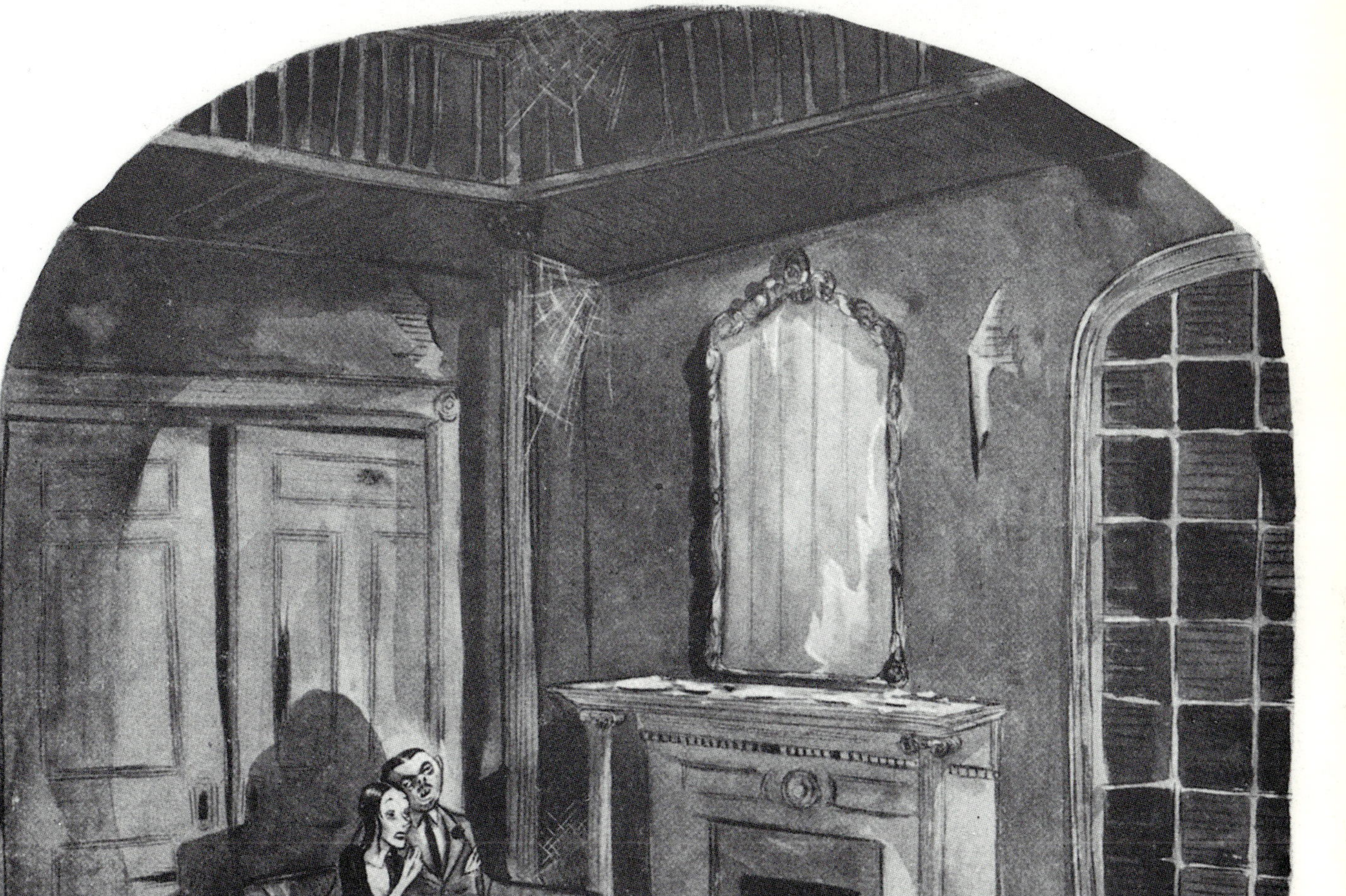

'Are you unhappy, darling?'
'Oh, yes, *yes*! Completely.'

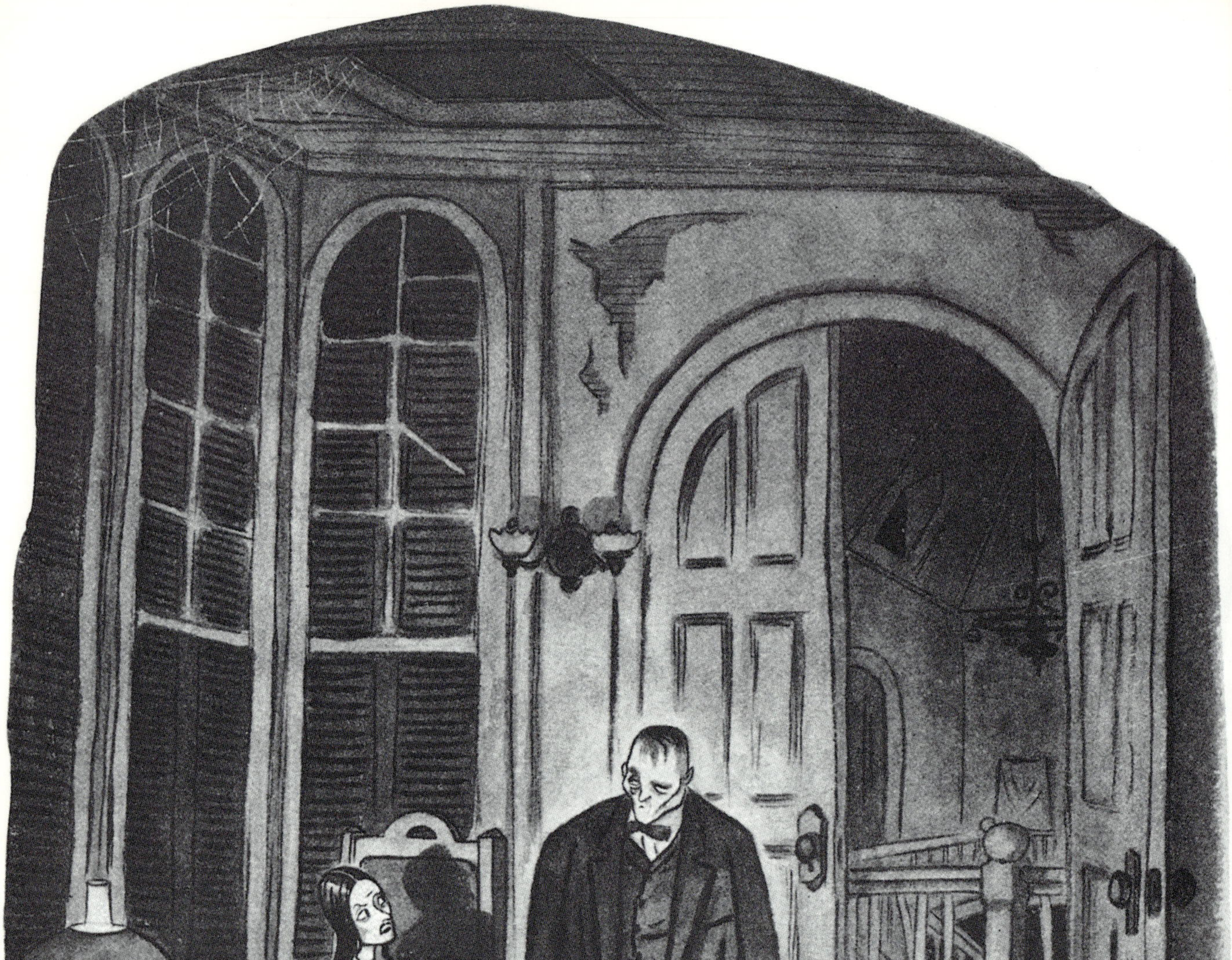

'Oh, it's *you*! For a moment you gave me quite a start.'

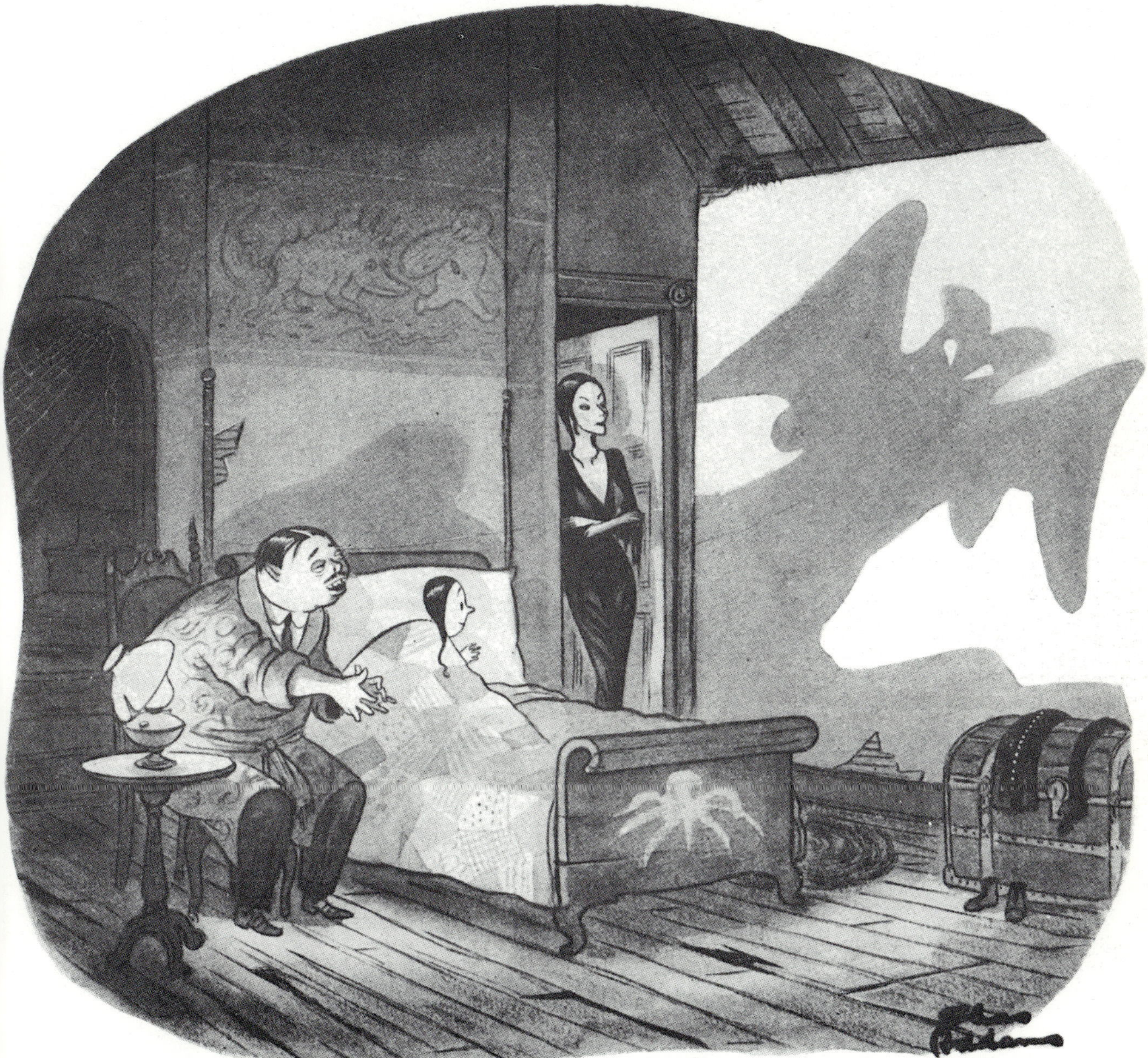

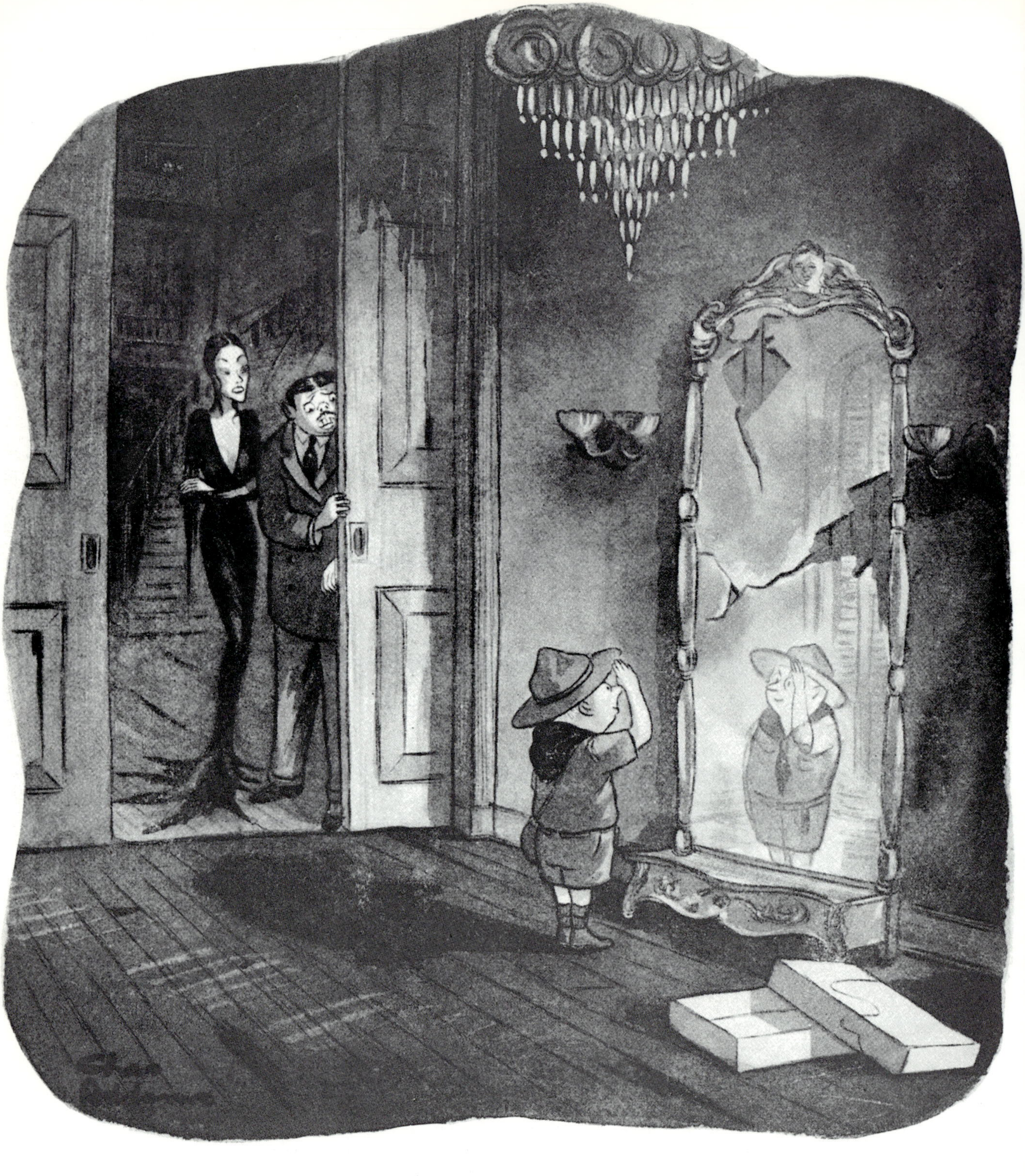

'Well, he certainly doesn't take after *my* side of the family.'

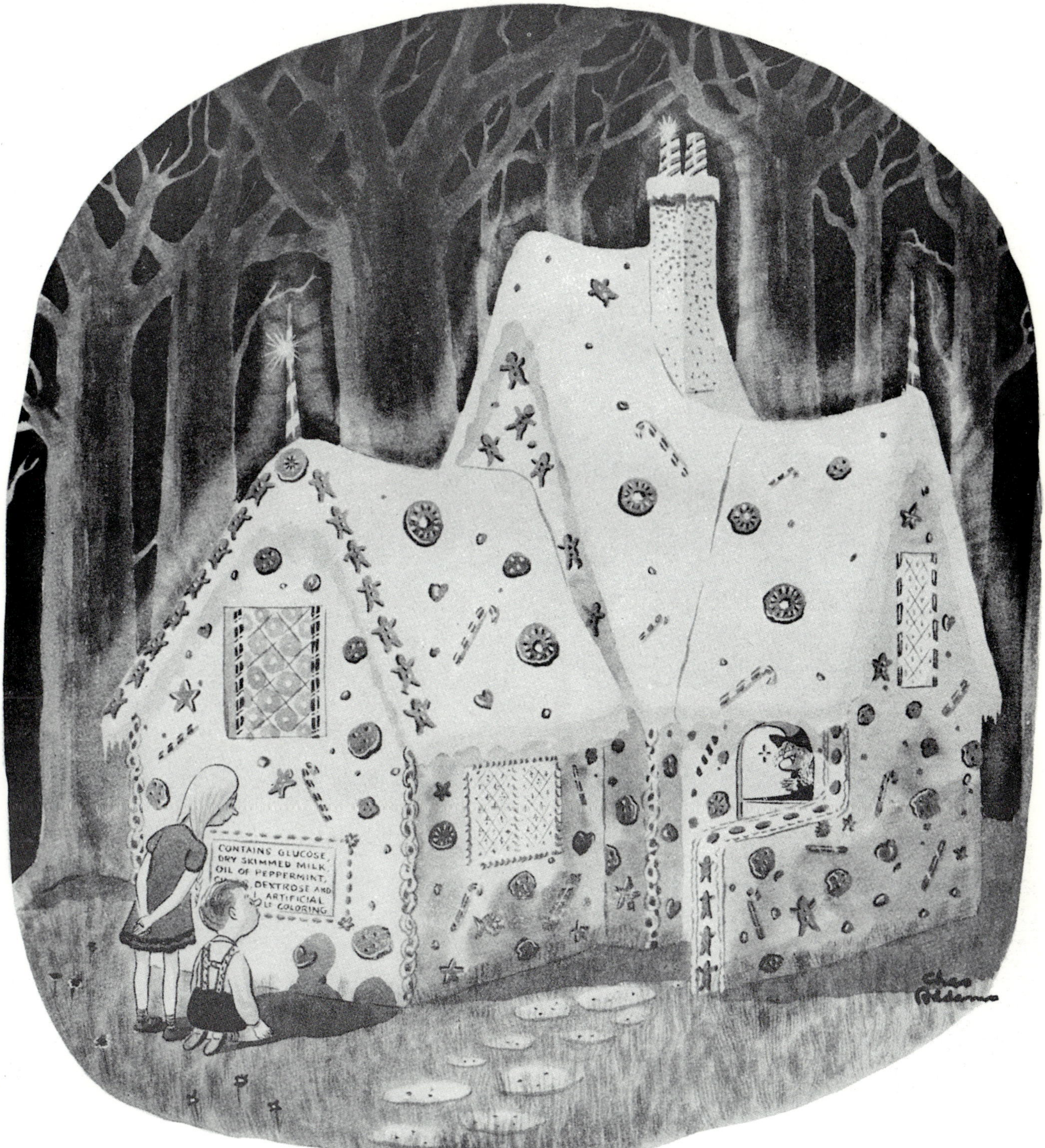
CONTAINS GLUCOSE,
DRY SKIMMED MILK,
OIL OF PEPPERMINT,
DEXTROSE AND
ARTIFICIAL
COLORING
Chas Addams

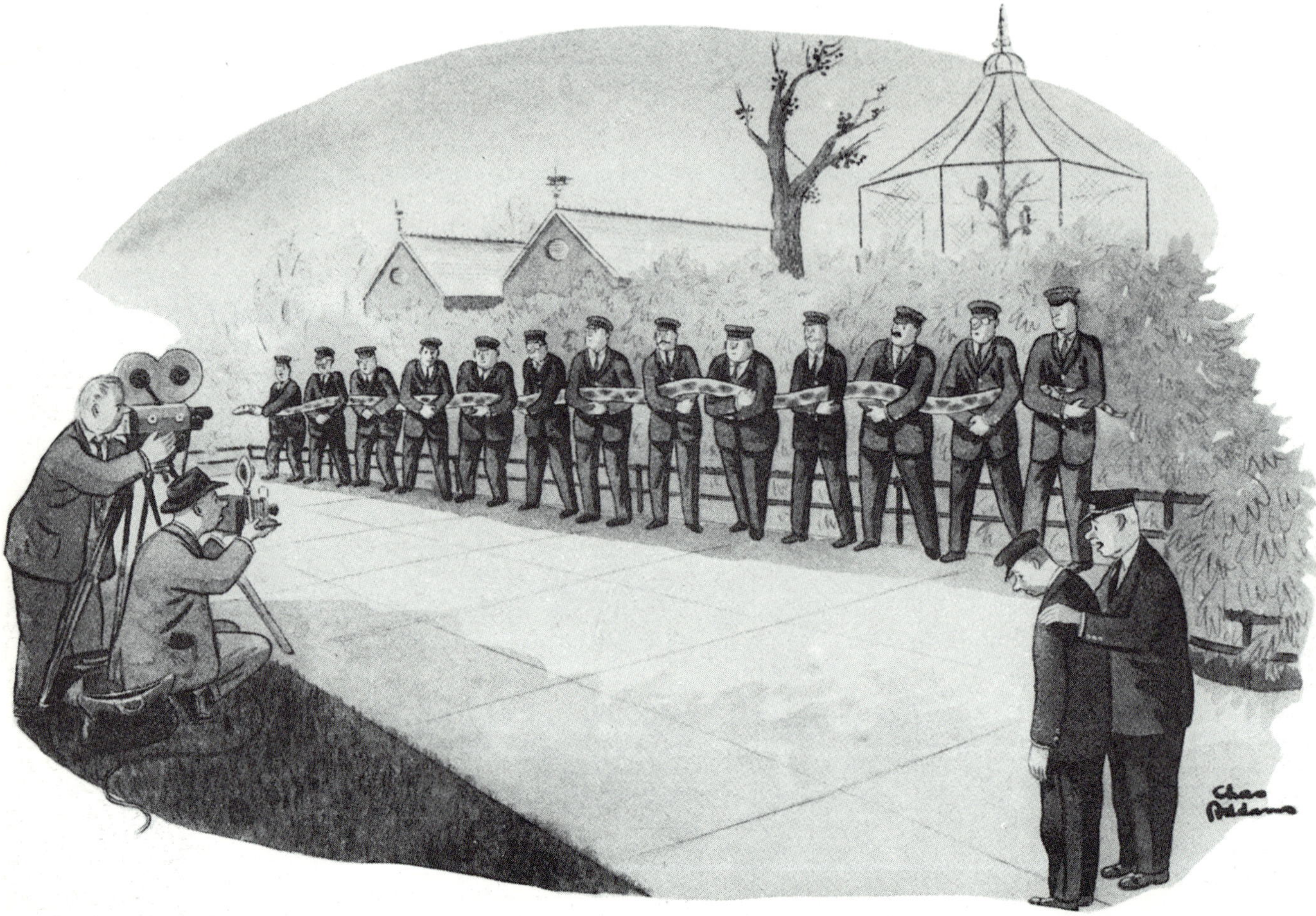

'Don't feel badly, Nelson. With normal growth, you'll be in there next year.'

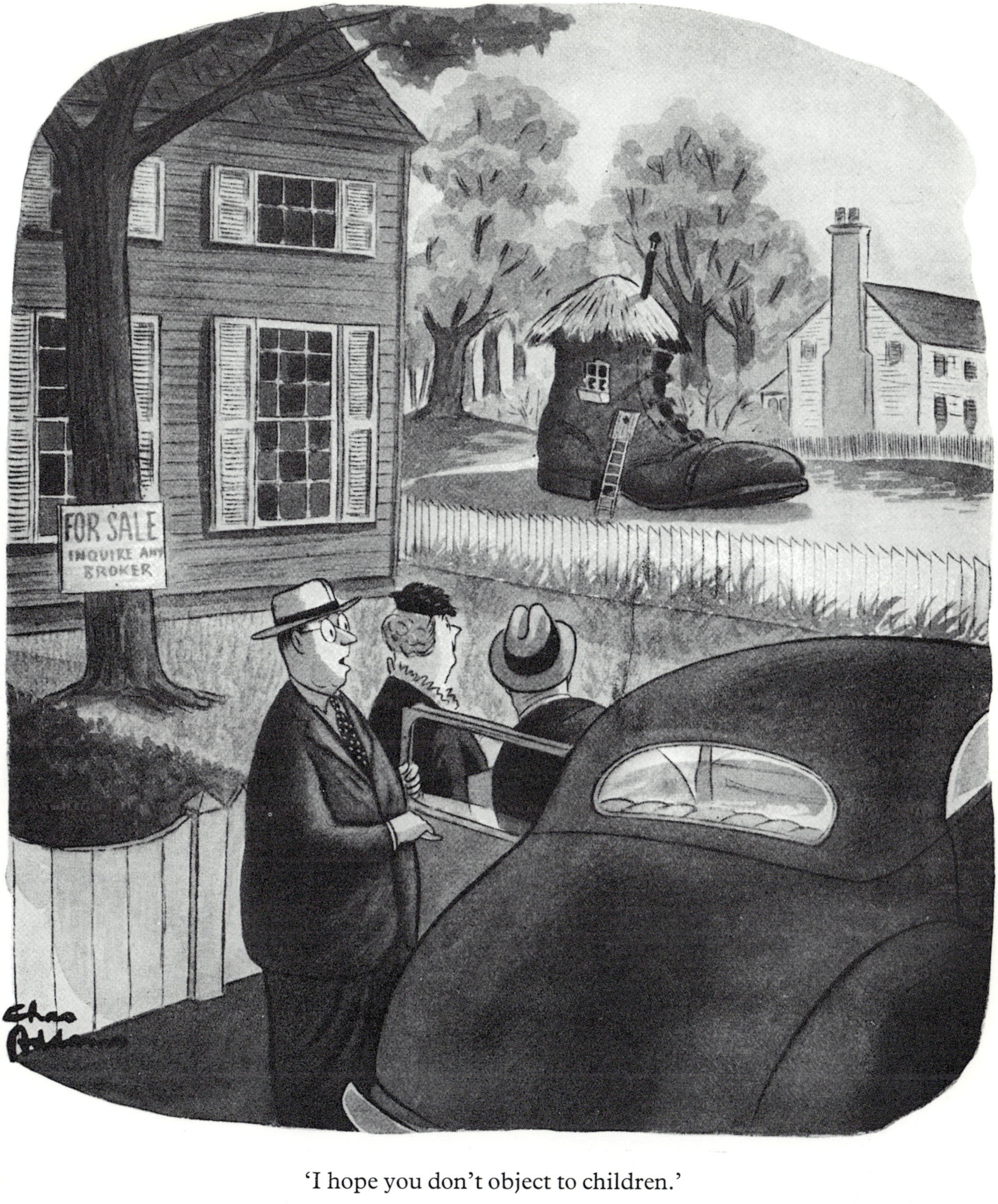

'I hope you don't object to children.'

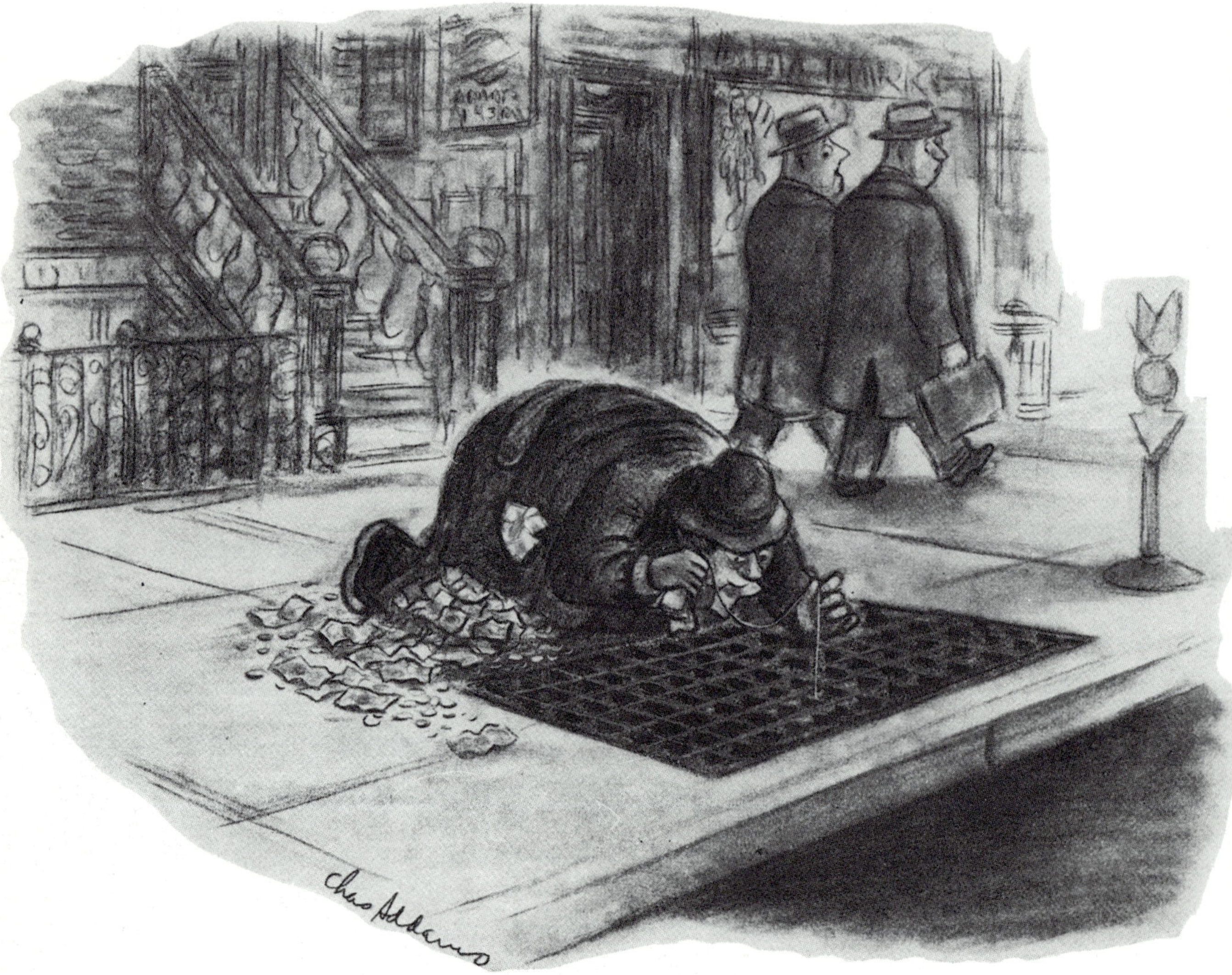

'Everybody's certainly cleaning up these days.'

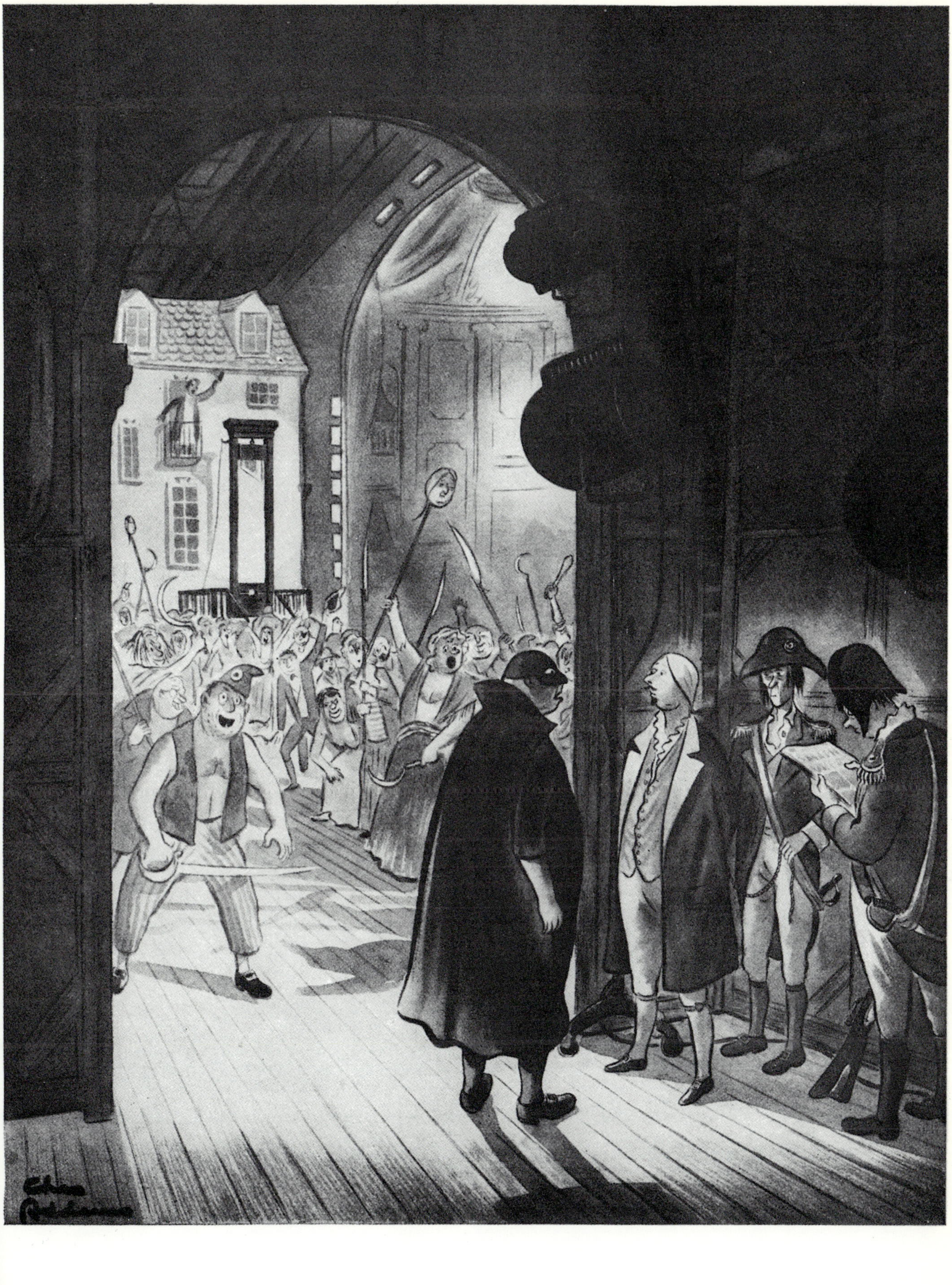

'Excuse me, Walter, that's my cue.'

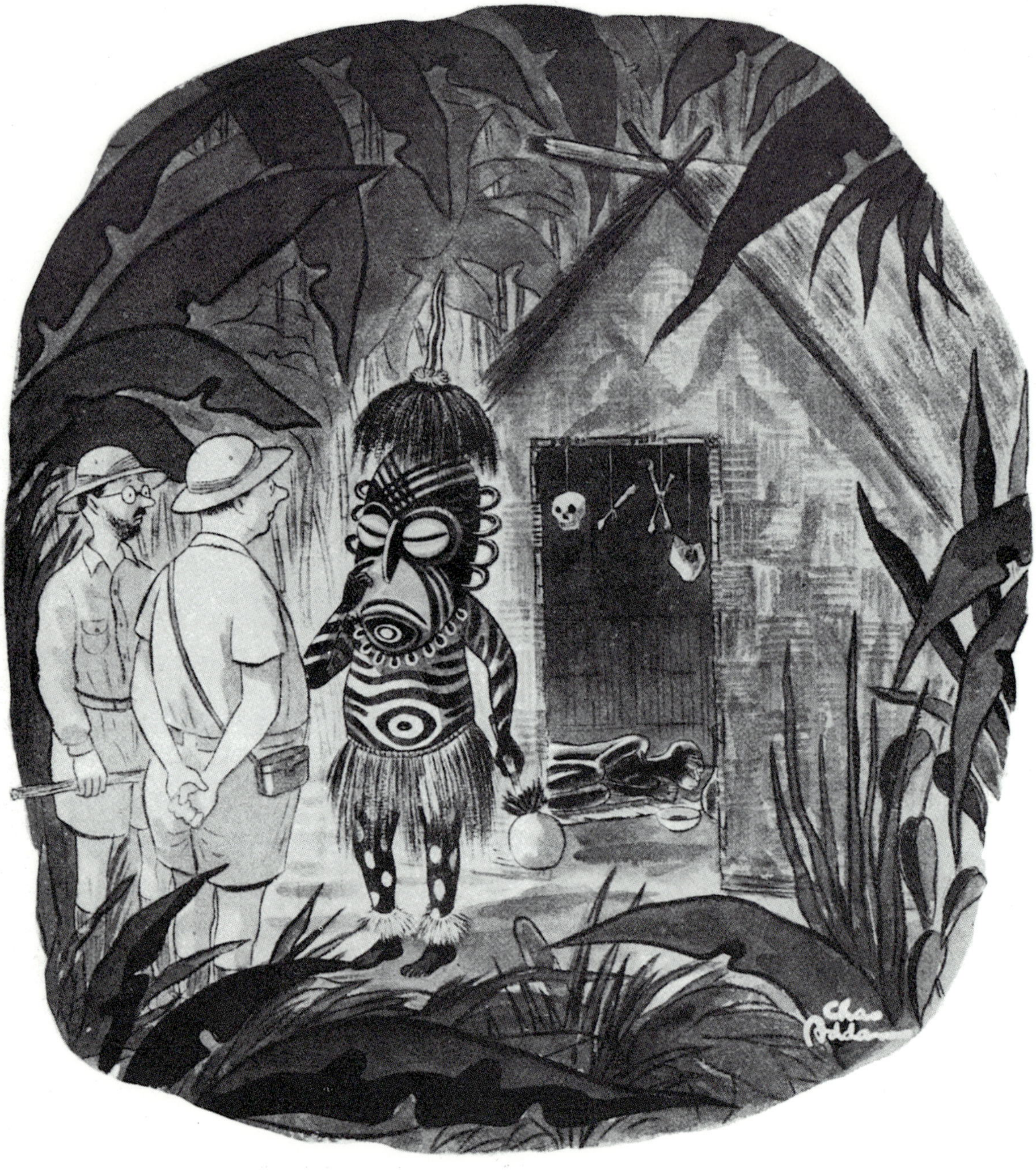

'This is just a front, you understand.
All I do, really, is slip sulfanilamide tablets into his drinking water.'

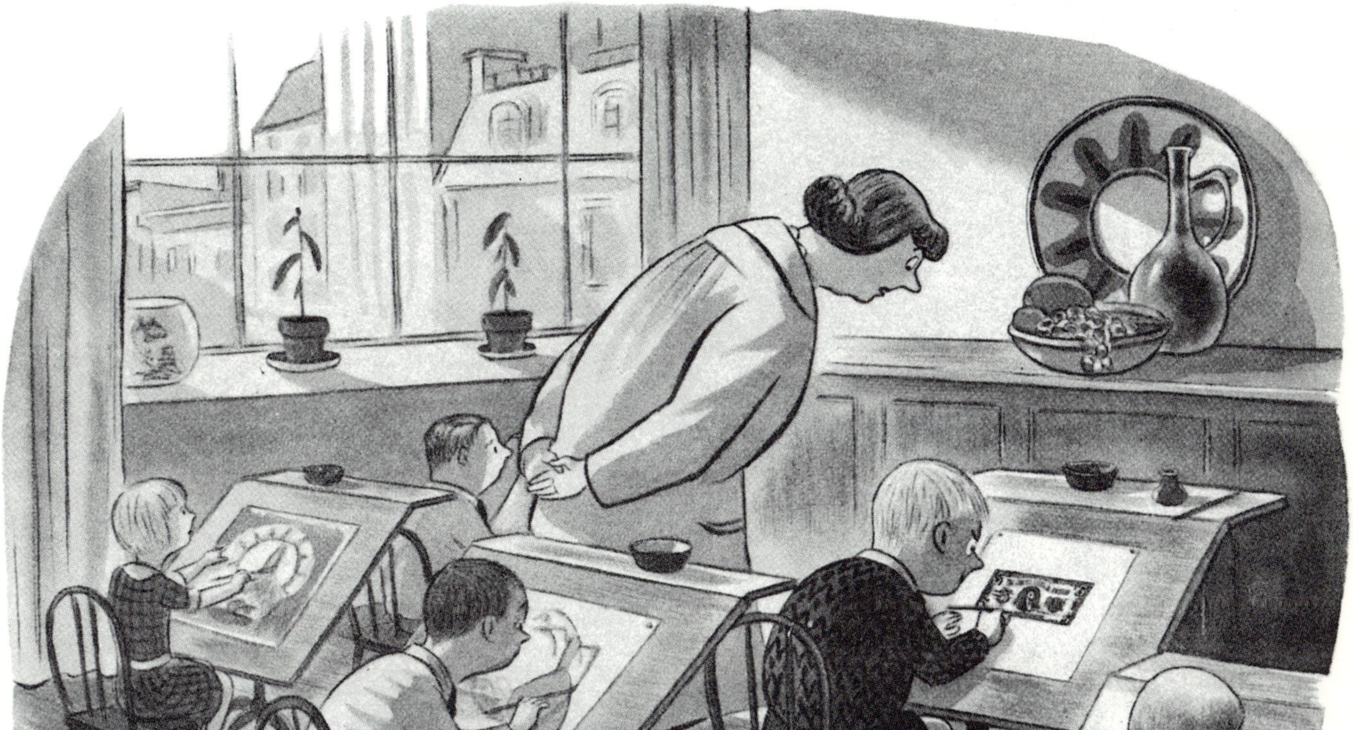
Chas Addams

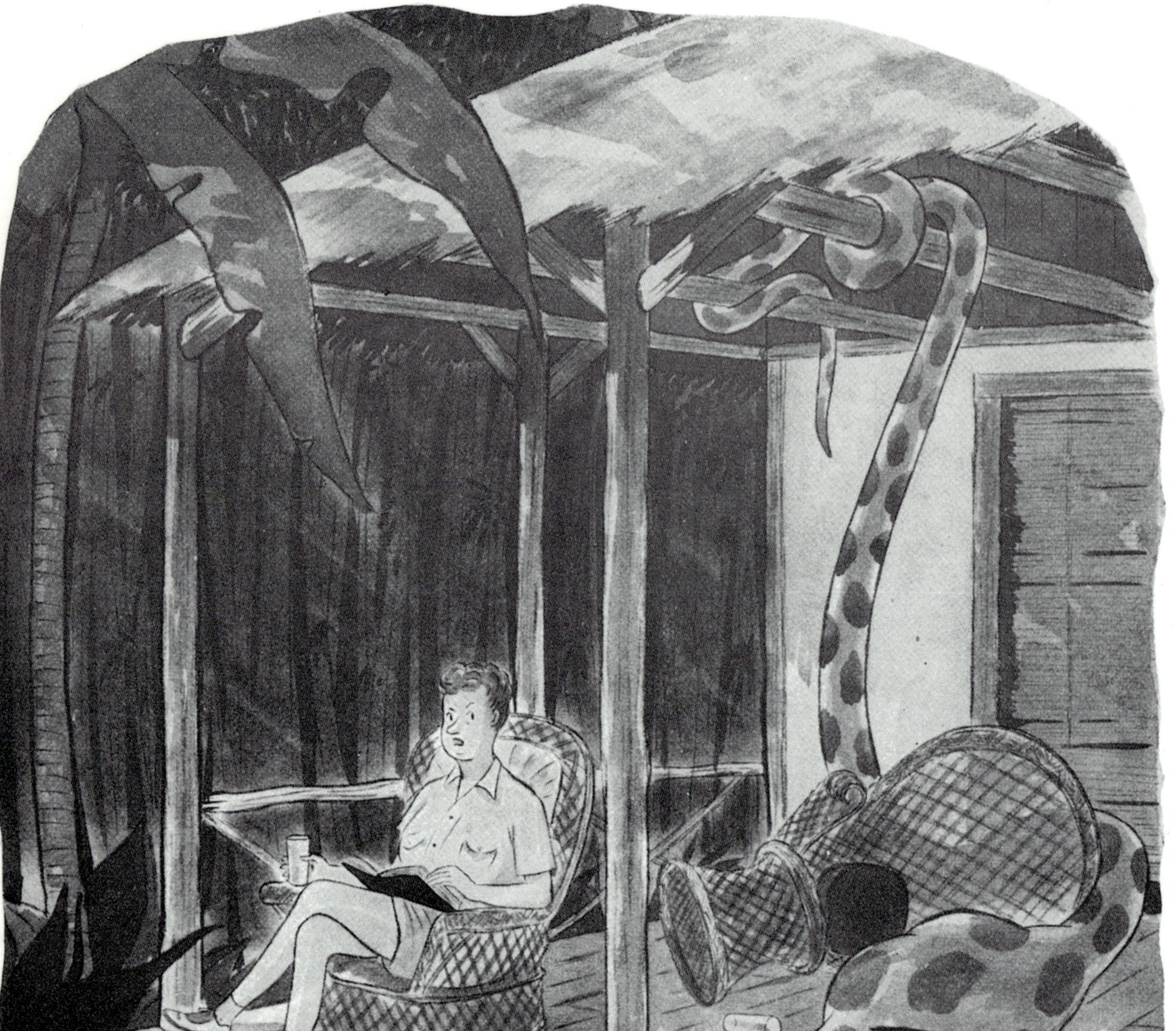

'Oh, speak up, George! Stop mumbling!'

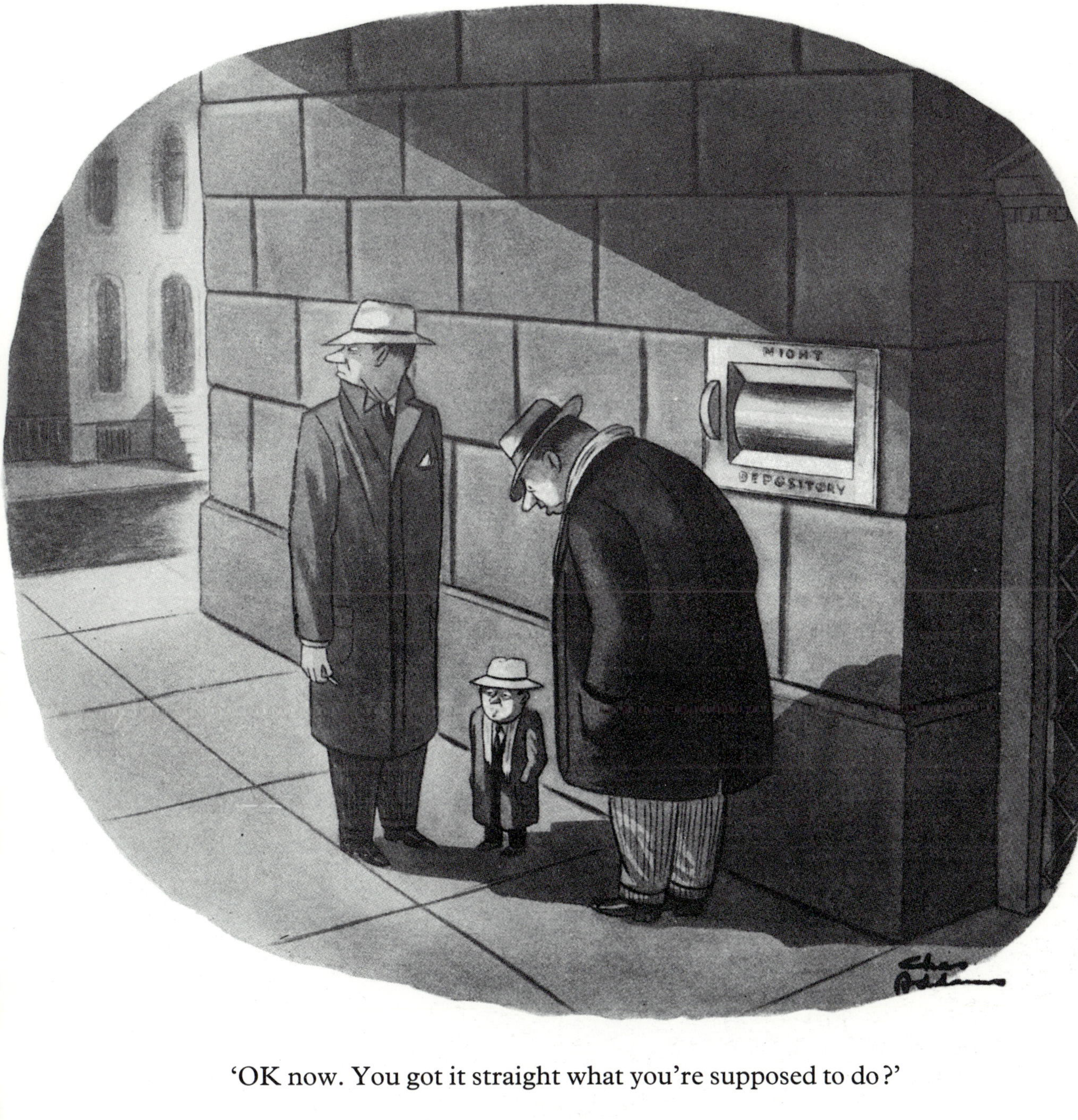

'OK now. You got it straight what you're supposed to do?'

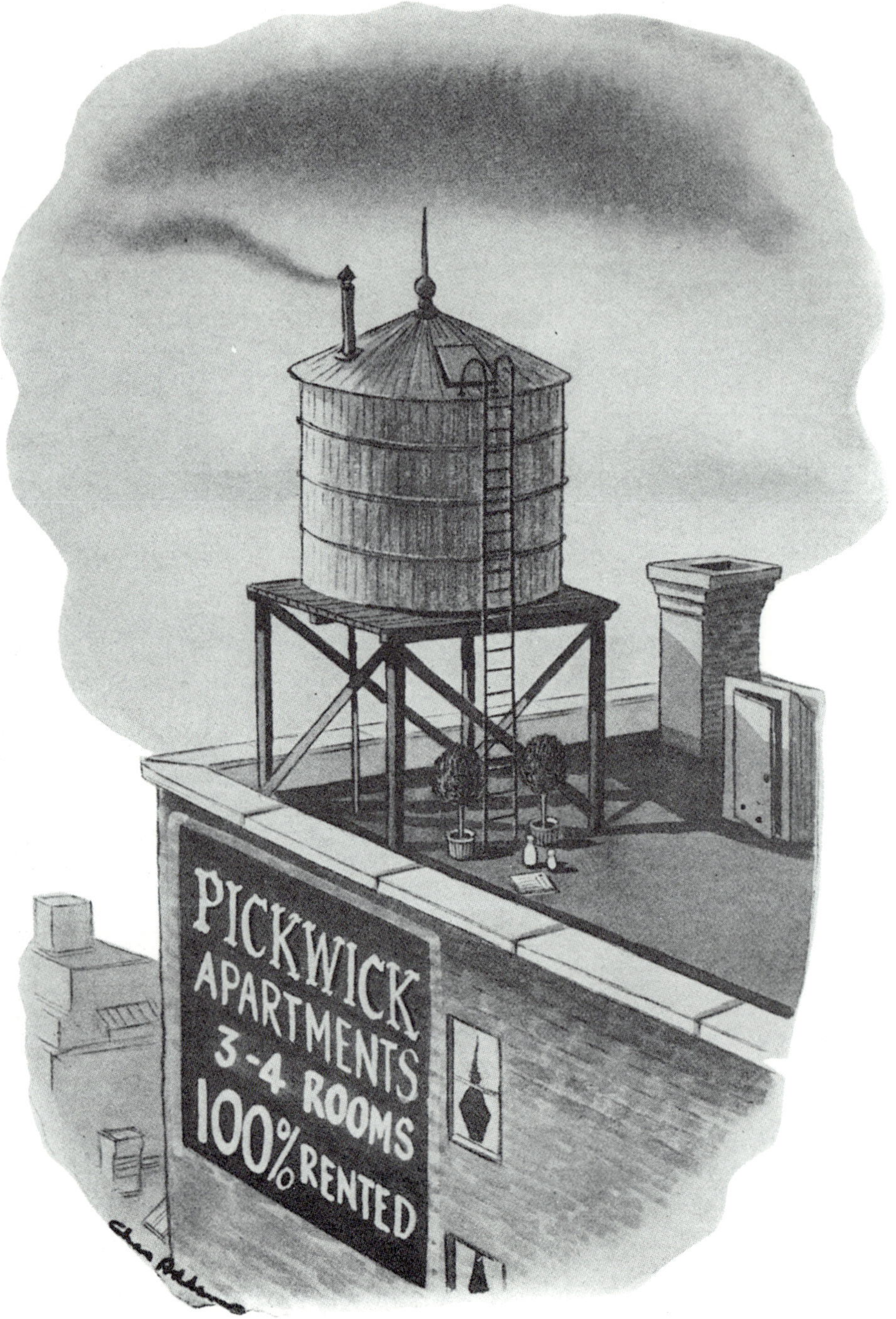
PICKWICK
APARTMENTS
3-4 ROOMS
100% RENTED

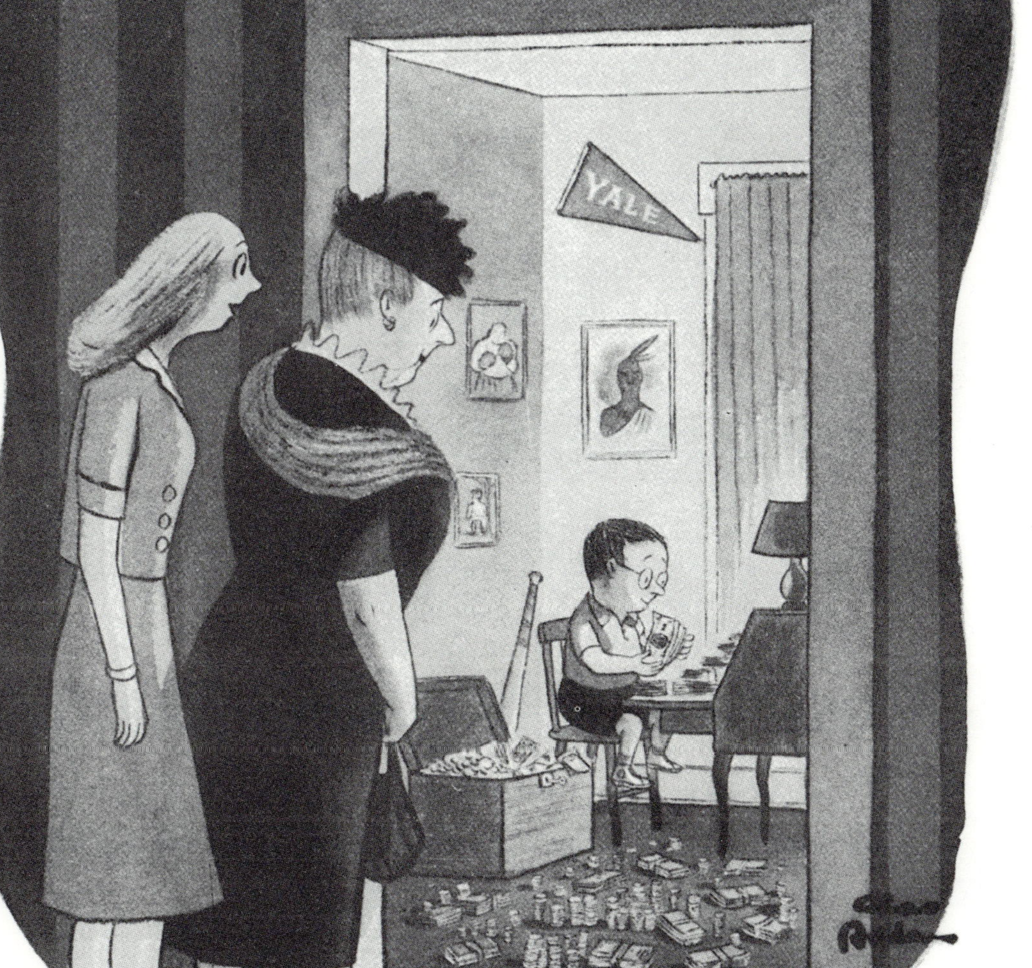

'As a matter of fact, it's a rather amusing story.
Do you remember last spring when Herbert was police commissioner
during Boys' Week? . . .'

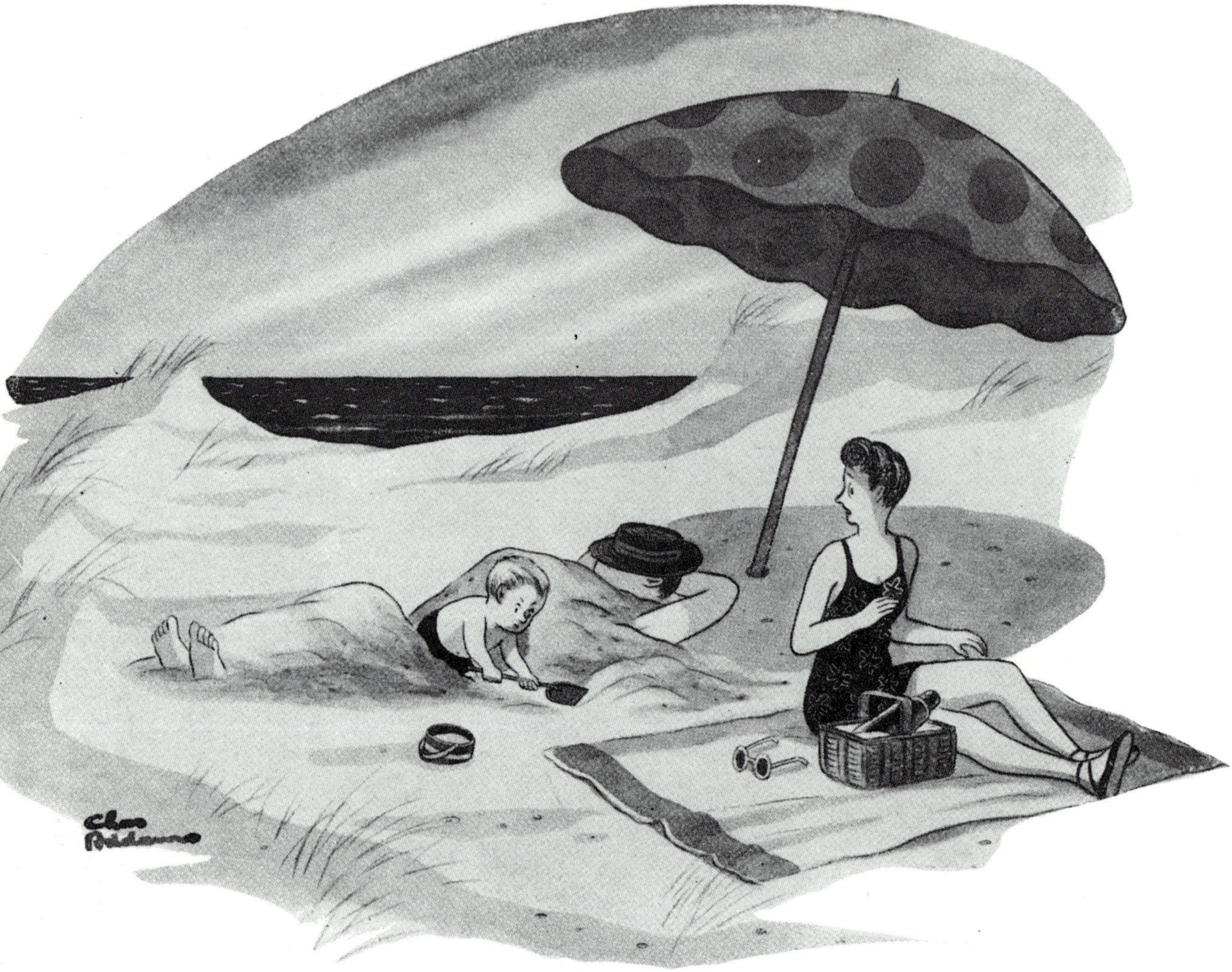
Chas Addams

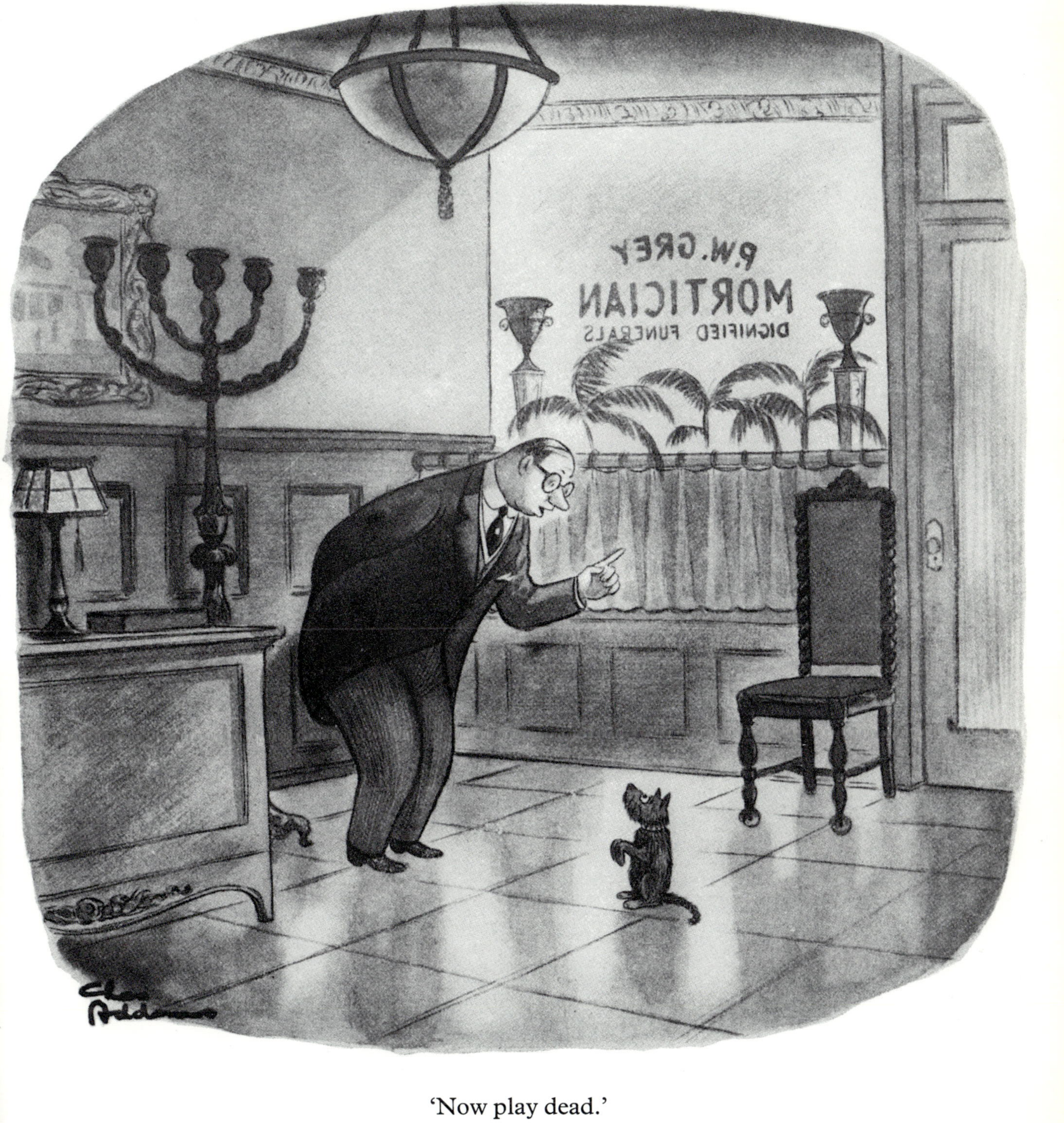

'Now play dead.'

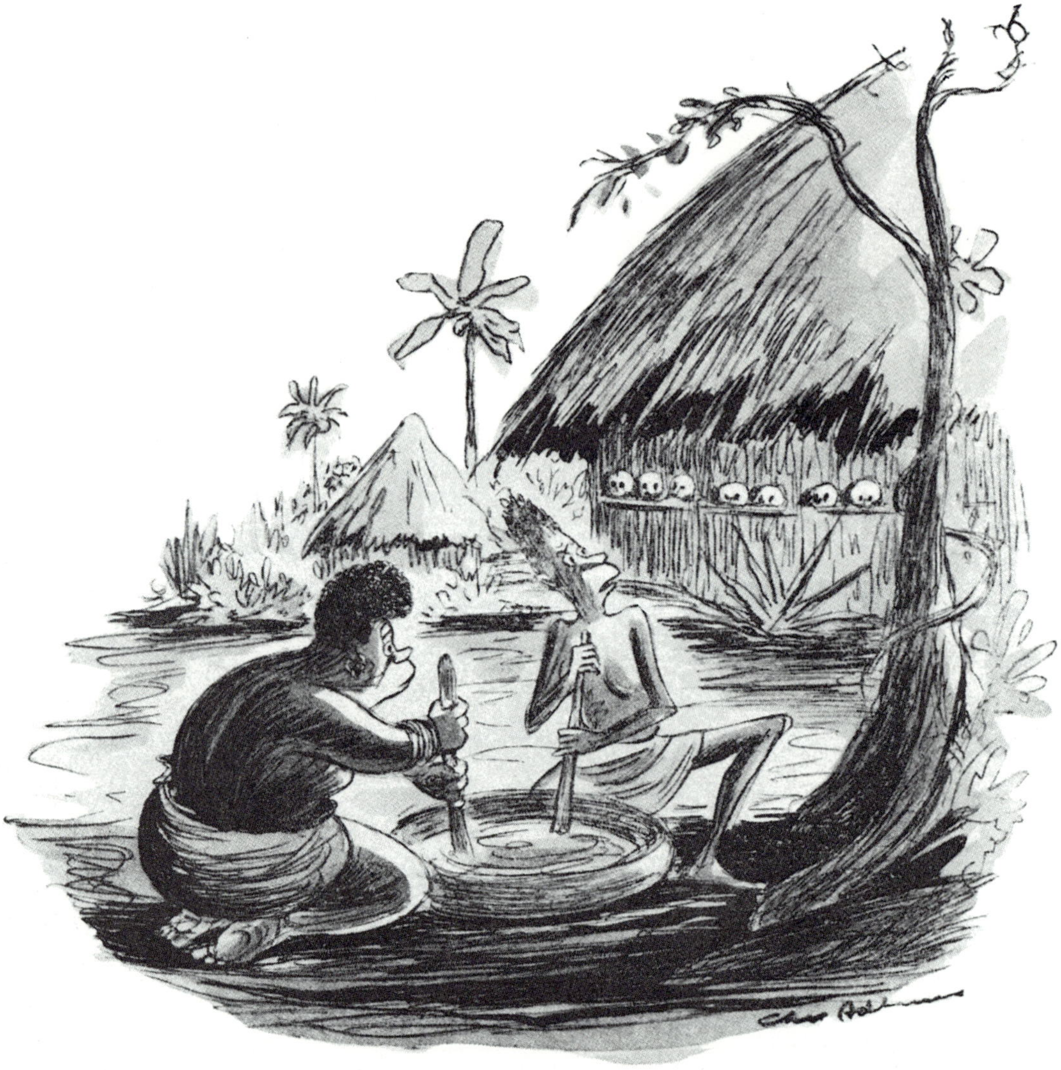

'Do you smell someone burning?'

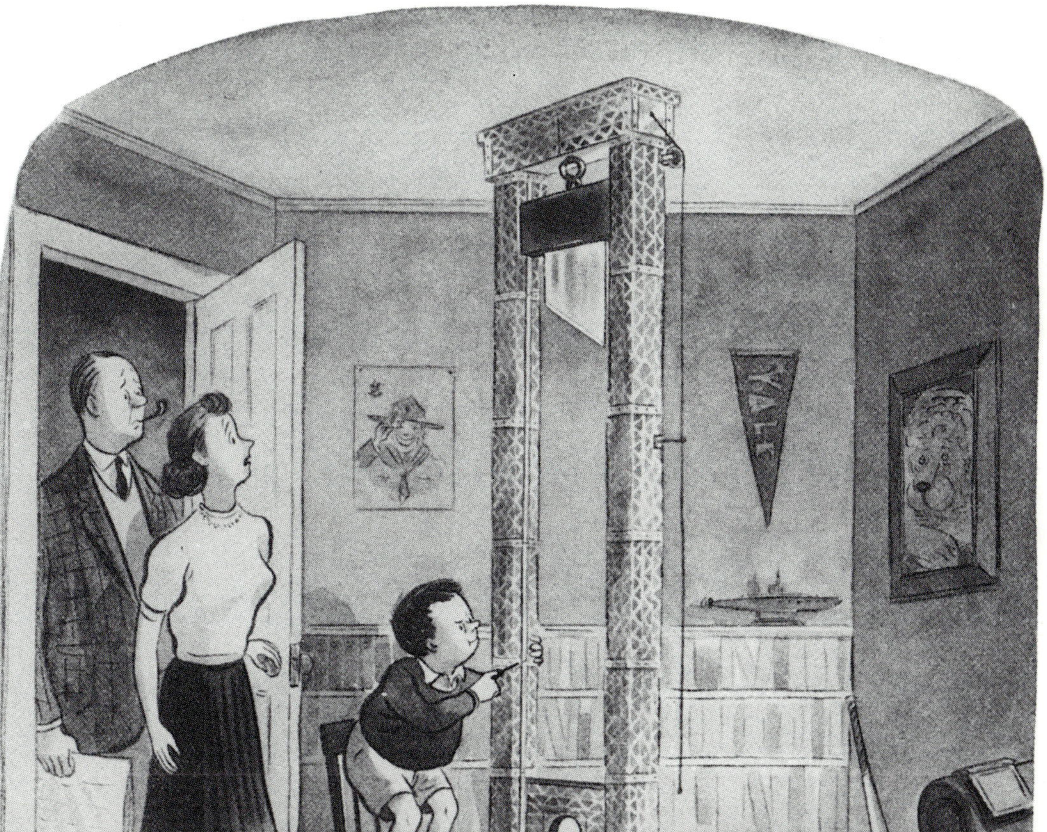
YALE
ERECTOR

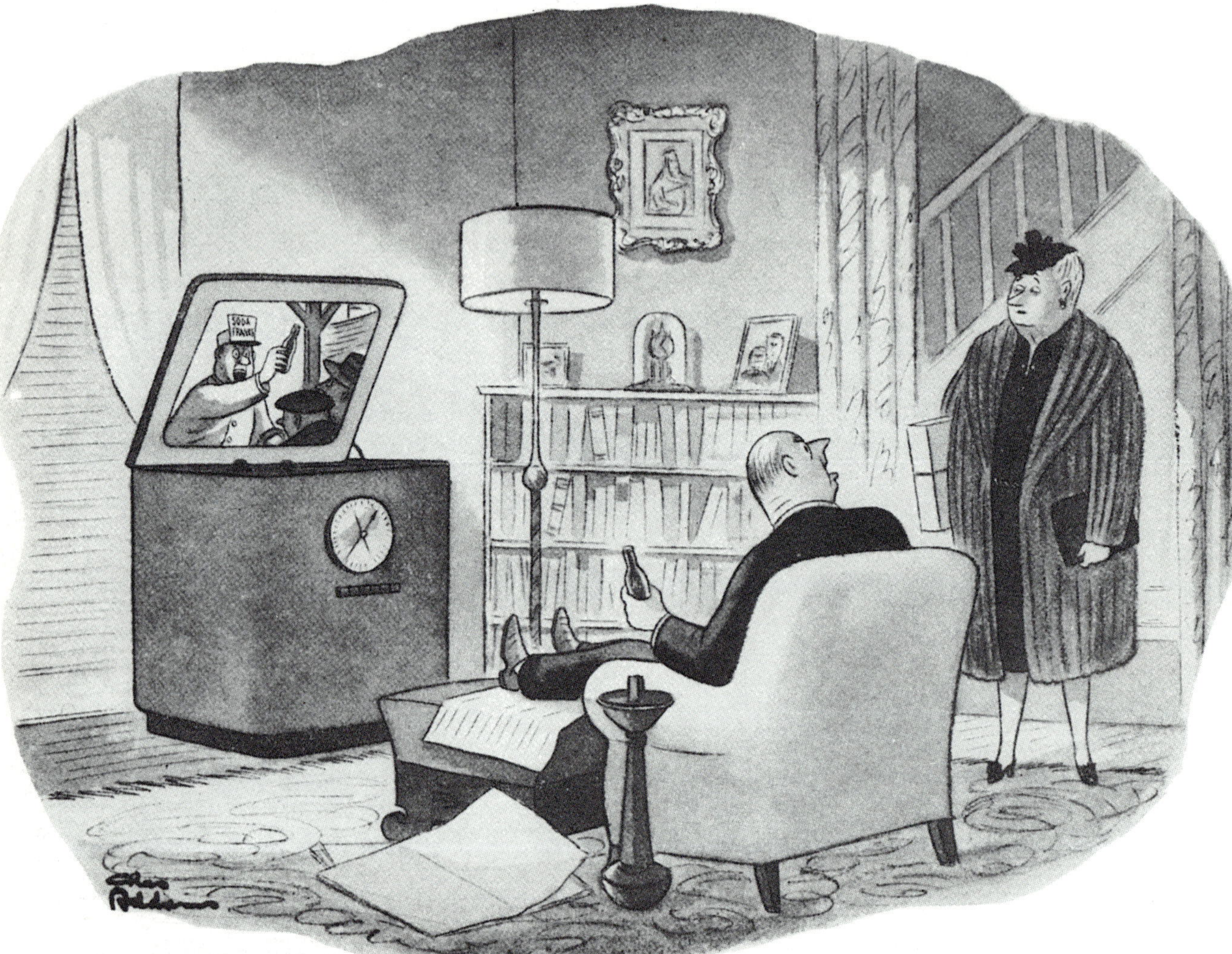

'I got it out of the refrigerator. Why?'

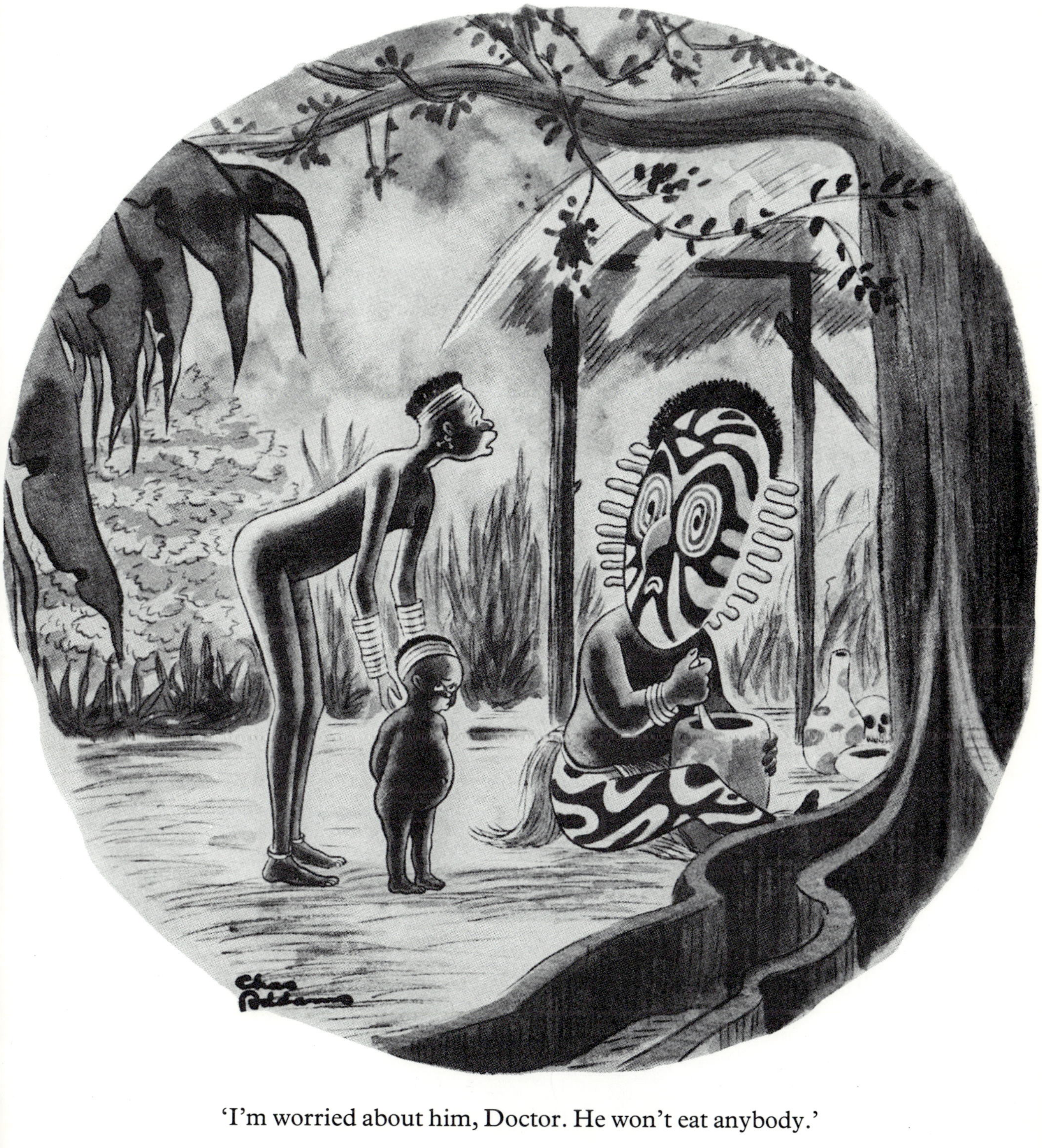

‘I’m worried about him, Doctor. He won’t eat anybody.’

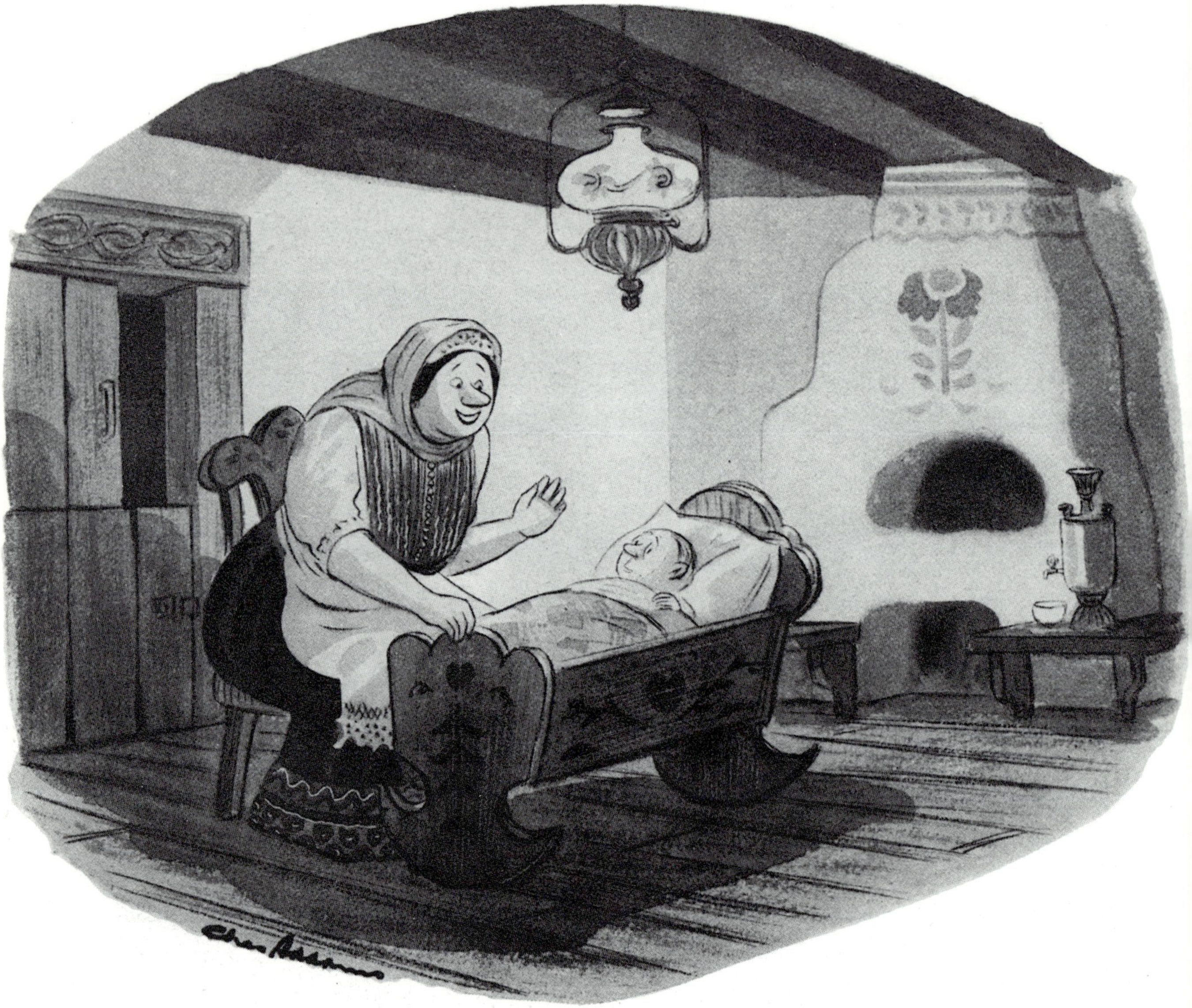

'. . . and so the poor peasant's daughter liquidated the handsome young prince, set up a people's government, and lived happily ever after.'

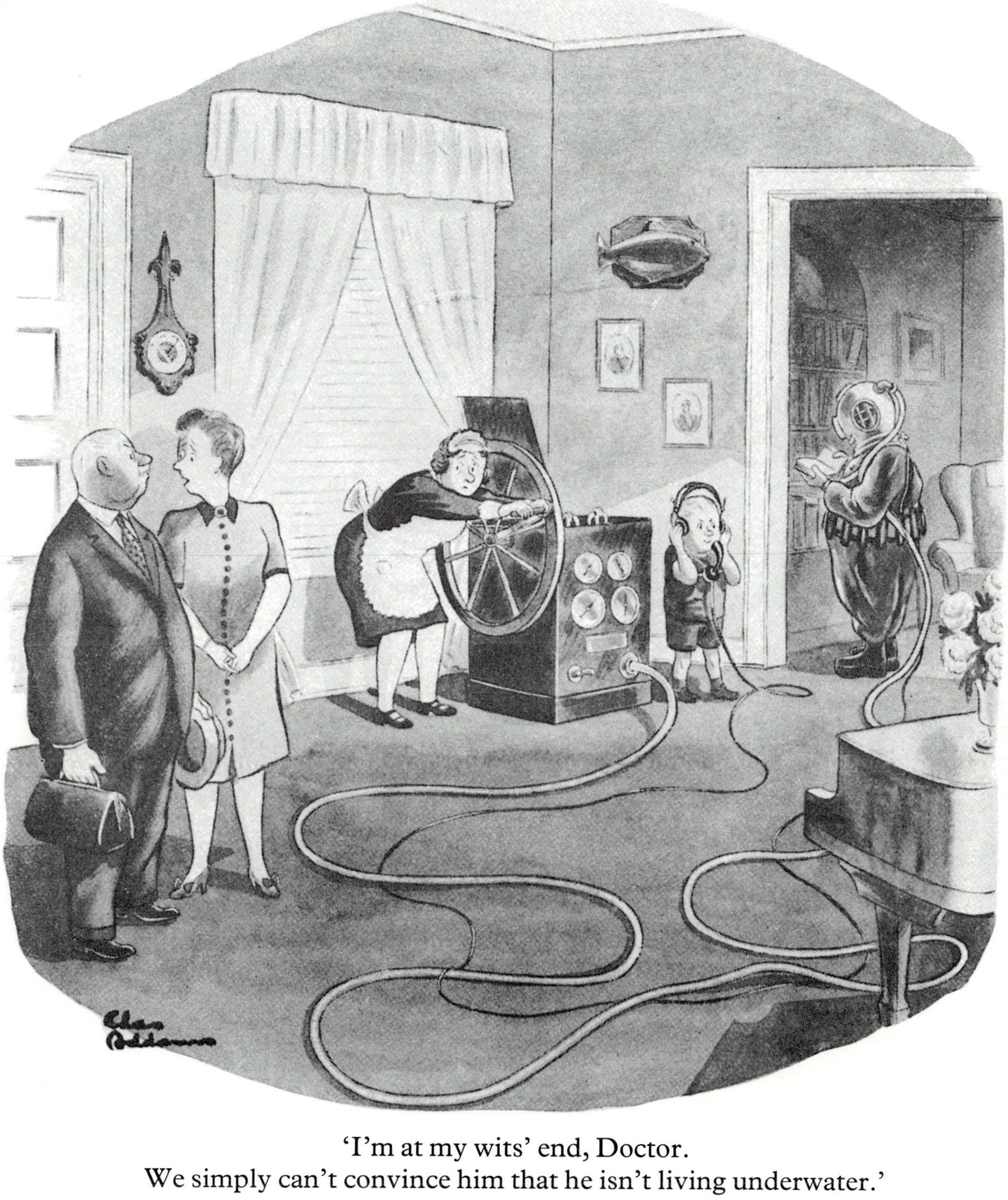

'I'm at my wits' end, Doctor.
We simply can't convince him that he isn't living underwater.'

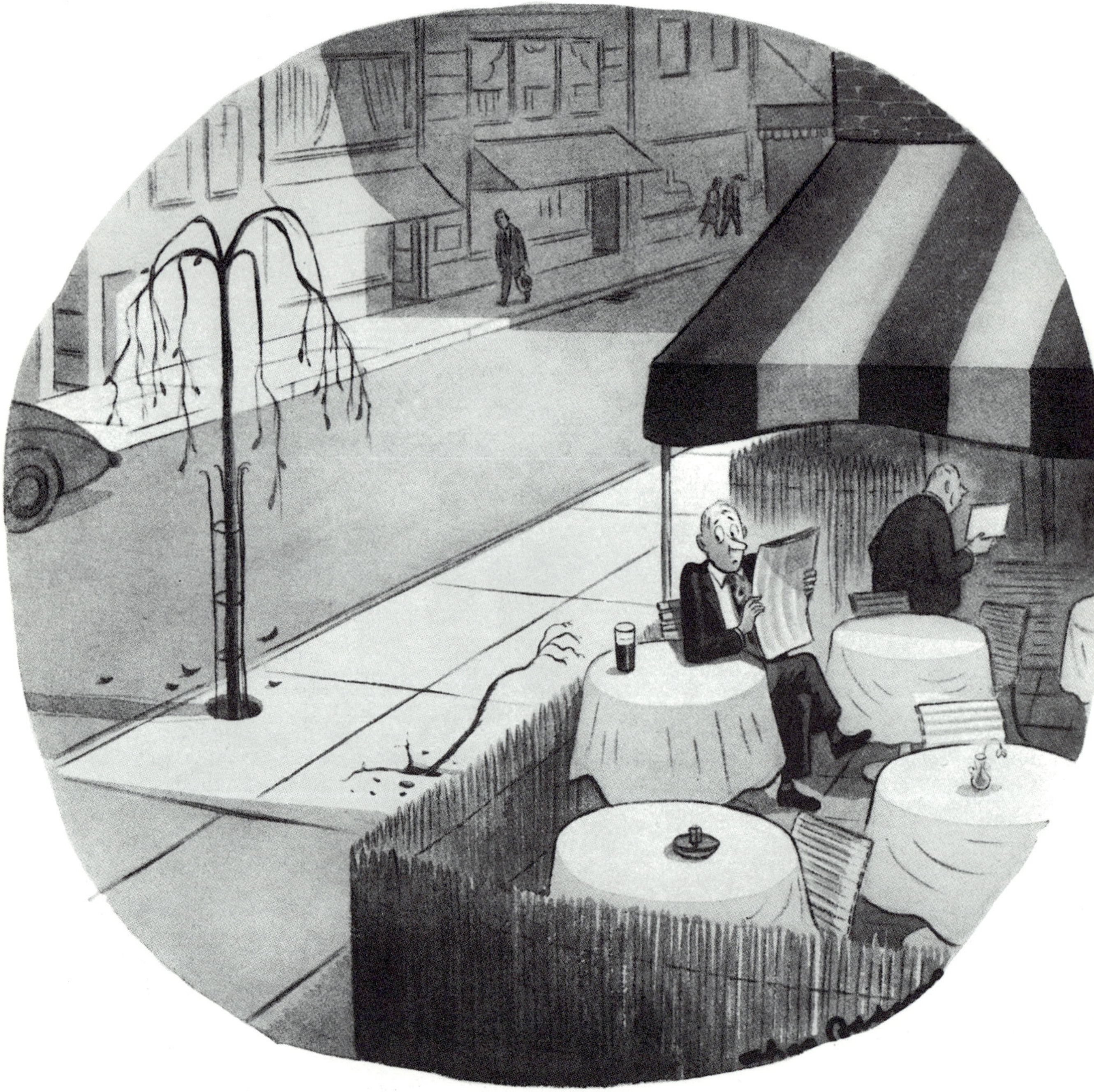

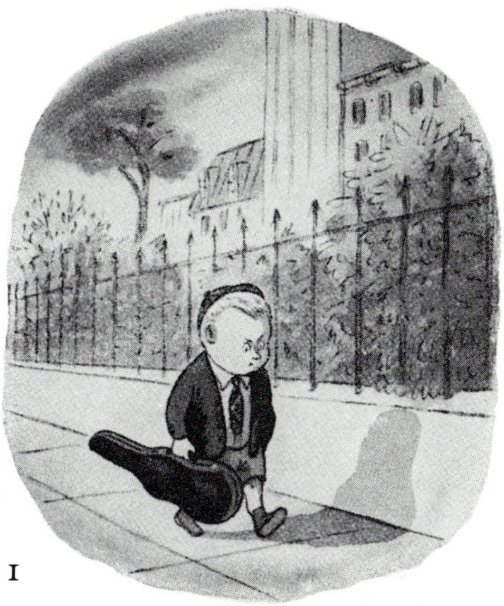

1

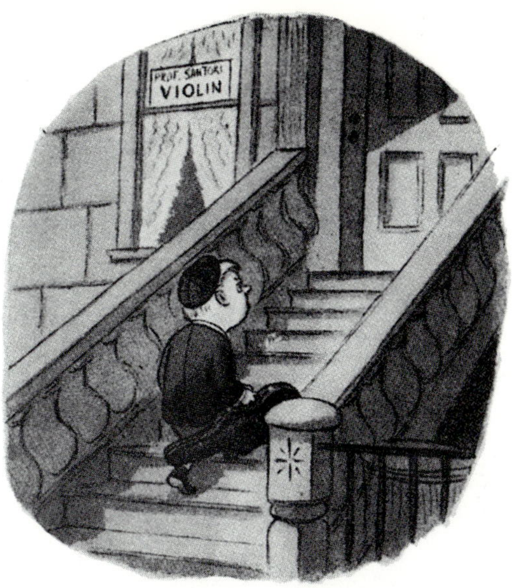

2

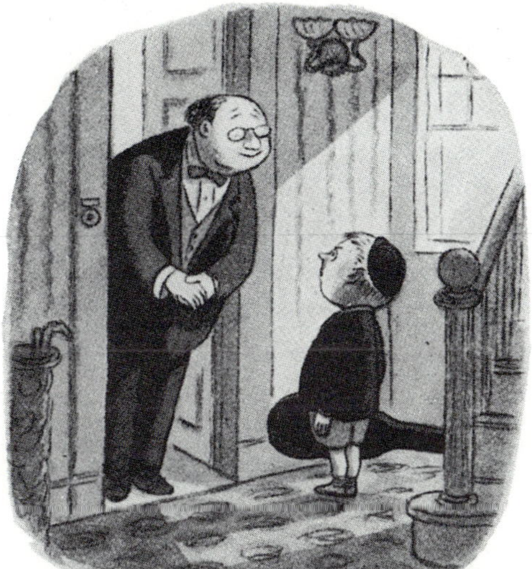

3

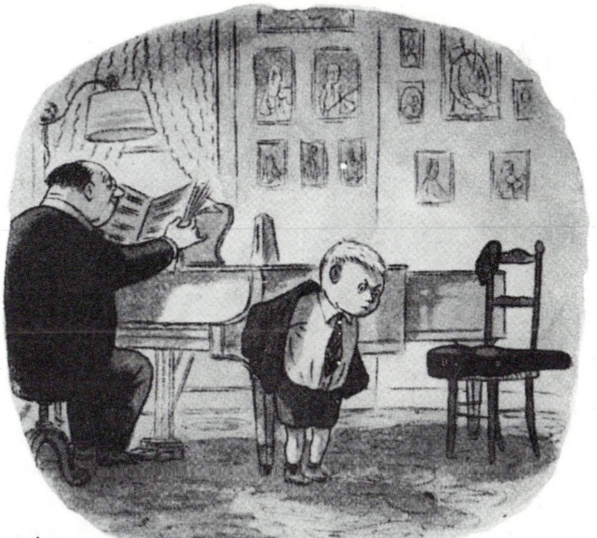

4

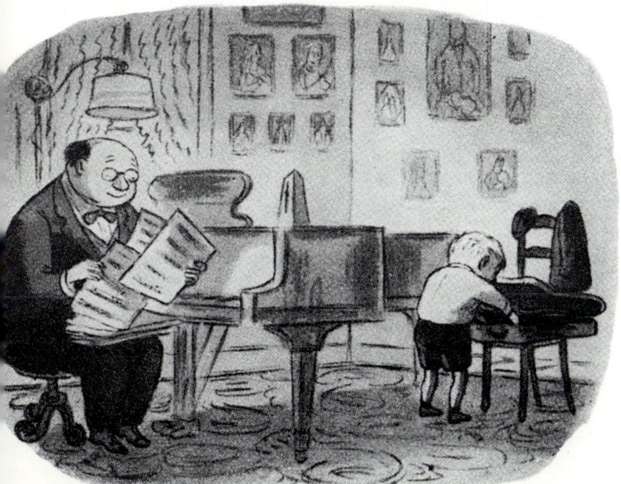

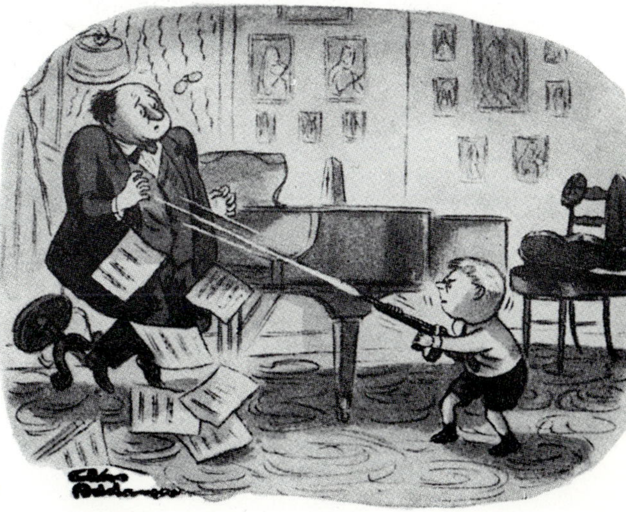

6

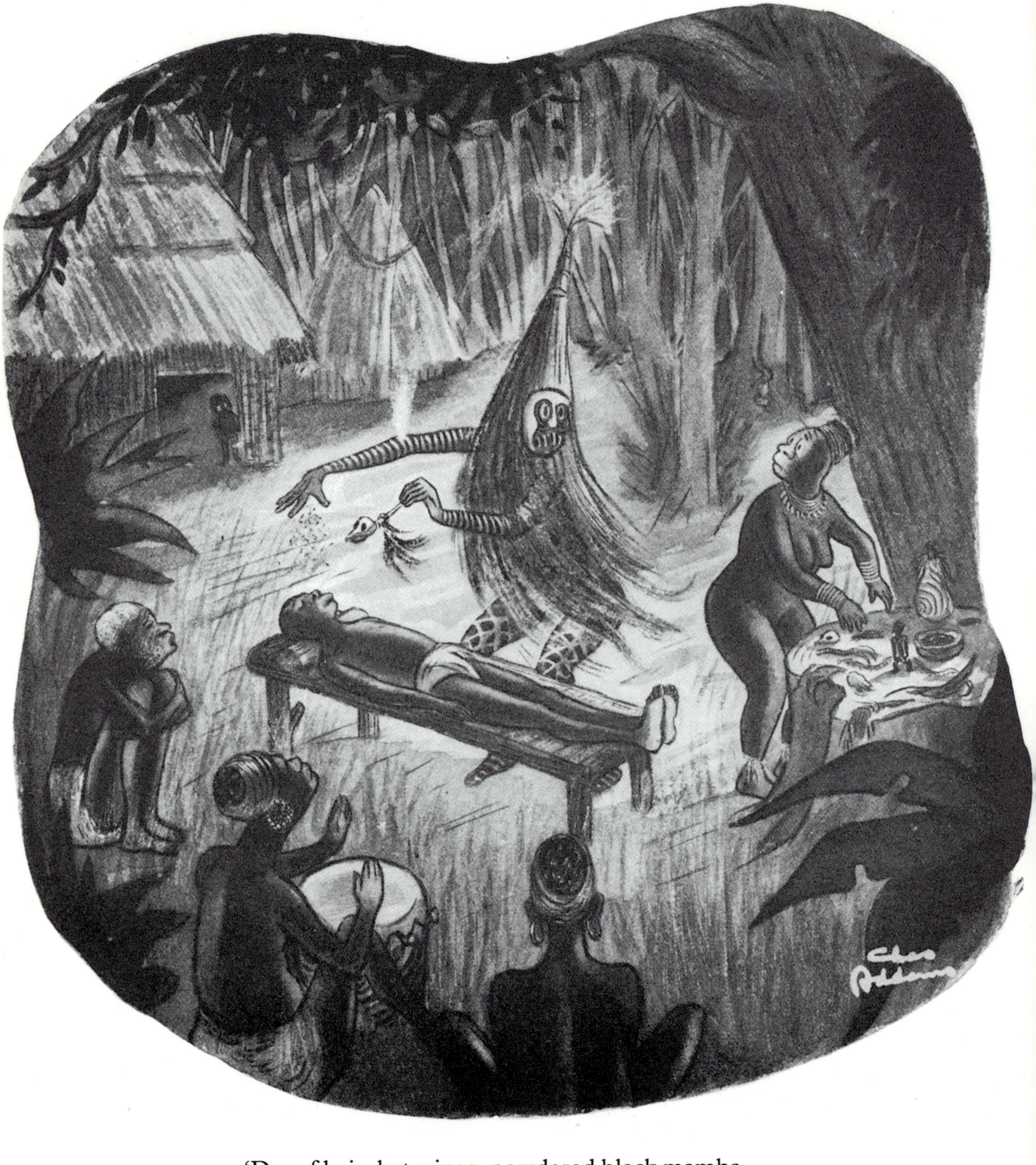

'Dwarf hair, bat wings, powdered black mamba . . . .
Quick, Miss Tonka!'

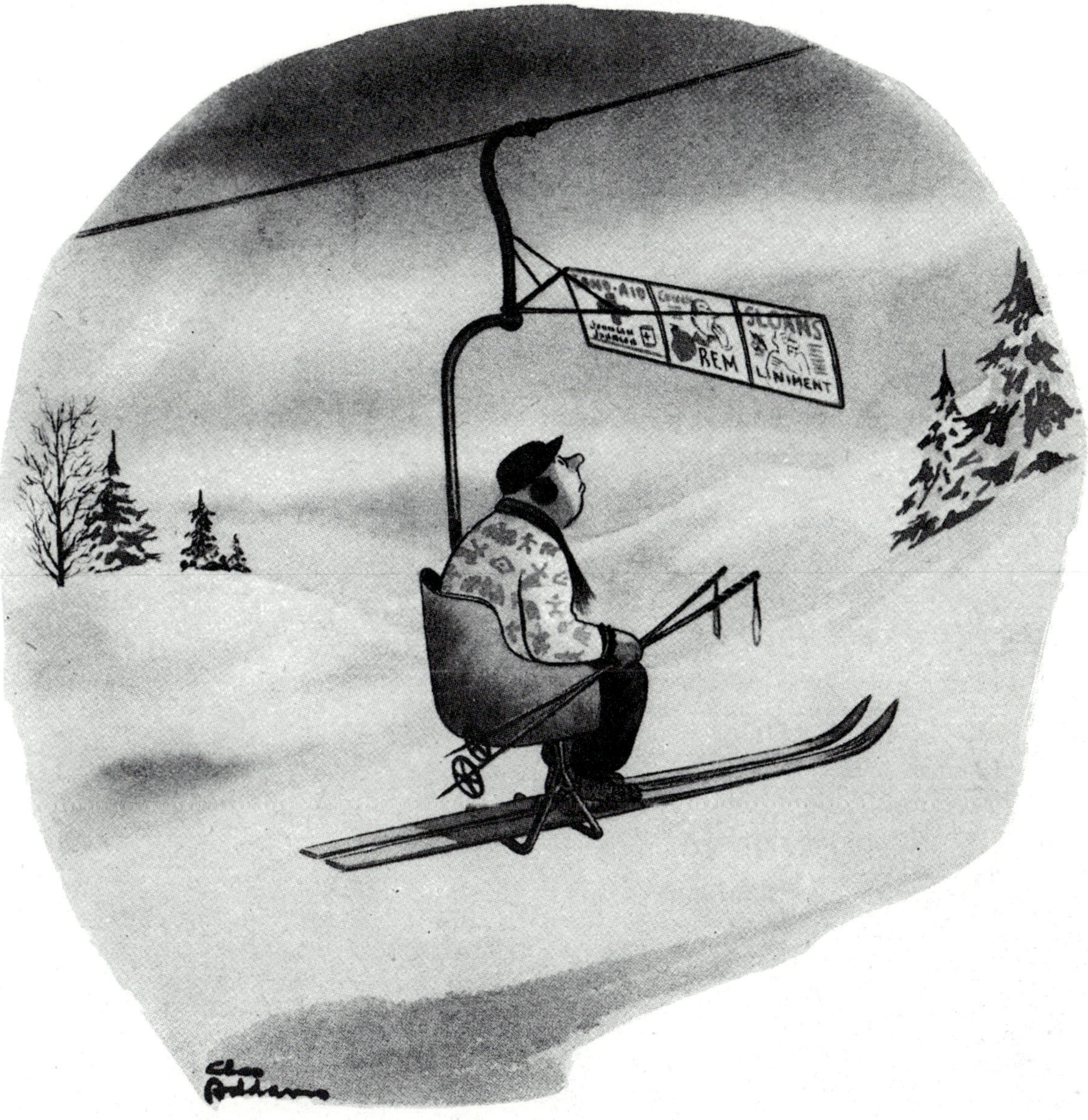
REM
SLOANS
LINIMENT
Chas Addams

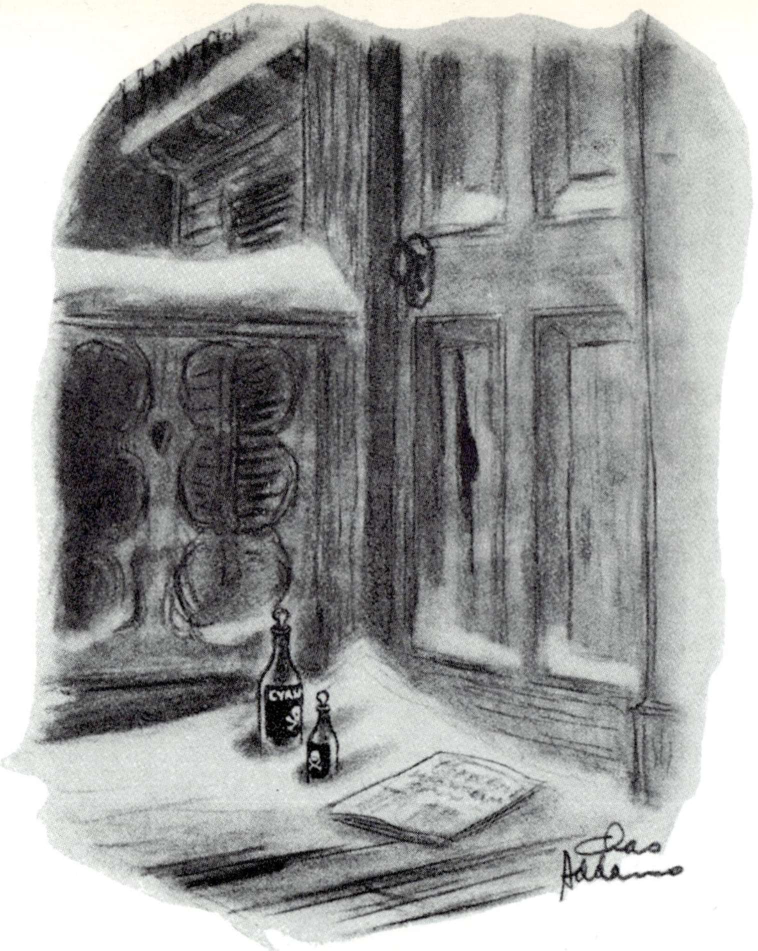

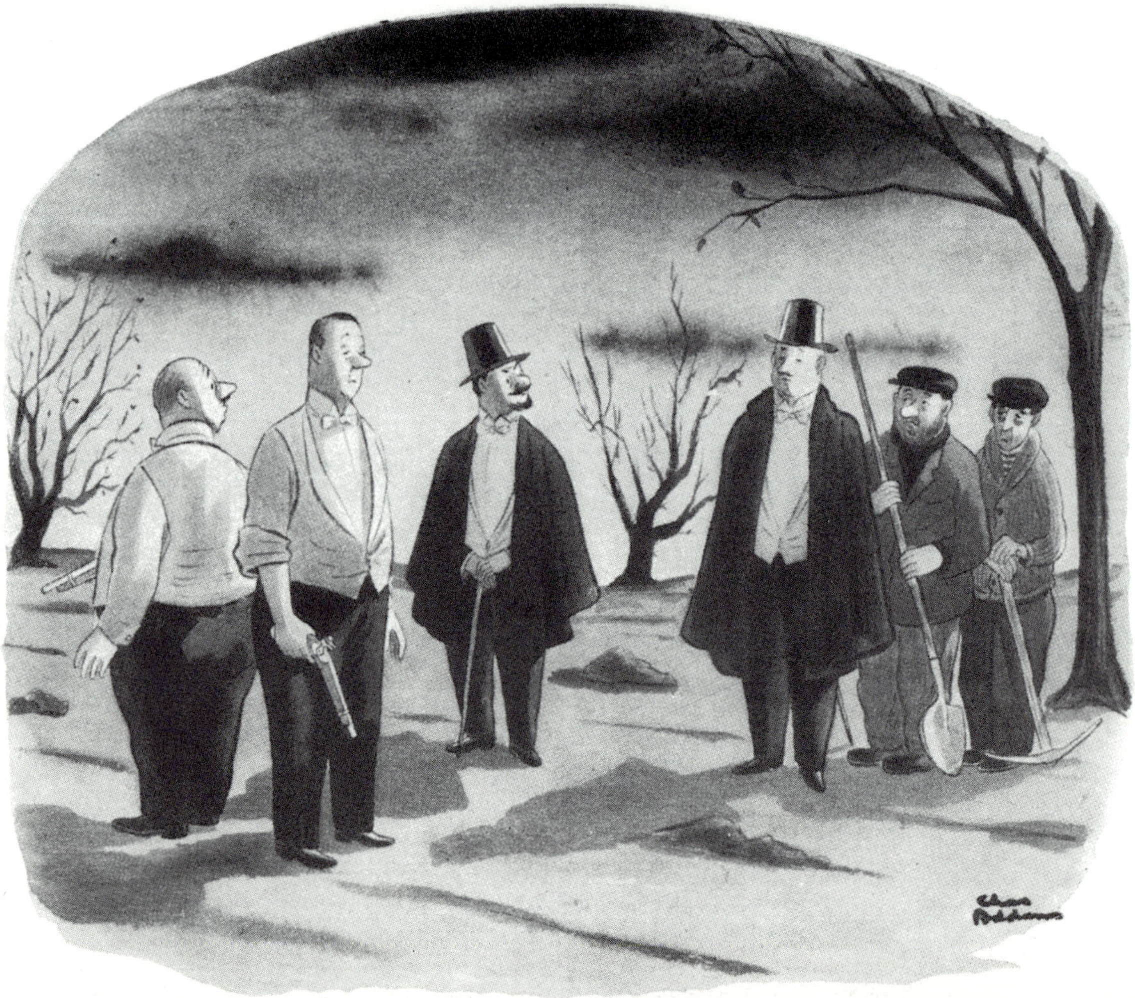

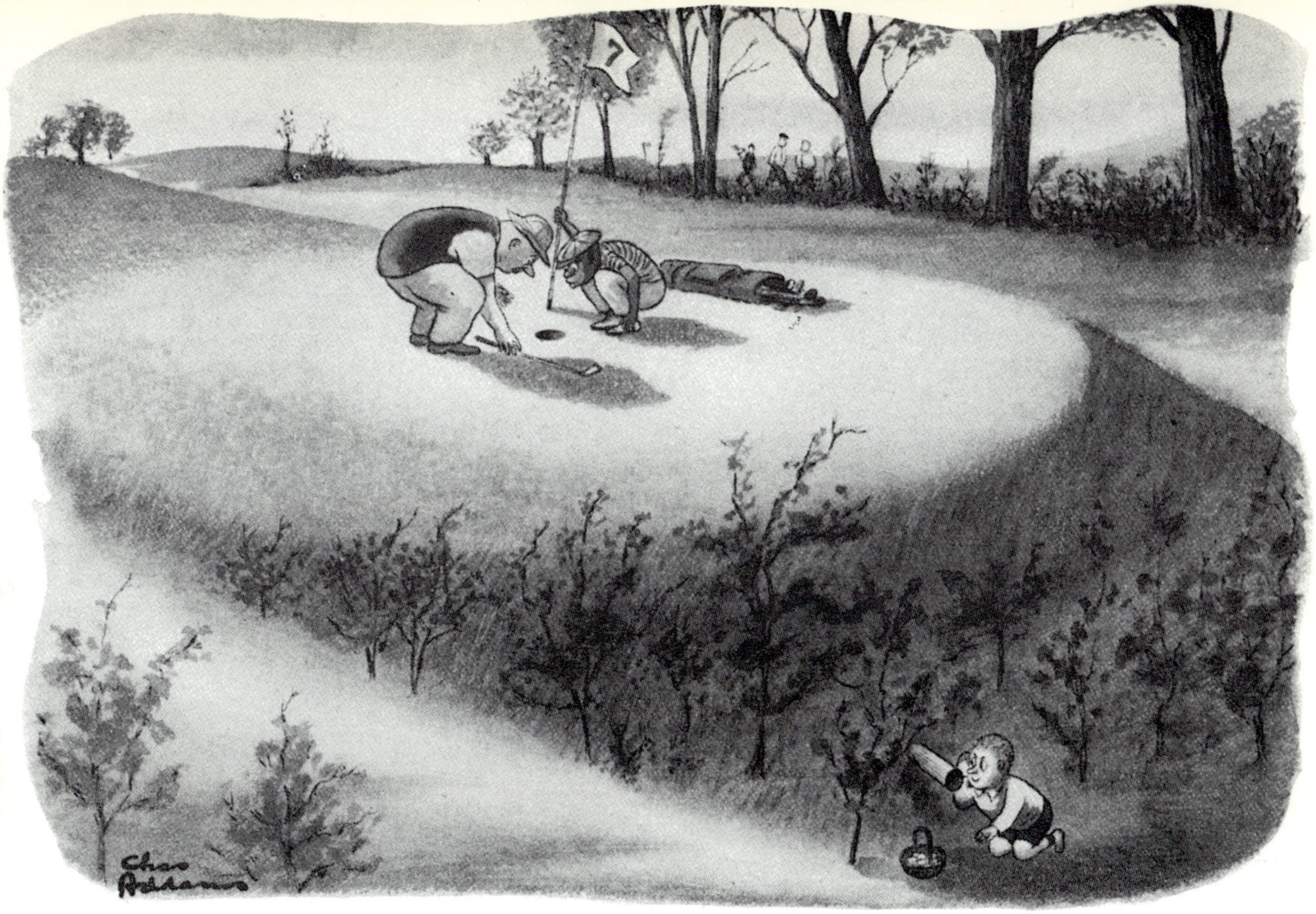

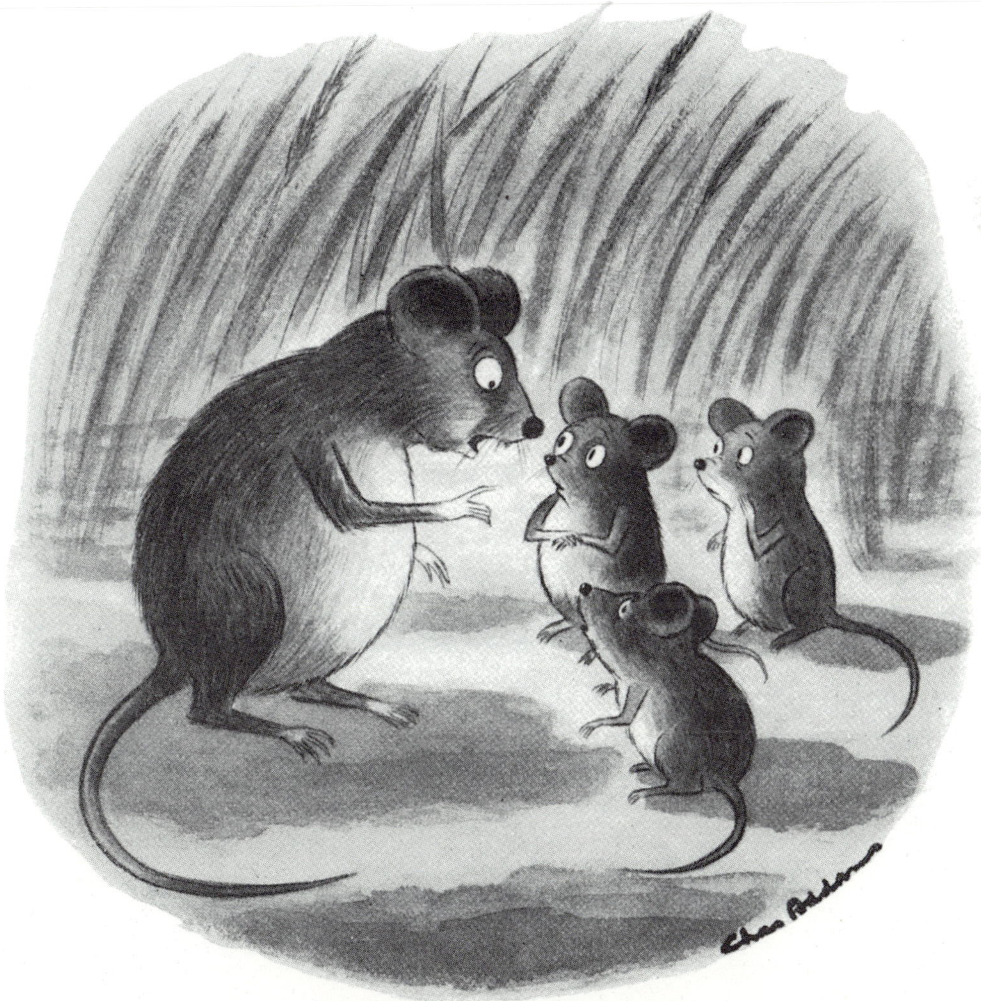

'. . . and never, never go near a house with a well-beaten path to the door.'

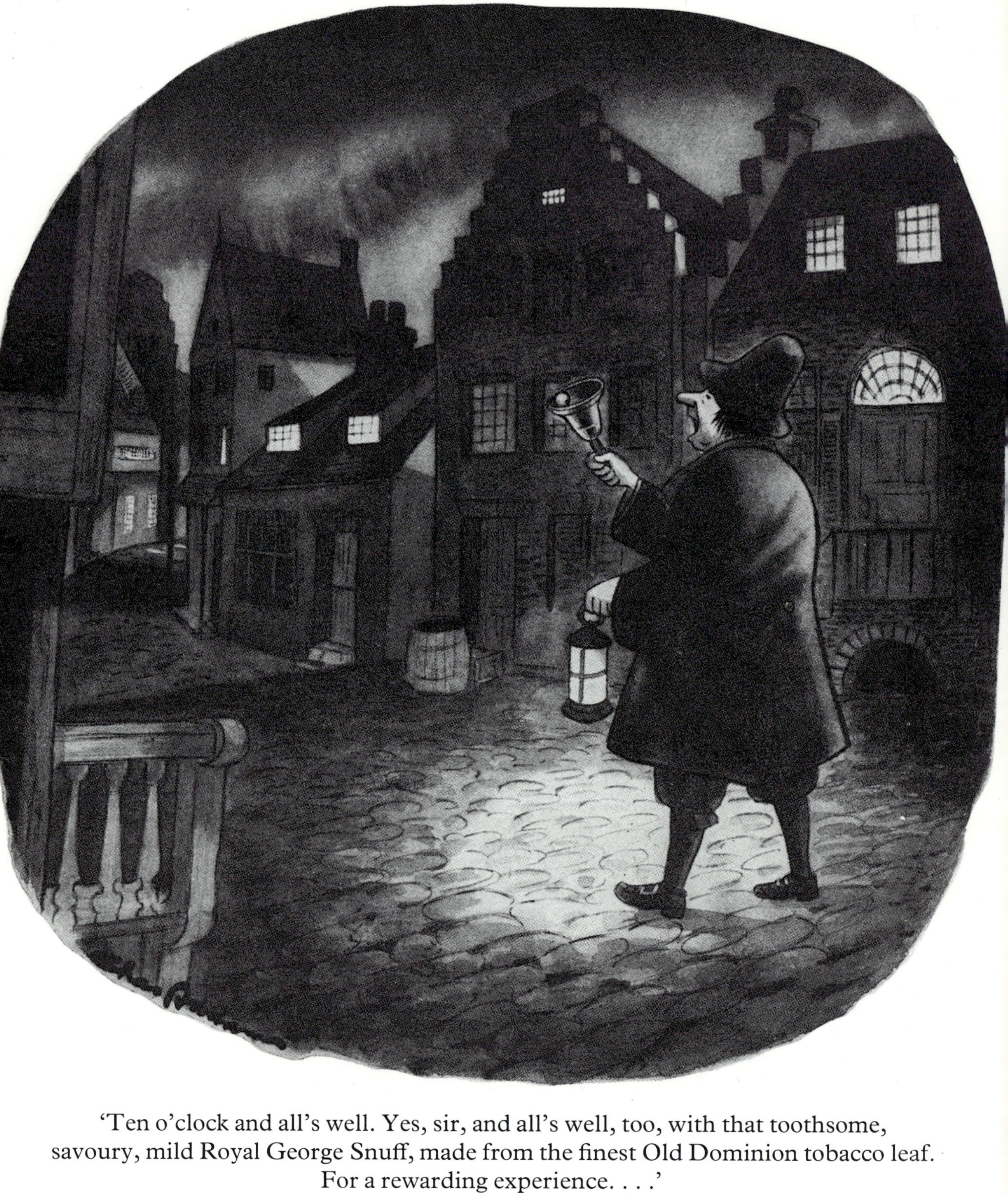

'Ten o'clock and all's well. Yes, sir, and all's well, too, with that toothsome, savoury, mild Royal George Snuff, made from the finest Old Dominion tobacco leaf. For a rewarding experience. . . .'

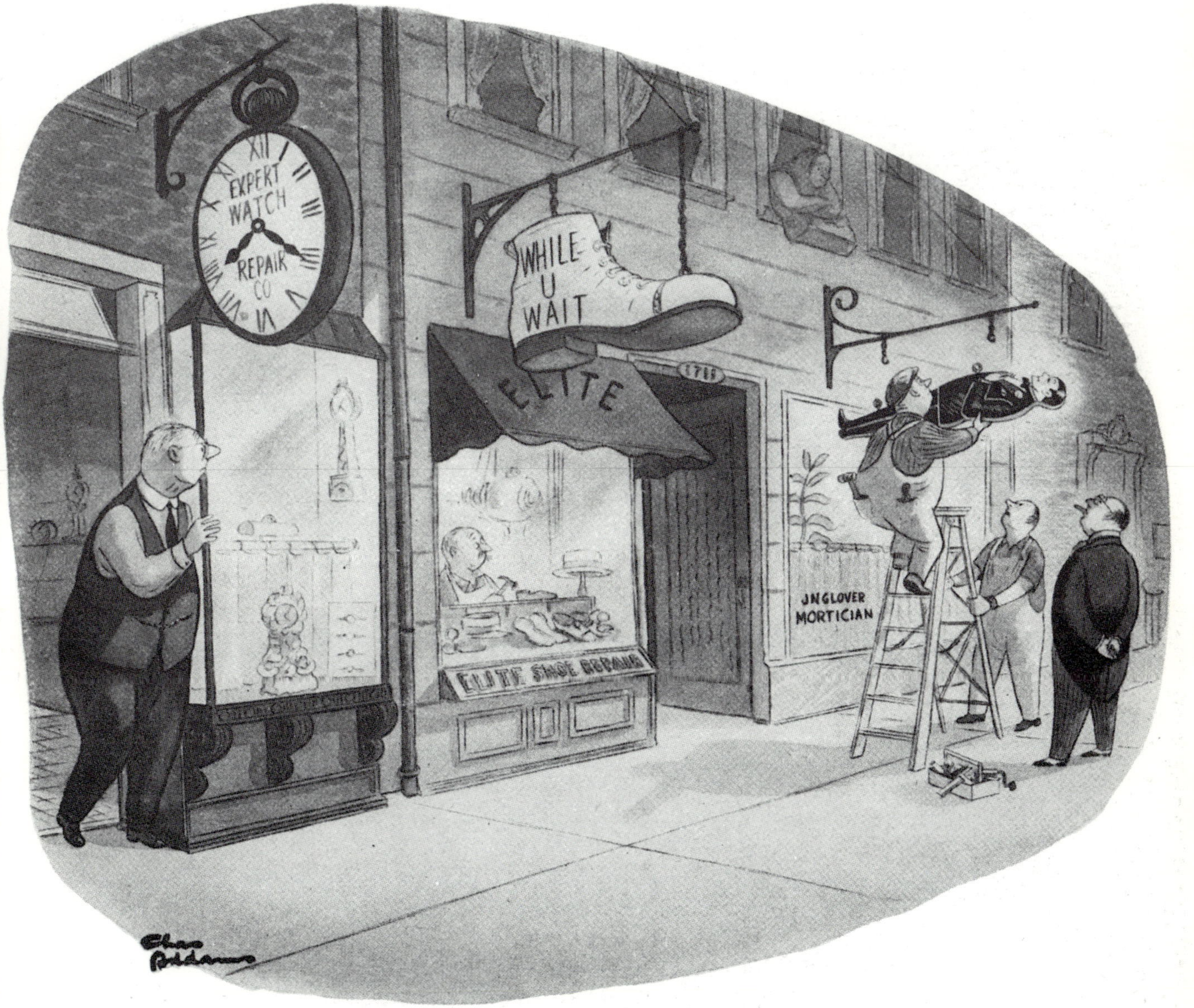
EXPERT WATCH REPAIR CO
WHILE U WAIT
ELITE
ELITE SHOE REPAIR
J N GLOVER MORTICIAN
Chas Addams

THE CREAKING SHUTTER

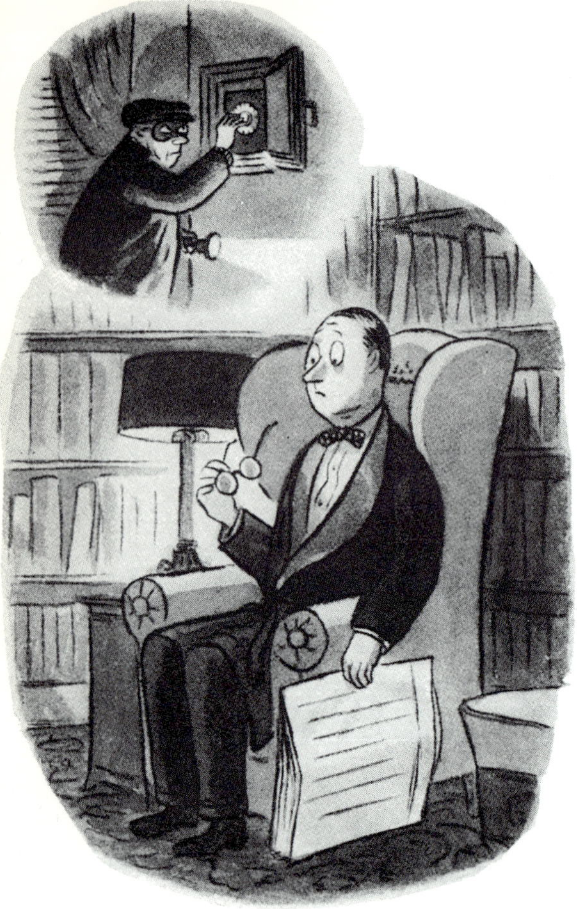

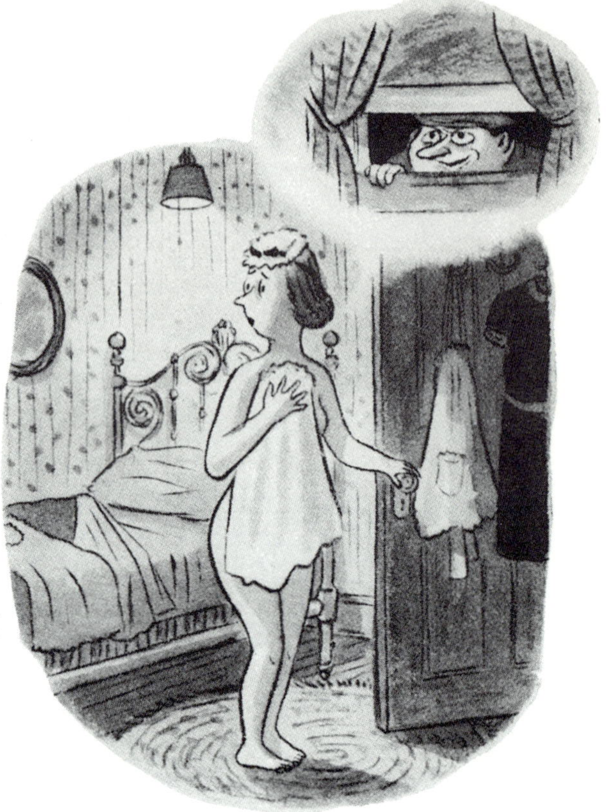

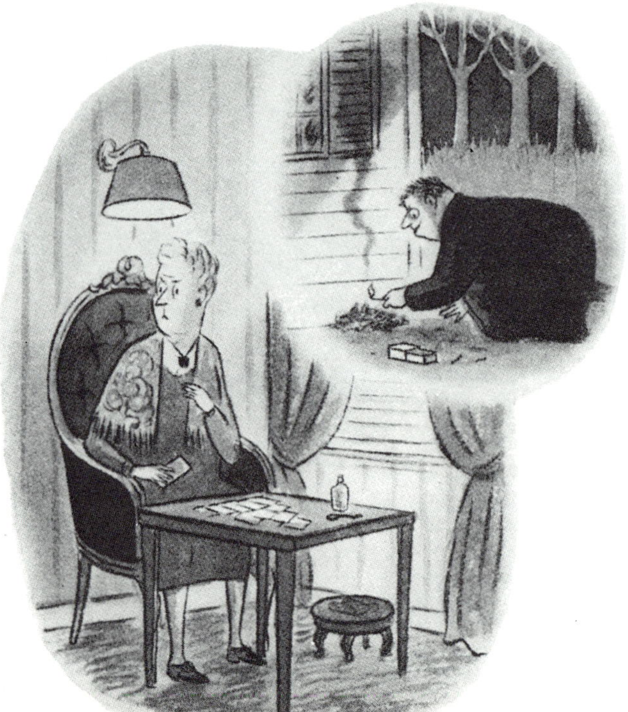

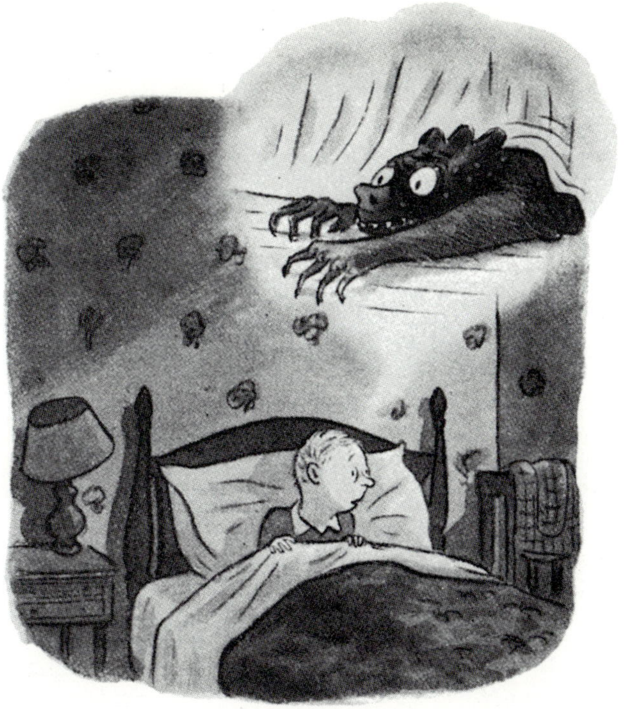

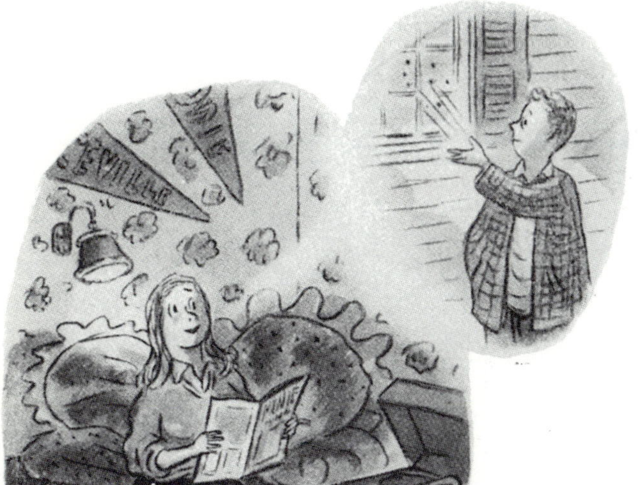

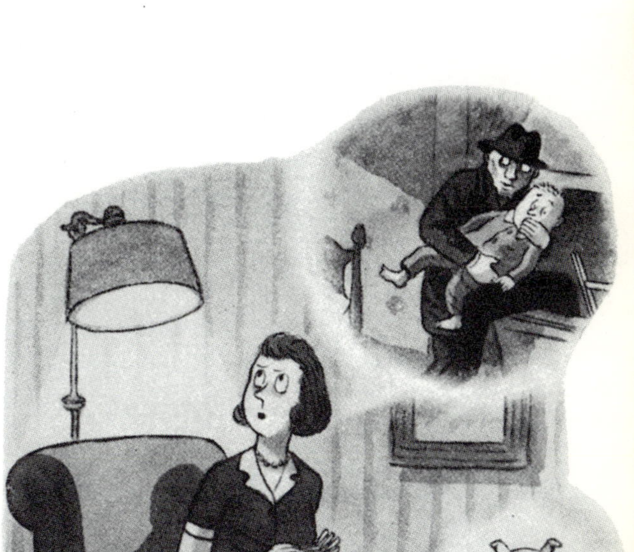

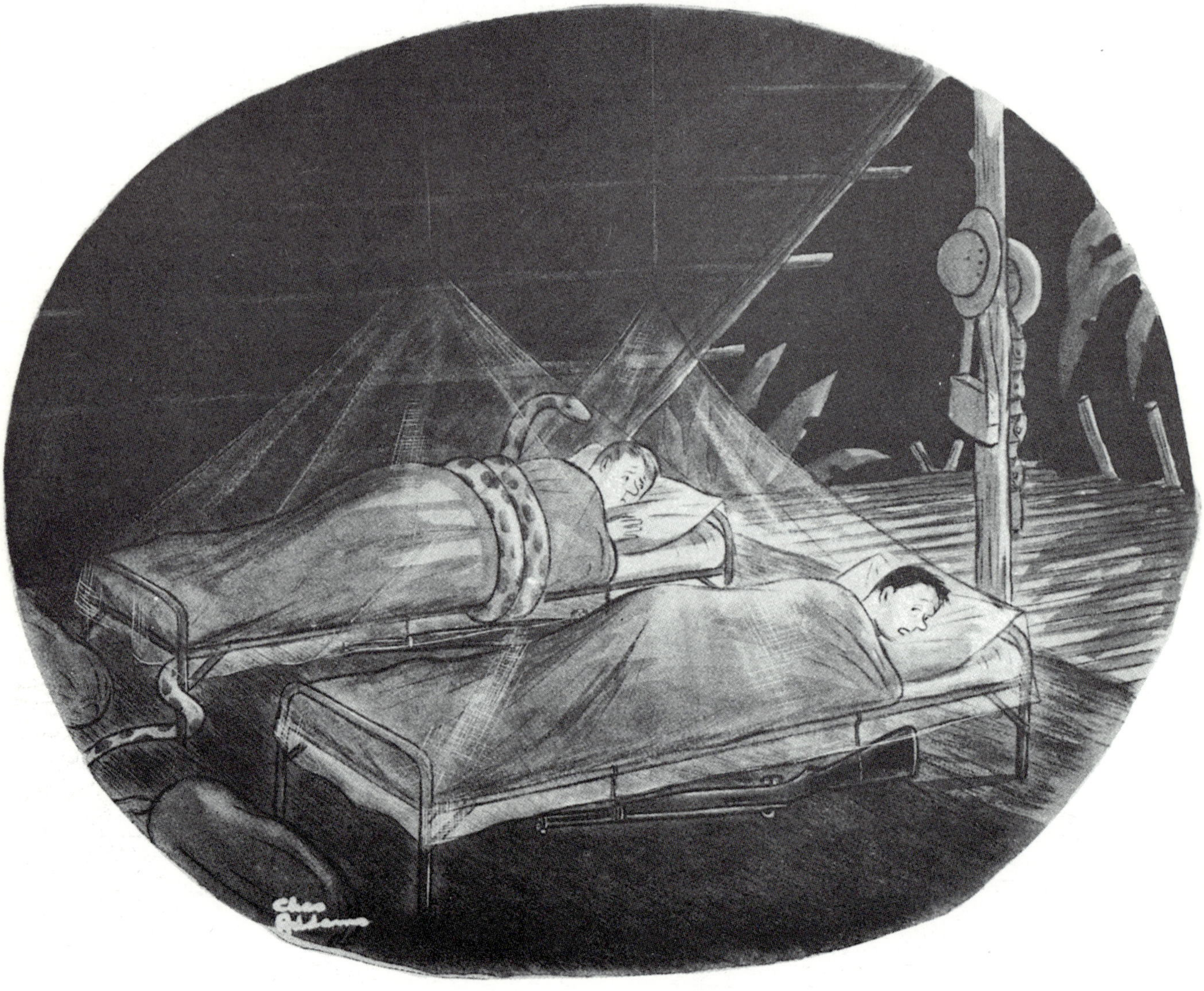

‘I wouldn’t worry about it, Ed – probably something you ate.’

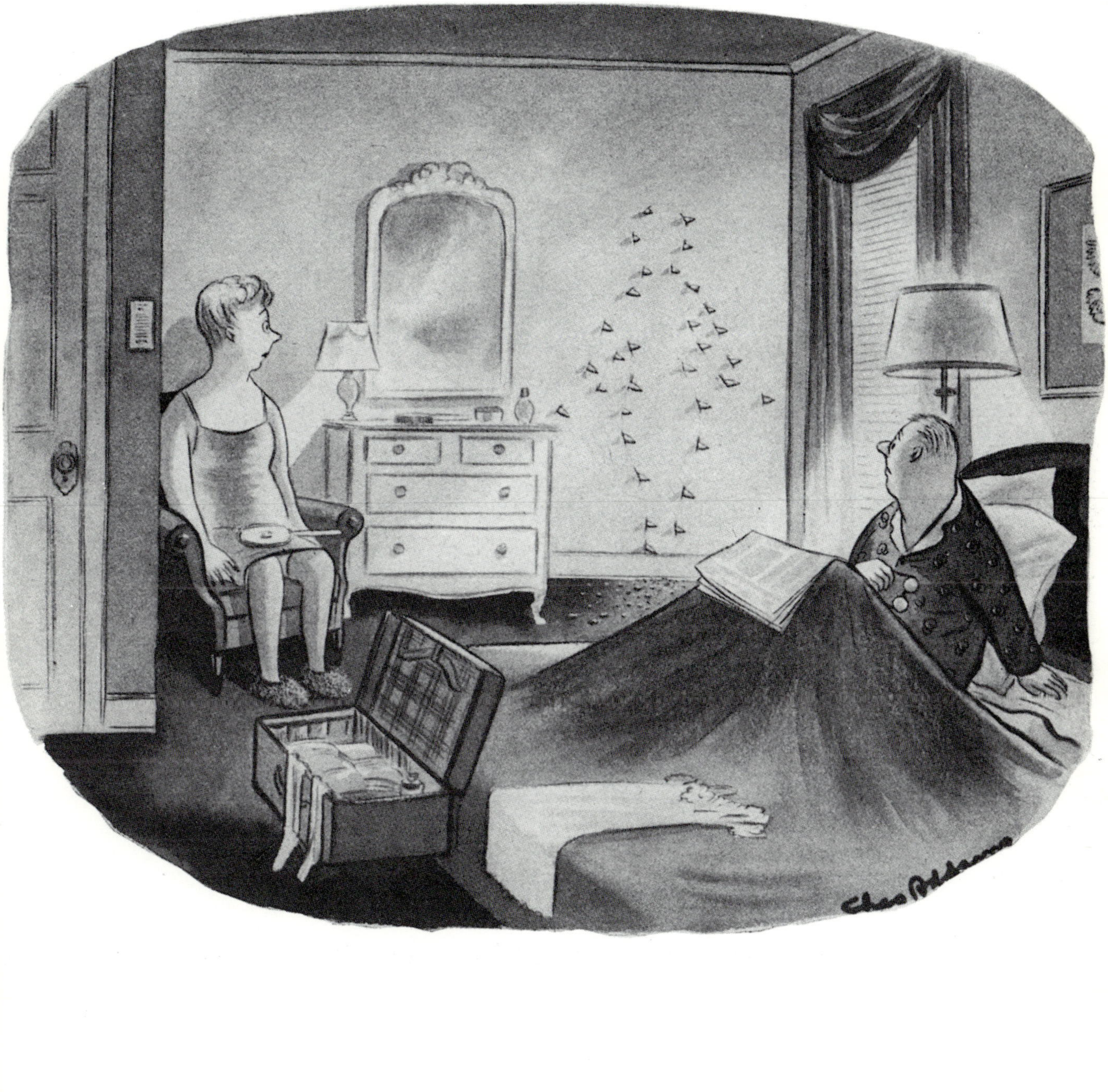

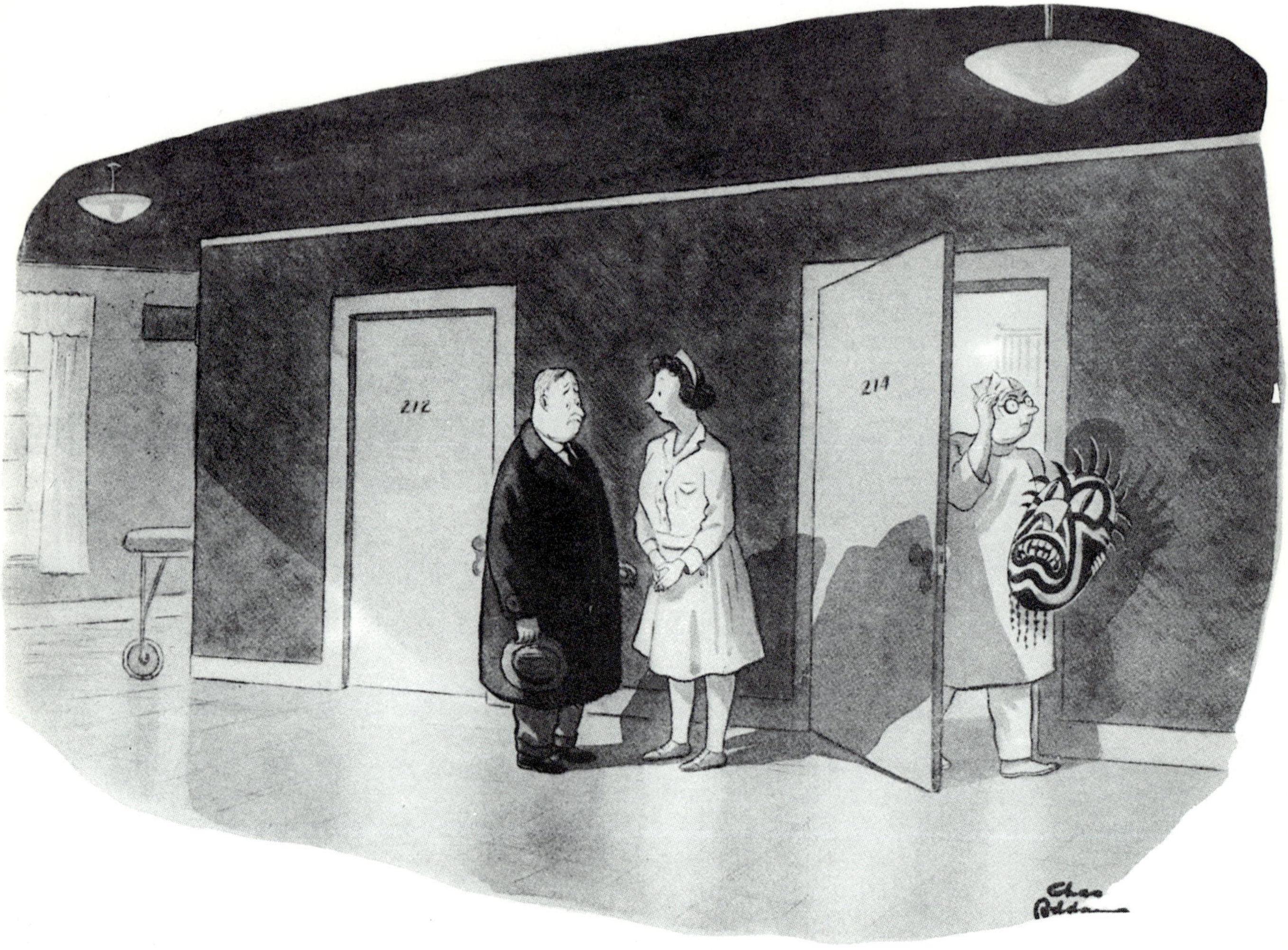

'You must try not to worry. Dr Perry is doing everything humanly possible.'

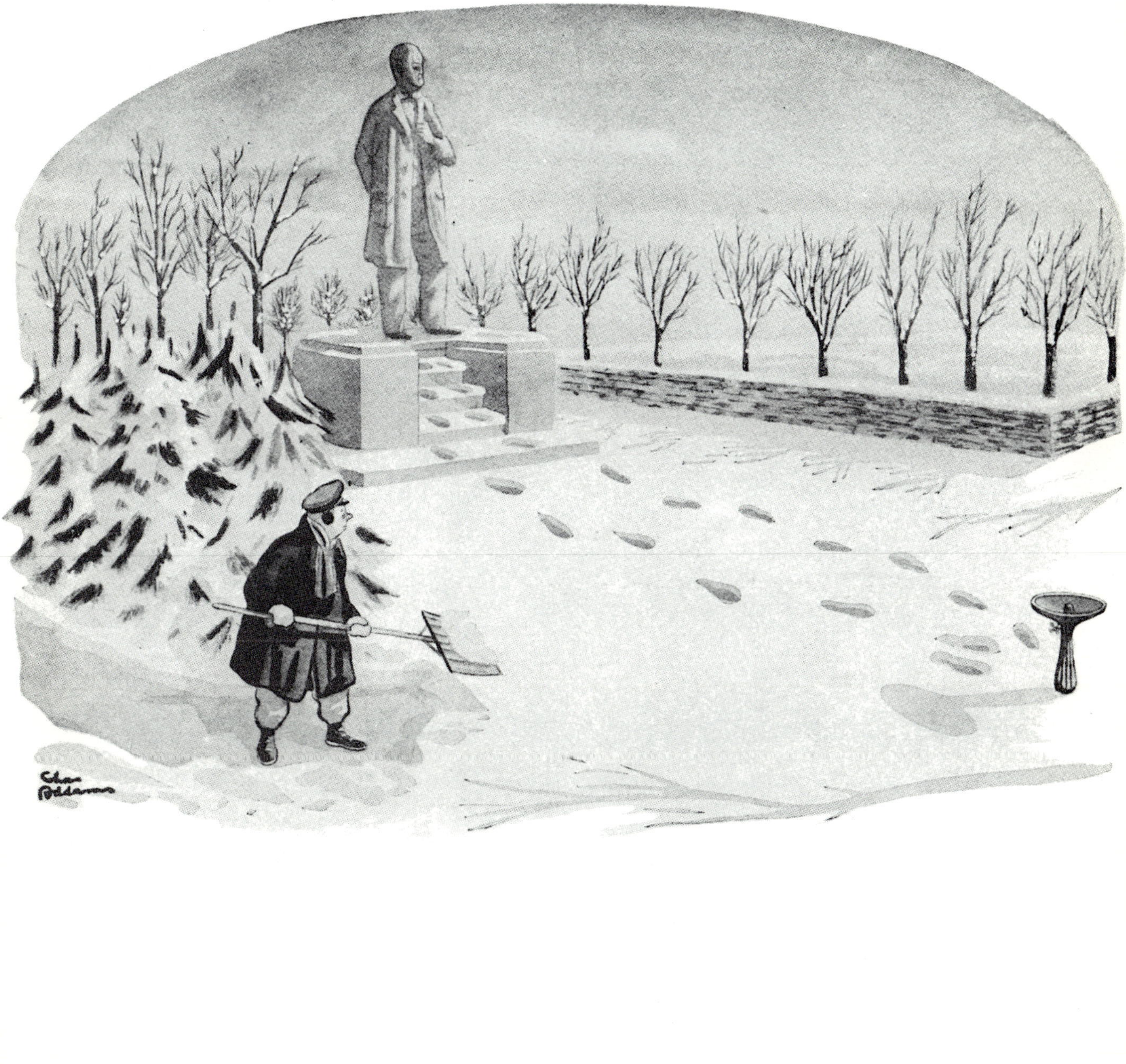
Chas Addams

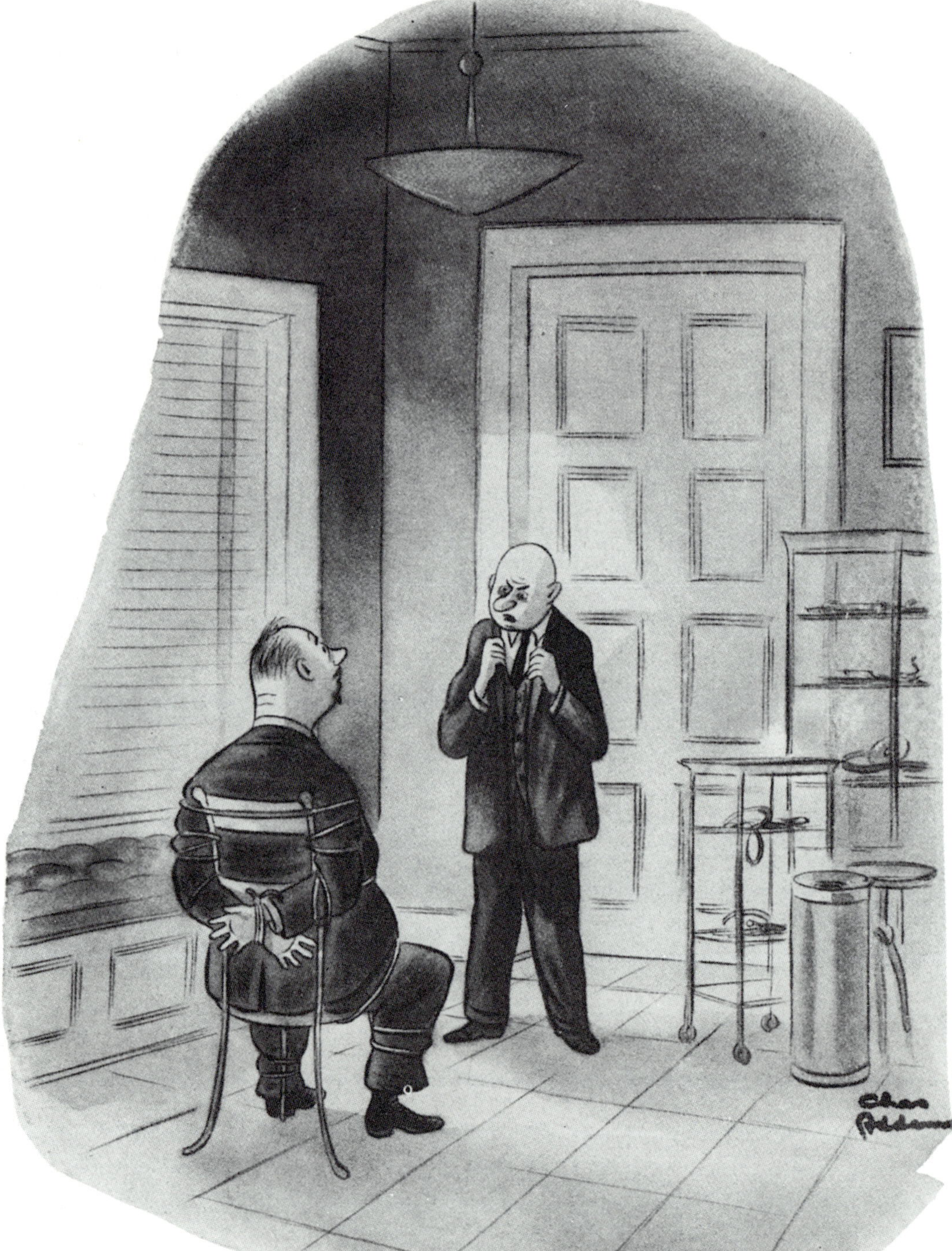

'Now tell me, Doctor, just when did you first
begin to notice this paranoia of mine?'

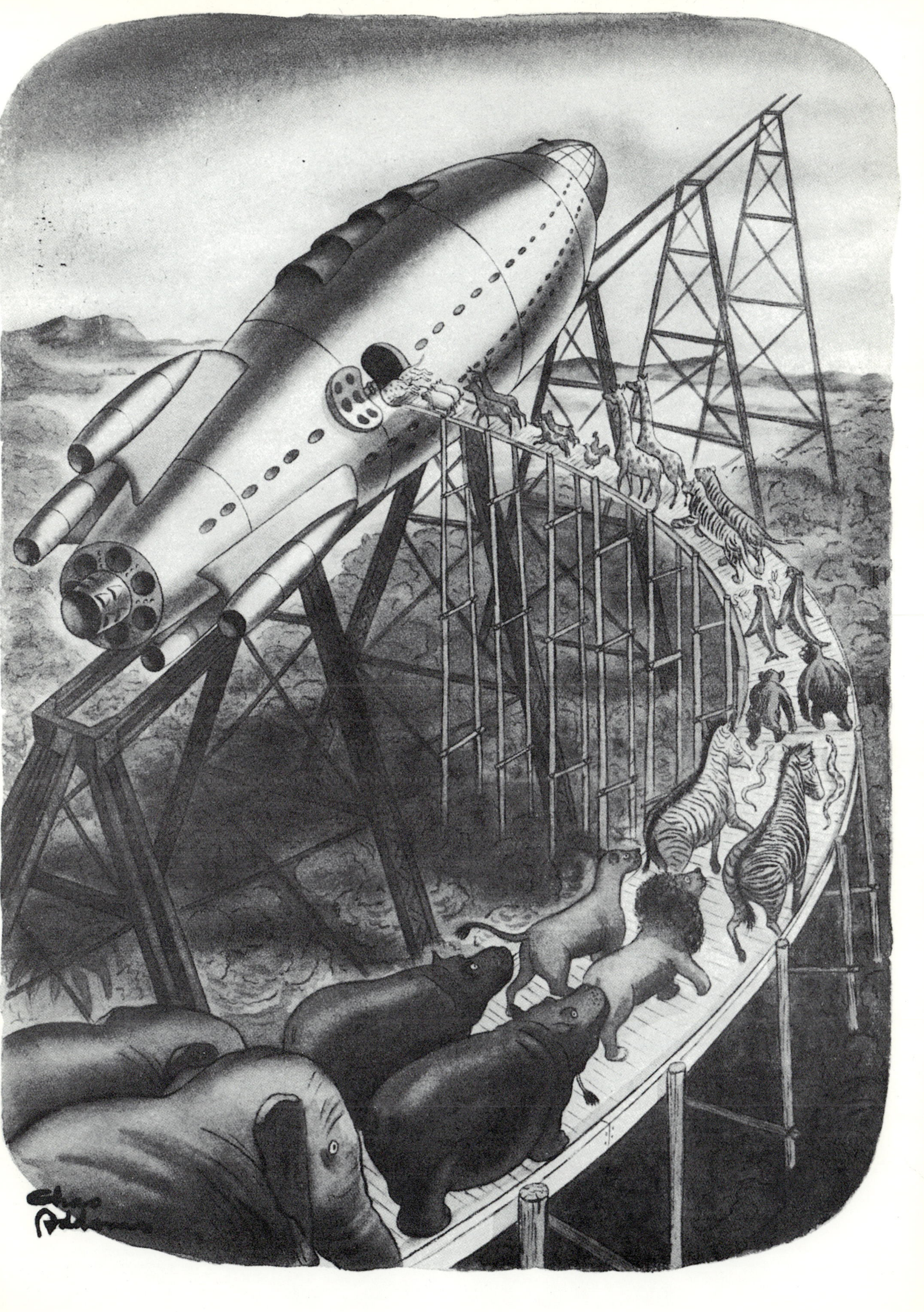

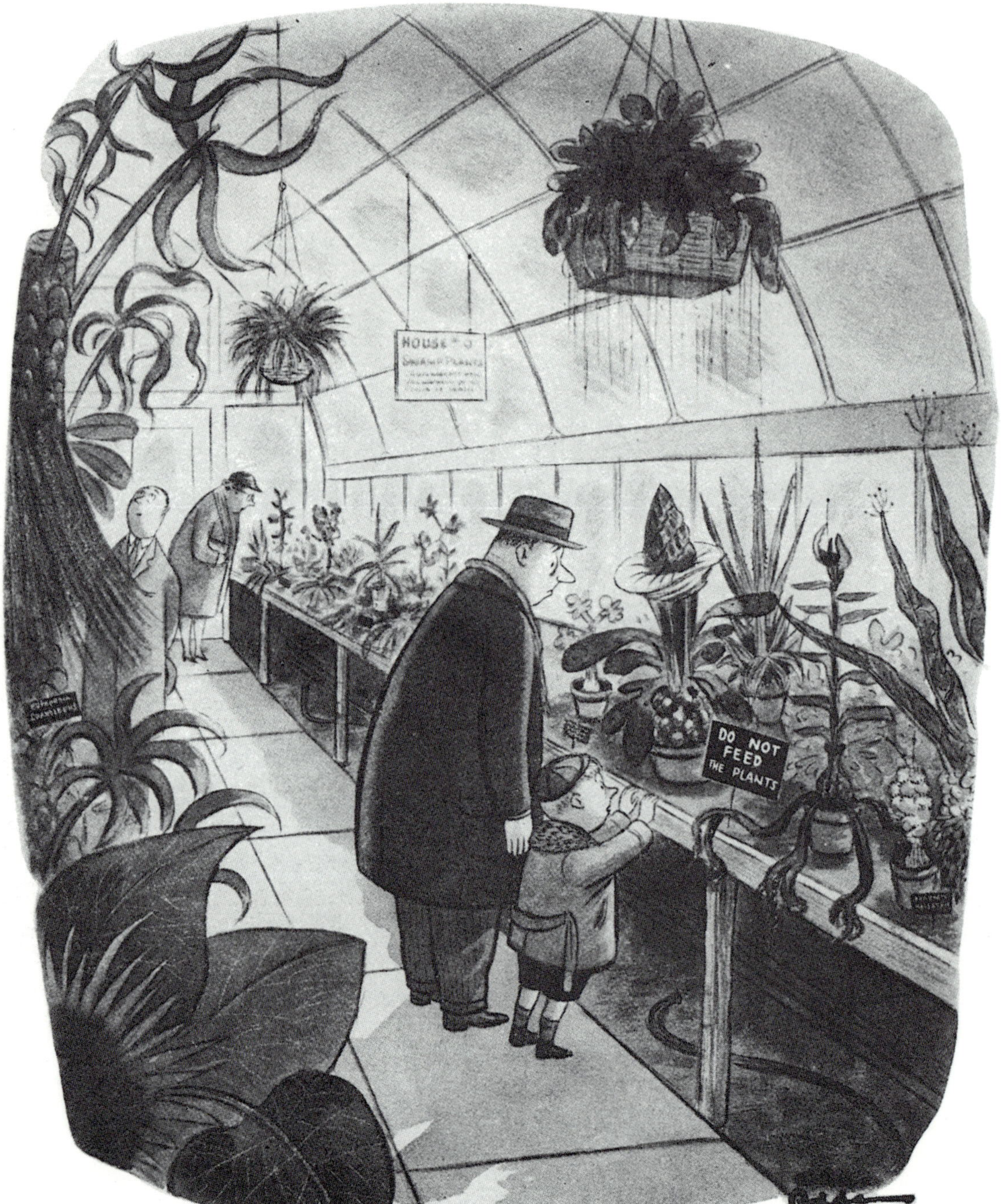
DO NOT
FEED
THE PLANTS

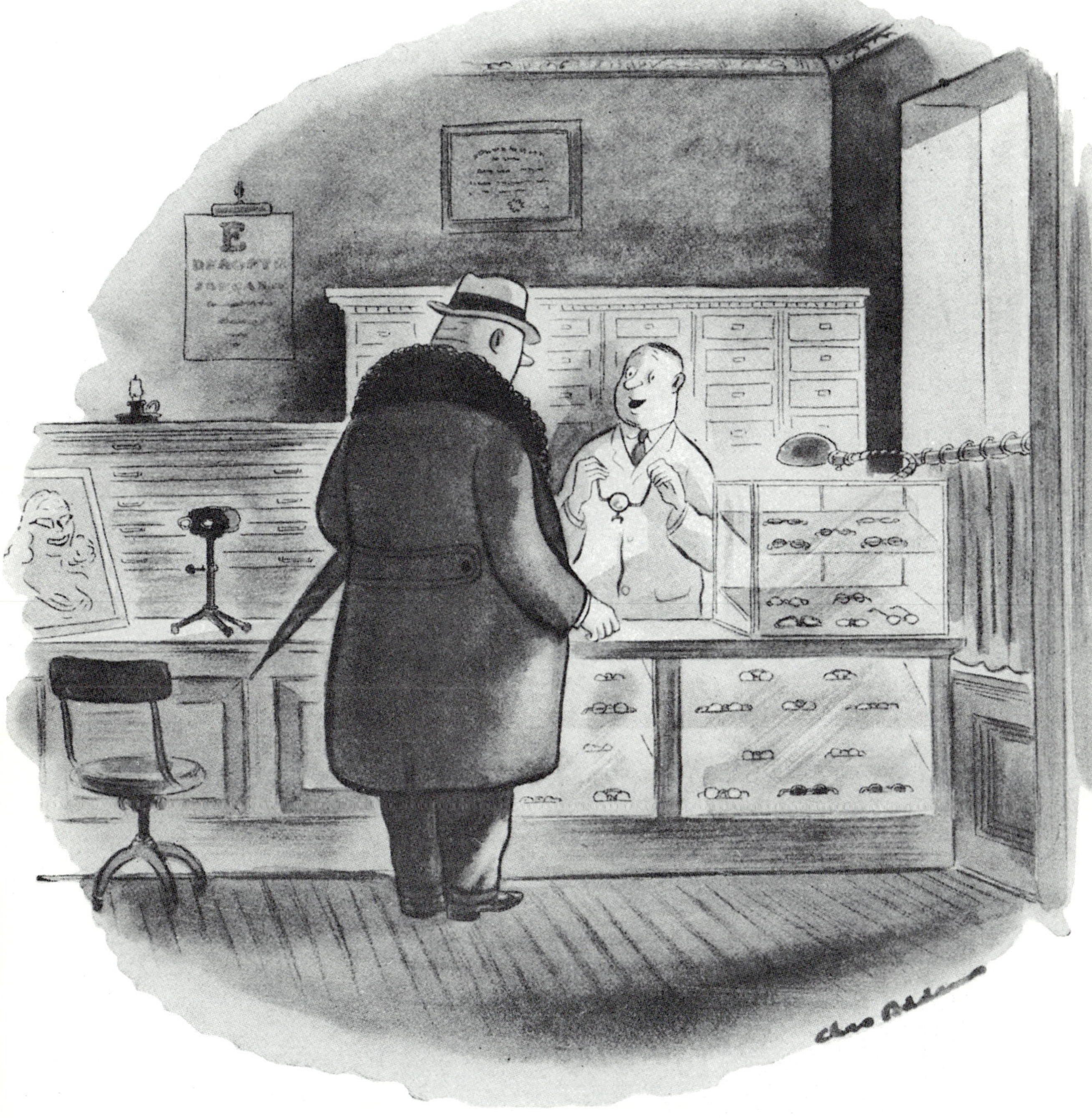

'Now, let's just slip it on and see how it fits.'

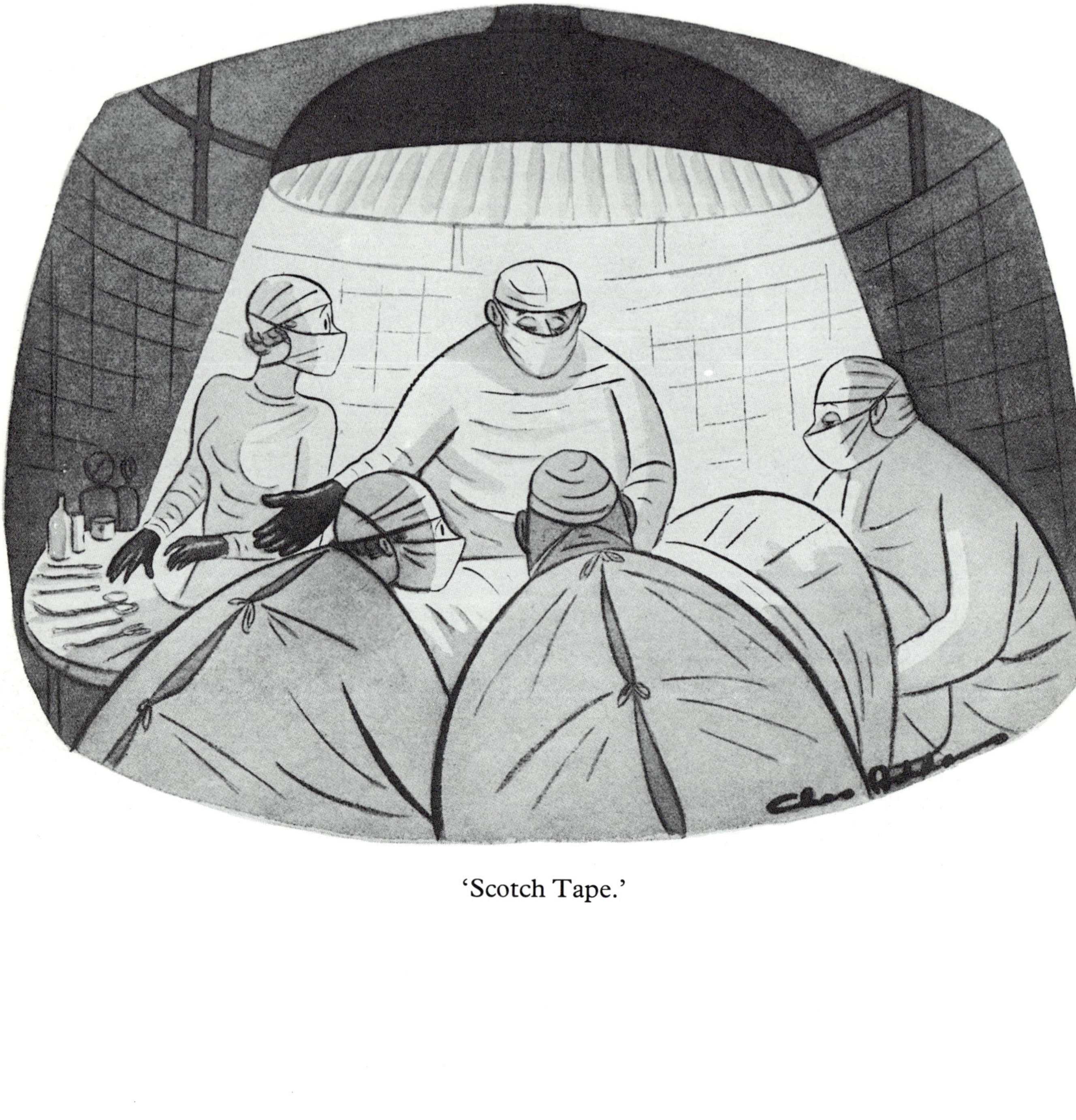

'Scotch Tape.'

THE REMODELLED HOUSE

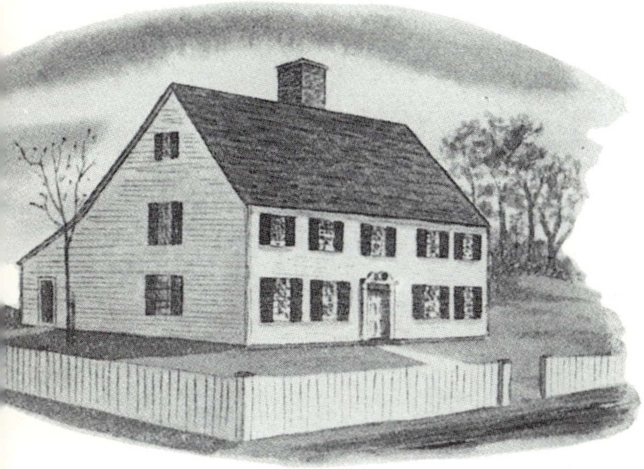

1790

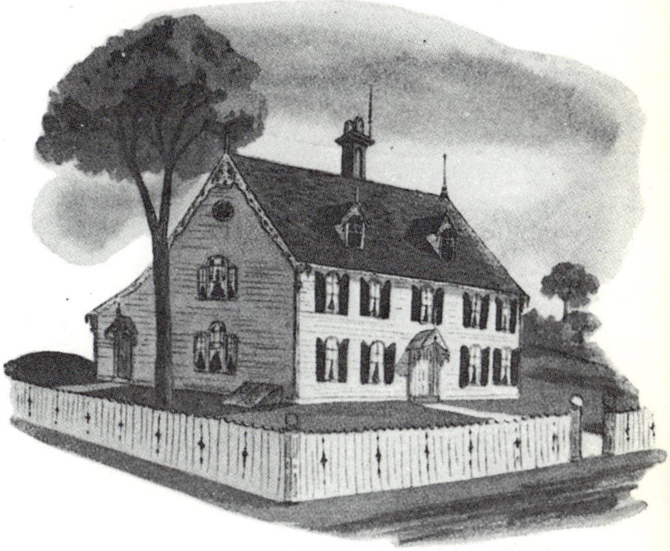

1840

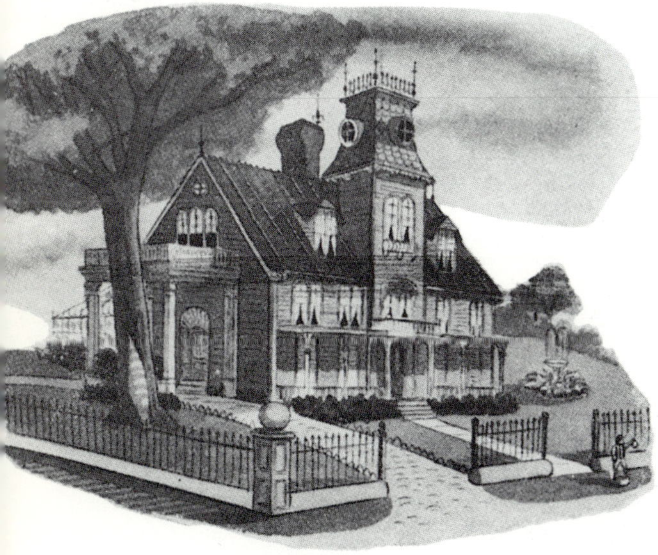

1870

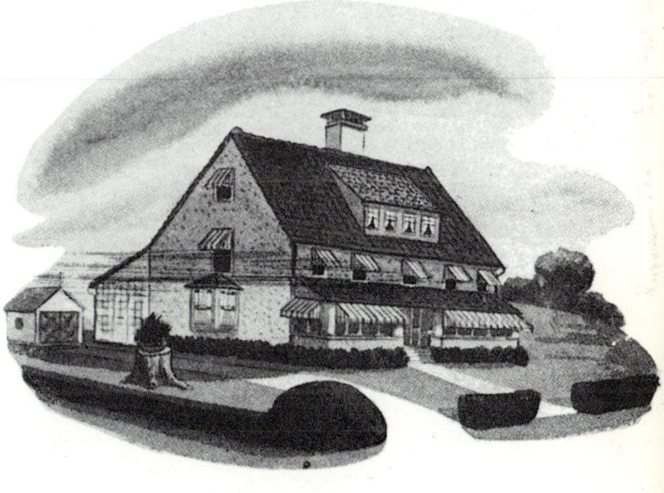

1910

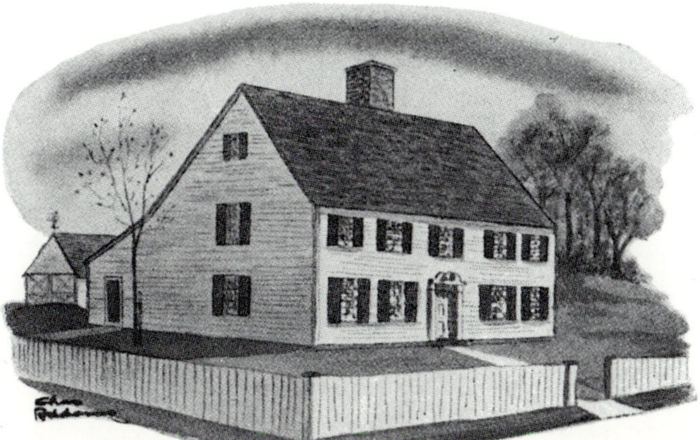

1946

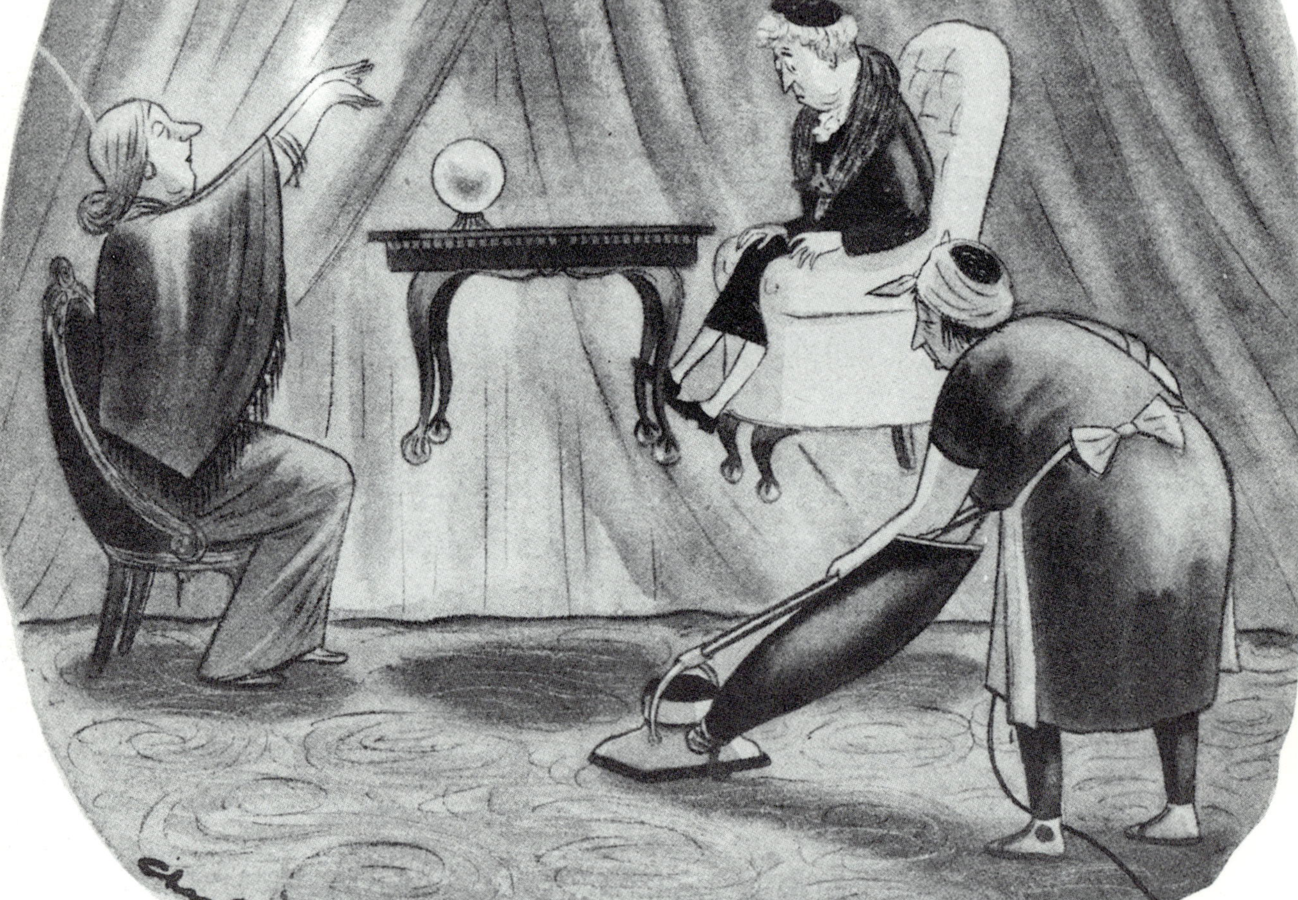
Chas Addams

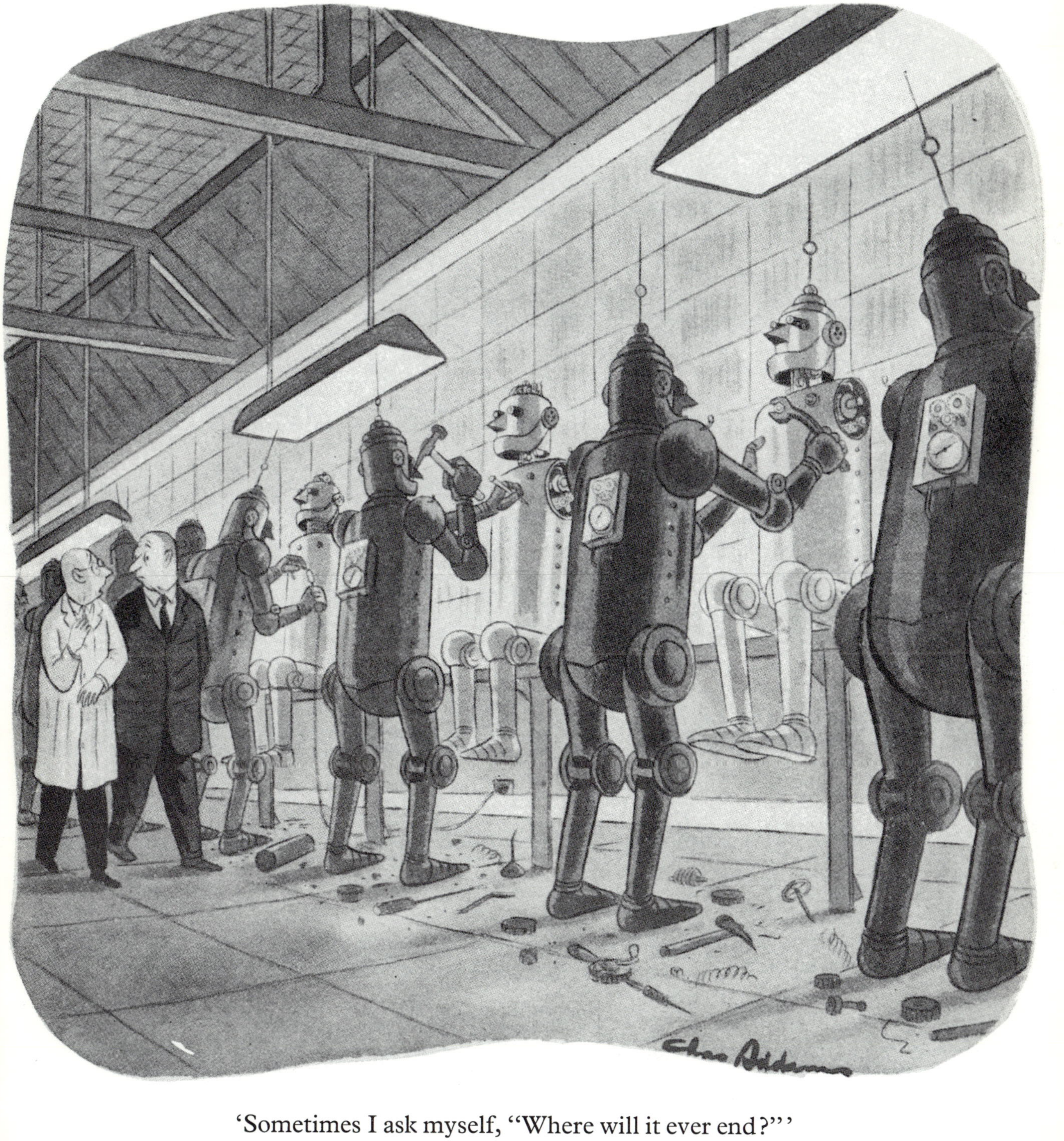

'Sometimes I ask myself, "Where will it ever end?"'

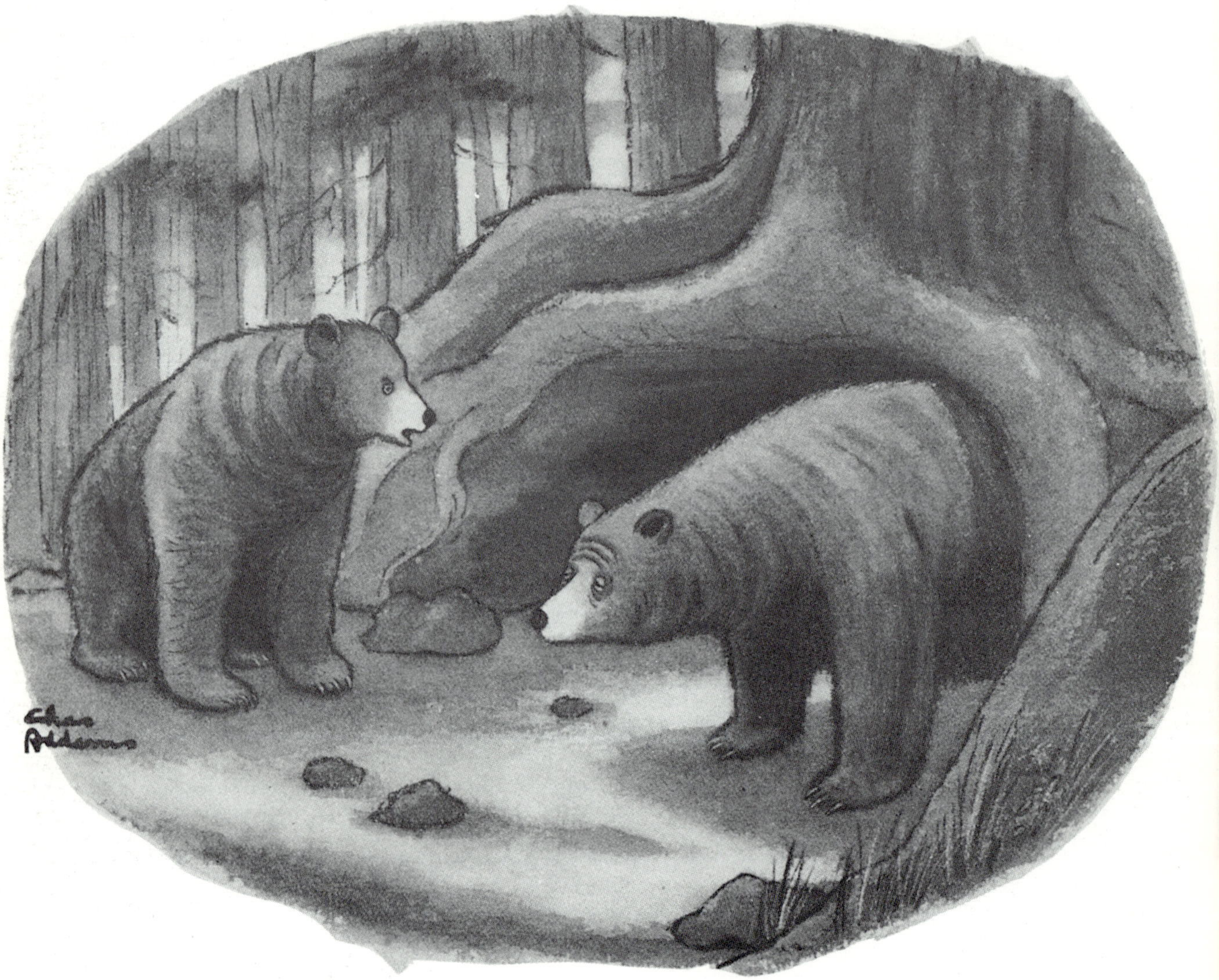

'What in the world was the matter? You tossed and turned all winter.'

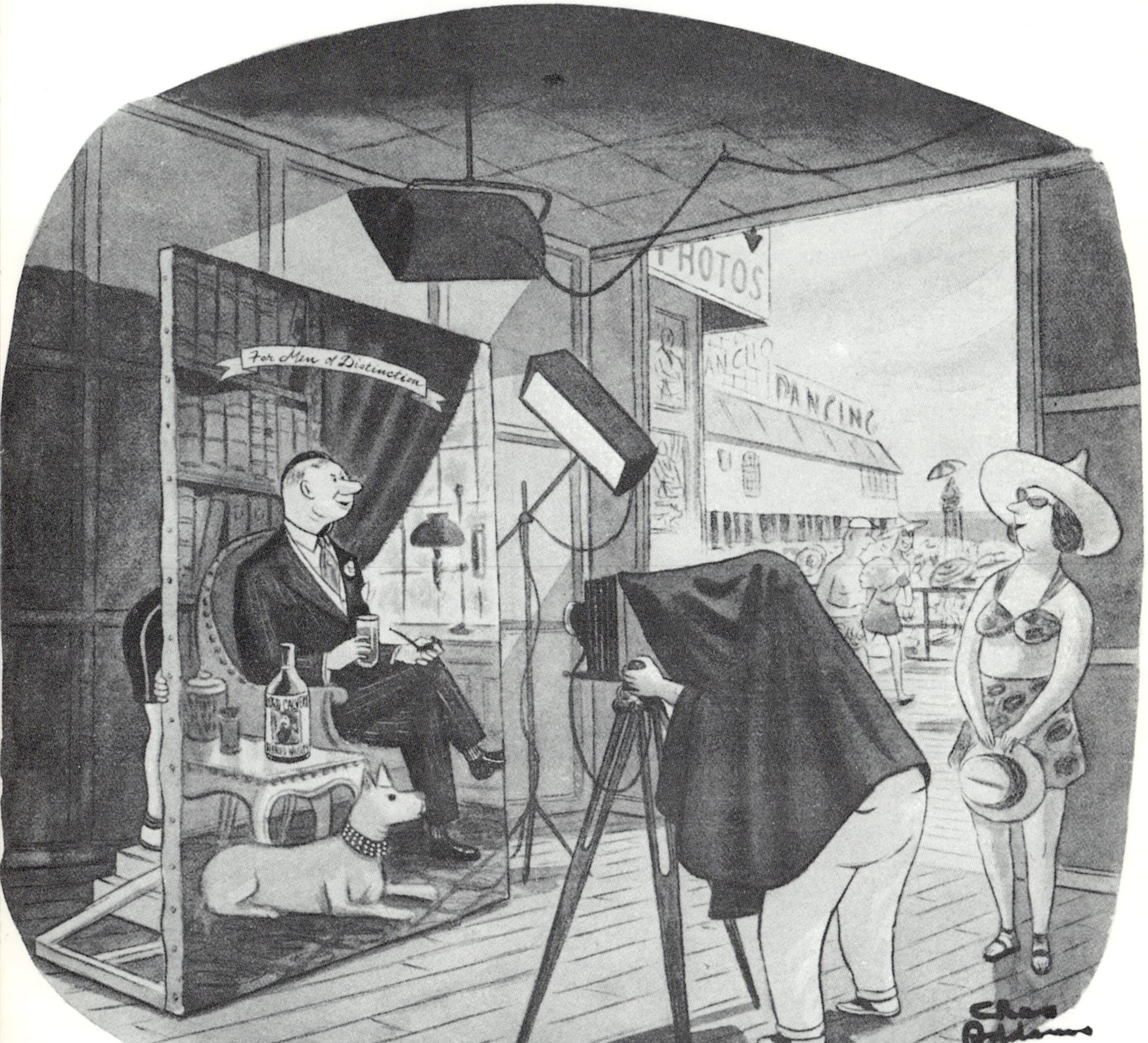
For Men of Distinction
PHOTOS
DANCING
Chas Addams

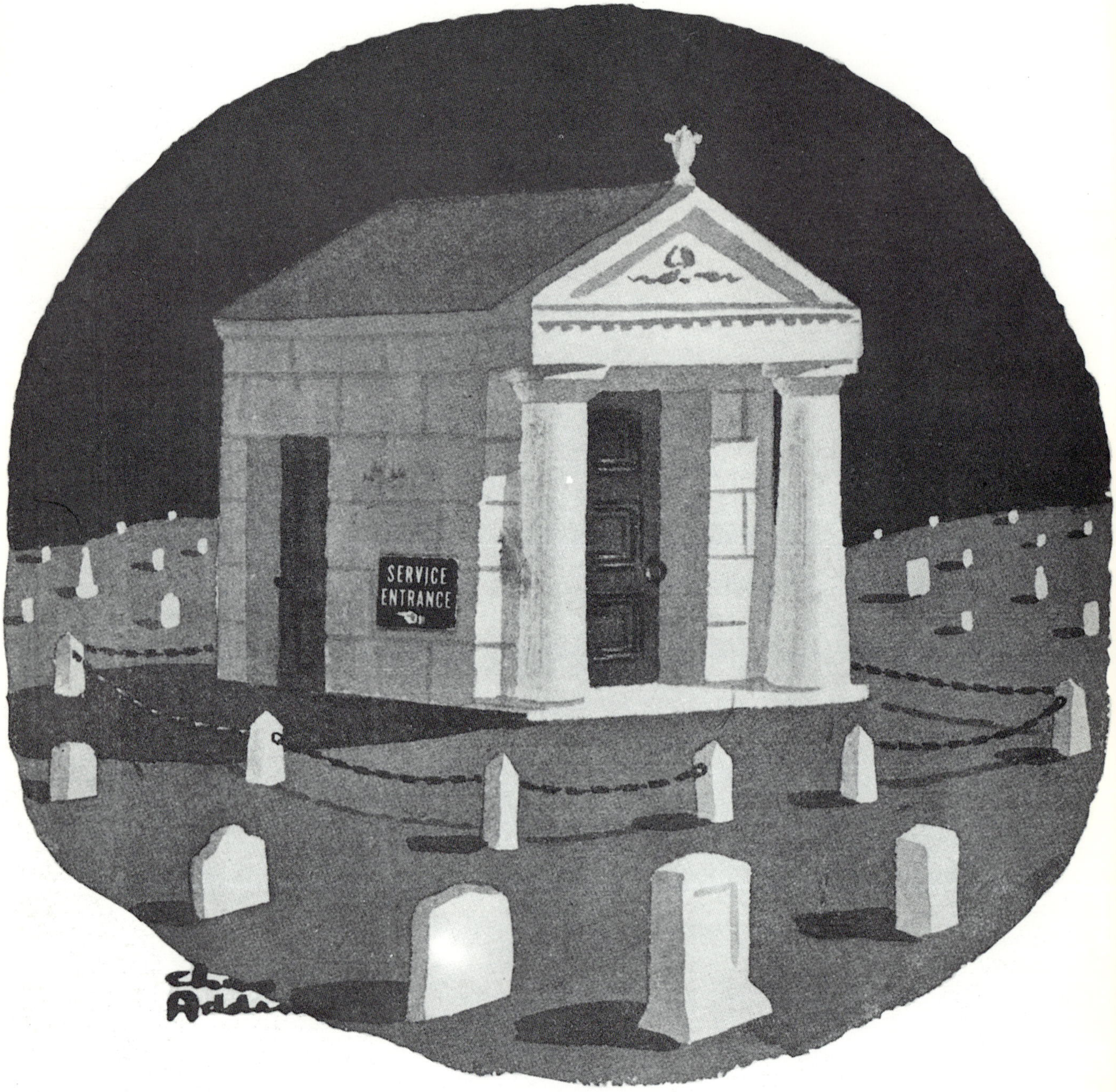
SERVICE
ENTRANCE

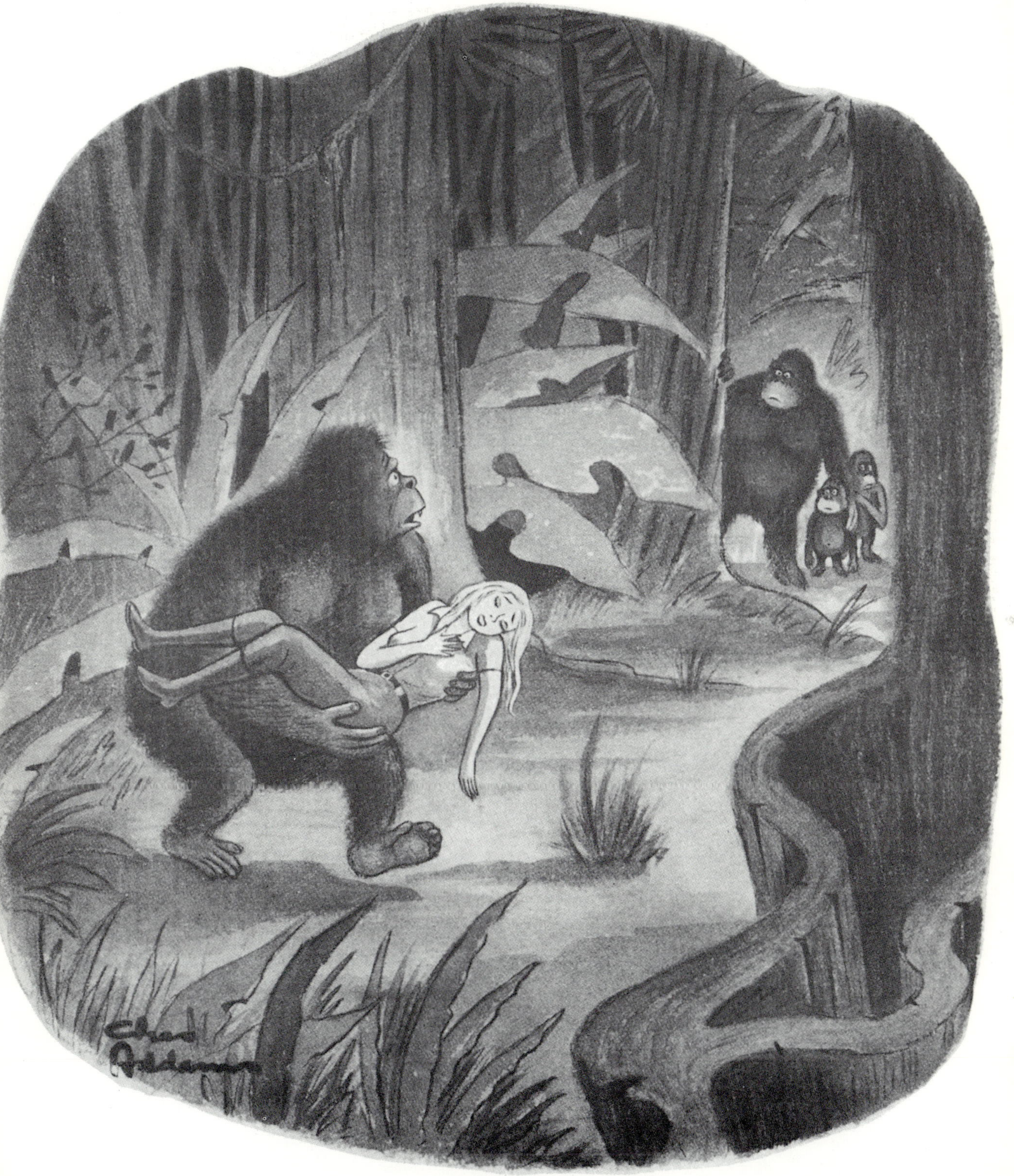

'Oh, oh!'

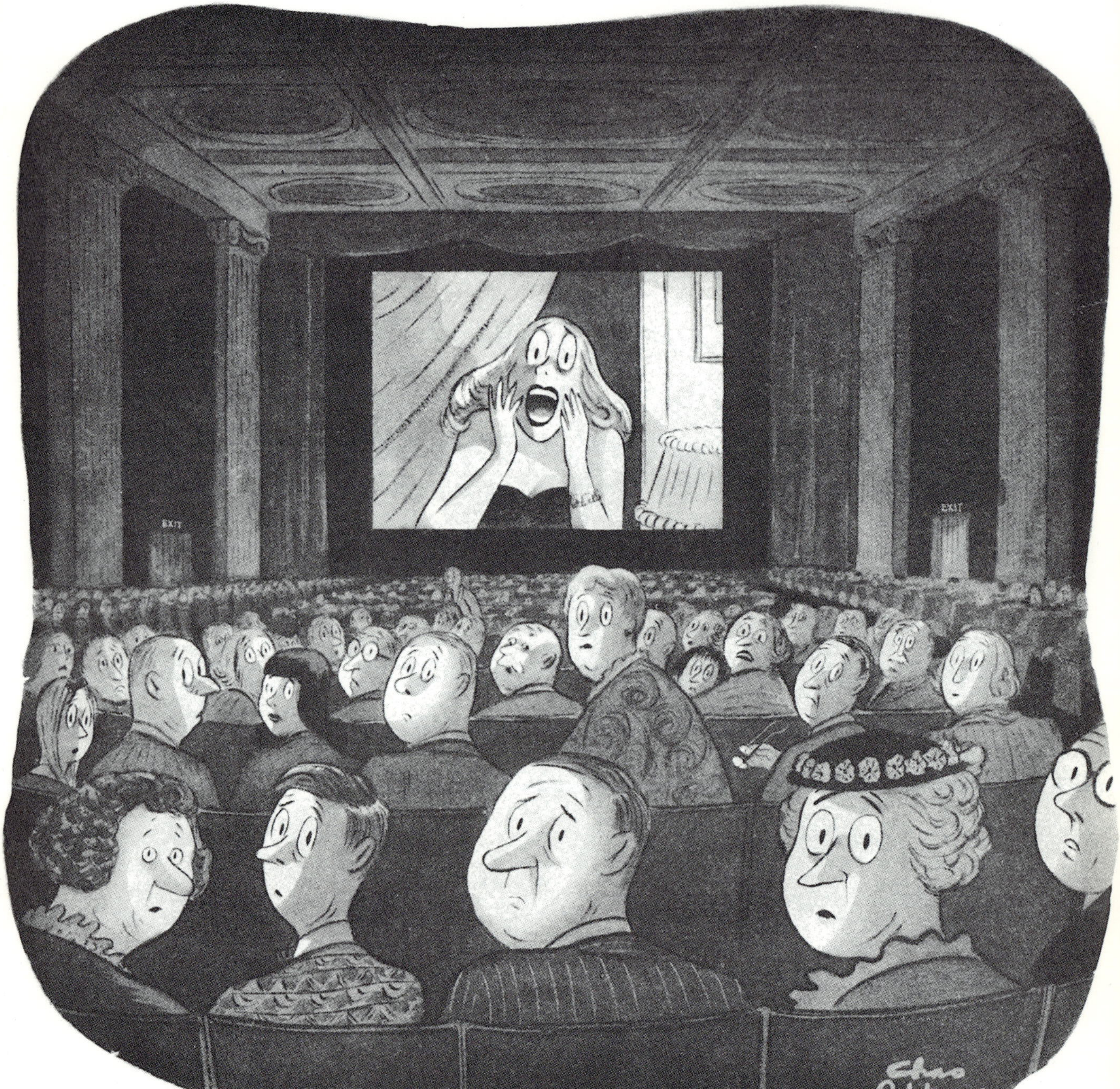
Chas Addams